eLmL 2016

The Eighth International Conference on Mobile, Hybrid, and On-line Learning

April 24 - 28, 2016

Venice, Italy

eLmL 2016 Editors

Stephen White, The University of Huddersfield - Queensgate, UK
Herwig Mannaert, University of Antwerp, Belgium
Jaime Lloret Mauri, Universidad Politecnica de Valencia, Spain

Printed from e-media with permission by:

Curran Associates, Inc.
57 Morehouse Lane
Red Hook, NY 12571

CURRAN ASSOCIATES INC. proceedings .com

Some format issues inherent in the e-media version may also appear in this print version.

Printed by Curran Associates, Inc. (2016)

International Academy, Research, and Industry Association (IARIA)
412 Derby Way
Wilmington, DE 19810

Phone: (408) 893-6407
Fax: (408) 527-6351

petre@iaria.org

Additional copies of this publication are available from:

Curran Associates, Inc.
57 Morehouse Lane
Red Hook, NY 12571 USA
Phone: 845-758-0400
Fax: 845-758-2633
Email: curran@proceedings.com
Web: www.proceedings.com

TABLE OF CONTENTS

ELML 1: TOOLS AND PLATFORMS

ELML 2: HYBRID LEARNING

ELML 3: MOBILE LEARNING, TEACHING, AND TRAINING

ELML 4: ONLINE LEARNING

ELML 5: CHALLENGING TECHNICAL ASPECTS

eLmL 2016

Forward

The Eighth International Conference on Mobile, Hybrid, and On-line Learning (eLmL 2016), held between April 24 and April 28, 2016 in Venice, Italy, continued bringing together federated views on mobileLearning, hybridLearning, and on-lineLearning. eLmL 2016 was dedicated to educators, eLearning experts, and students to exchange their ideas, experiences and lessons learnt in different facets of modern learning.

eLearning refers to on-line learning delivered over the World Wide Web via the public Internet or the private, corporate intranet. The conference was intended to provide an overview of technologies, approaches, and trends that are happening right now. The constraints of e-learning are diminishing and options are increasing as the Web becomes increasingly easy to use and the technology becomes better and less expensive.

As the ease of execution increases, more and more institutions are discovering the benefits of delivering training via the Web. Interest in e-learning is at an all-time high, and the workshop wants to serve as a stimulus to accelerate collaboration and dialog among the e-learning providers, trainers, IT researchers and the lifelong, self-directed learners. Such business trends as an increased global economy, the pressures for rapid development, and the necessity of teamwork are shaping the present state and the future of eLearning.

Employees are increasingly aware that they must continue to update and advance their skills if they want to understand the state-of-the-art technologies and remain valuable to their organizations. This means that learners will be more and more self-directed, and they will want access to what they need when they need it. The Internet based educational materials and the e-learning providers have to meet this demand.

The conference focuses on the latest trends in e-learning and also on the latest IT technology alternatives that are poised to become mainstream strategies in the near future and will influence the e-learning environment. Ubiquitous systems proliferate quickly due to the latest achievements in the industry of telecommunications, electronics, wireless, and economical globalization.

Wireless and mobility allow any user to timely use resources using various access technologies under (assumed) secured and guaranteed privacy. The family of mobile devices expands dramatically, allowing a user to have a portable office everywhere, every time. Mobile learning became a fact, due to the technical accessibility and Internet communications. Many online classes, learning systems, university curricula, remote education, and virtual training classes are now part of the corporate education and use.

Progress is made in user modeling and adaptive learning models. The generalization of successful practices on mobile learning is favored by many national and international projects and policy synchronization boards. Adaptation implies also the use of the classical methods, still in use and useful in some contexts and for some categories of users. Hybrid learning is an increasing trend in education today. The traditional classroom learning has been historically proven beneficial. Hybrid learning is rather a series of different learning strategies going from teacher-centric to student-centric. This improves the critical thinking, creativity, self-management, self-study, and advance problem solving thinking of the student.

The conference had the following tracks:

- Tools and platforms
- Hybrid learning
- Mobile learning, teaching, and training
- Online learning
- Challenging technical aspects

We take here the opportunity to warmly thank all the members of the eLmL 2016 technical program committee, as well as the numerous reviewers. The creation of such a high quality conference program would not have been possible without their involvement. We also kindly thank all the authors that dedicated much of their time and effort to contribute to eLmL 2016. We truly believe that, thanks to all these efforts, the final conference program consisted of top quality contributions.

Also, this event could not have been a reality without the support of many individuals, organizations and sponsors. We also gratefully thank the members of the eLmL 2016 organizing committee for their help in handling the logistics and for their work that made this professional meeting a success.

We hope eLmL 2016 was a successful international forum for the exchange of ideas and results between academia and industry and to promote further progress in the field of mobile, hybrid and on-line learning. We also hope that Venice, Italy, provided a pleasant environment during the conference and everyone saved some time to enjoy the unique charm of the city.

eLmL Advisory Committee

eLmL 2016

Committee

eLmL Advisory Committee

Herwig Mannaert, University of Antwerp, Belgium
Dumitru Dan Burdescu, University of Craiova, Romania
Bernd Krämer, FernUniversität in Hagen, Germany
Stephen White, The University of Huddersfield - Queensgate, UK
Maiga Chang, Athabasca University - Edmonton, Canada
Adam M. Gadomski, ENEA, Italy
Michelle Marquard, Independent Researcher, USA
Murtuza Ali Lakhani, Adecco for Cisco Systems, Inc., USA

eLmL 2016 Technical Program Committee

Ignacio Aedo, Universidad Carlos III de Madrid, Spain
Esma Aimeur, Université de Montréal, Canada
Ali Ahmad Alawneh, Philadelphia University, Jordan
Luis Alberto Álvarez-González, Universidad Austral de Chile - Valdivia, Chile
Tomaz Amon, Amnim, center for scientific visualization (CSV) – Ljubljana, Slovenia
George Anastassakis, University of Piraeus, Greece
Trish Andrew, The University of Queensland-Brisbane, Australia
Miquel Àngel Prats, Universitat Ramon Llull, Spain
Sergio Assis Rodrigues, Federal University of Rio de Janeiro, Brazil
Anders Avdic, Dalarna University, Sweden
Cristina Azevedo Gomes, Polytechnics Institute of Viseu, Portugal
Panagiotis D. Bamidis, Aristotle University of Thessaloniki, Greece
Antonio R. Bartolomé, University of Barcelona, Spain
Karla Bastos Guedes, Universidade Federal Fluminense, Brazil
Patrícia Behar, The Federal University of Rio Grande do Sul, Brazil
Juarez Bento da Silva, Universidade Federal de Santa Catarina - UFSC, Brazil
Ilham Benyahia, Université du Québec en Outaouais, Canada
Werner Beuschel, Institute of Business Application Systems, Brandenburg, Germany
Franz X. Bogner, University of Bayreuth, Germany
Luis Borges Gouveia, University Fernando Pessoa, Portugal
Christos Bouras, University of Patras and Computer Technology Institute & Press «Diophantus», Greece
Maria Helena Braz, Technical University of Lisbon, Portugal
Julien Broisin, IRIT, France
Dumitru Dan Burdescu, University of Craiova, Romania

Egle Butkeviciene, Kaunas University of Technology, Lithuania
Maria-Dolores Cano, Universidad Politécnica de Cartagena, Spain
Manuel Cebrian de la Serna, Universidad de Málaga, Spain
Maiga Chang, Athabasca University, Canada
Mohamed Amine Chatti, RWTH Aachen University, Germany
Olga Cherednichenko, National Technical University "KhPI" - Kharkiv, Ukraine
Satyadhyan Chickerur , B V Bhoomaraddi College of Engineering and Technology, India
Bee Bee Chua, University of Technology, Sydney, Australia
Ritesh Chugh, CQUniversity Melbourne, Australia
Lorraine Cleeton, Northcentral University / Walden University, USA
David Comiskey, Ulster University, UK
Andre Constantino da Silva, Instituto Federal de São Paulo, Brazil
Felice Corona, University of Salerno, Italy
Richard Dabrowski, George C. Marshall European Center for Security Studies, Germany
Angélica de Antonio, Universidad Politecnica de Madrid, Spain
Claudia de Witt, FernUniversität in Hagen, Germany
Giuliana Dettori, ITD-CNR Genoa, Italy
Mihaela Dinsoreanu, Technical University of Cluj-Napoca, Romania
Gabriella Dodero, Free University of Bozen-Bolzano, Italy
Hamide Dogan, University of Texas at El Paso, USA
Roza Dumbraveanu, State Pedagogical University "Ion Creanga", Chisinau, Moldova
Martin Ebner, Graz University of Technology, Austria
Ruben Edel-Navarro, Universidad Veracruzana, Mexico
Paula Escudeiro, ISEP, Porto, Portugal
Pascal Estraillier, Université de La Rochelle, France
Ramon Fabregat , Universitat de Girona, Spain
Bekim Fetaji, South East European University - Tetovo, Republic of Macedonia
Joseph Finkelstein, The Johns Hopkins Medical Institutions, USA
Sue Folley, University of Huddersfield, UK
Rita Francese, Università di Salerno, Italy
Adam M. Gadomski, ENEA, Italy
Ivan Ganchev, University of Limerick, Ireland
Leonardo Garrido, Tecnológico de Monterrey, Mexico
Isabela Gasparini, UDESC - Santa Catarina State University, Brazil
Mercè Gisbert, Universitat Rovira i Virgili, Spain
Giuliana Guazzaroni, Università Politecnica delle Marche, Italy
Angela Guercio, Kent State University, USA
Christian Guetl, Institute for Information Systems and Computer Media (IICM) - Graz University of Technology, Austria
David Guralnick, Kaleidoscope Learning - New York, Columbia University - New York, USA
Ibrahim A. Hameed, University College of Alesund, Norway
Imed Hammouda, Tampere University of Technology, Finland
Felix Hamza-Lup, Armstrong State University, USA
Mais Hasan, Ilmenau University of Technology, Germany

Thanos Hatziapostolou, University of Sheffield International Faculty - CITY College, Greece
Misook Heo, Duquesne University, USA
Oriel Herrera, Universidad Católica de Temuco, Chile
Carmen Holotescu, "Politehnica" University of Timisoara, Romania
Jozef Hvorecky, Vysoká škola manažmentu, Slovakia
Siew Pei Hwa, Universiti Tunku Abdul Rahman, Malaysia
Eun Jin Hwang, Indiana University of Pennsylvania, USA
Taketoshi Inaba, Tokyo University of Technology, Japan
Tsunenori Ishioka, The National Center for University Entrance Examinations, Japan
Larisa Ismailova, NRNU MEPhI, Russia
Tomayess Issa, Curtin University, Australia
Mirjana Ivanovic, University of Novi Sad, Serbia
Dinesh C. Jain, Dept. of CSE, SVITS - Indore, India
Naxhije Jakupi, South East European University Ilindenska - Tetovo, Macedonia
Marc Jansen, University of Applied Sciences Ruhr West, Germany
Klaus P. Jantke, Fraunhofer IDMT, Germany
Athanassios Jimoyiannis, University of Peloponnese, Greece
Mike Joy, University of Warwick, UK
Katerina Kabassi, TEI of Ionian Islands, Greece
Konstantinos Kalemis, National Centre for Public Administration and Local Government (E.K.D.D.A.) / National and Kapodistrian University of Athens, Greece
Michail Kalogiannakis, University of Crete, Greece
Keiichi Kaneko, Tokyo University of Agriculture and Technology, Japan
Marja Kankaanranta, University of Jyväskylä, Finland
Jai Kang, Rochester Institute of Technology, USA
Atis Kapenieks, Riga Technical University, Latvia
Ilias Karasavvidis, University of Thessaly, Greece
Charalampos Karagiannidis, University of Thessaly, Greece
David Kaufman, Simon Fraser University, Canada
Mizue Kayama, Shinshu University, Japan
Cristian Kop, Alpen-Adria-Universitaet Klagenfurt, Austria
Rob Koper, Open University of the Netherlands, Netherlands
Eugenia Kovatcheva, State University of Library Studies and Information Technologies, Bulgaria
Bernd Krämer, FernUniversität in Hagen, Germany
Miroslav Kulich, Czech Technical University in Prague, Czech Republic
Joe Kush, Duquesne University, USA
Jan Kusiak, AGH University of Science and Technology, Poland
Ivan Kuzio, Technical Trainers College, Kingdom of Saudi Arabia
Murtuza Ali Lakhani, Adecco for Cisco Systems, Inc., USA
Niki Lambropoulos, University of Patras, Greece
Asterios Leonidis, University of Crete, Greece
Cynthia Lester, Georgia Perimeter College, USA
Ken W. Li, Hong Kong Institute of Vocational Education (Tsing Yi), Hong Kong
Andreas Lingnau, SGM - Solutions & Global Media GmbH | CSES group - Humboldt University

Lorne Thompson, Loyalist College, Canada
Katya Toneva, Mirandanet, UK
Guglielmo Trentin, Institute of Educational Technology of the Italian National Research Council (ITD-CNR), Italy
Thrasyvoulos Tsiatsos, Aristotle University of Thessaloniki, Greece
George Tsihrintzis, University of Piraeus, Greece
Doru Ursutiu, University "Transilvania" of Brasov, Romania
Ioannis O. Vardiambasis, Technological Educational Institute (TEI) of Crete, Greece
Emmanouel Varvarigos, University of Patras, Greece
Carlos Vaz de Carvalho, Instituto Superior de Engenharia do Porto, Portugal
Esteban Vázquez Cano, Spanish National University of Distance Education, Spain
Ioanna Vekiri, independent writer and researcher, Greece
Michael Verhaart, School of Computing EIT, New Zealand
Martine Verjans, Universiteit Hasselt, Belgium
Genny Villa, Université de Montreal, Canada
Amali Weerasinghe, University of Canterbury, New Zealand
Steve Wheeler, University of Plymouth, UK
Stephen White, The University of Huddersfield - Queensgate, UK
Nicola Whitton, Manchester Metropolitan University, UK
Penne L. Wilson, Ralph J. Bunche Academy Charter, USA
Martin Wolpers, Fraunhofer-Institut für Angewandte Informationstechnik FIT - Sankt Augustin, Germany
Lung-Hsiang Wong, Nanyang Technological University, Singapore
Mudasser F. Wyne, National University, - San Diego, USA
Jie Chi Yang, National Central University, Taiwan
Ahmed Mohamed Fahmy Yousef, Fayoum University, Egypt
Katarina Zakova, Slovak University of Technology, Slovakia
Diego Zapata-Rivera, Educational Testing Service, USA
Miguel Zapata Ros, Universidad de Alcalá, Spain
Qinglong Zhan, Tianjin University of Technology and Education, China
Xiangmin Zhang, School of Library and Information Science - Wayne State University, USA
Grygoriy Zholtkevych, V.N. Karazin Kharkiv National University, Ukraine
Leyla Zhuhadar, Western Kentucky University, USA

Copyright Information

Micro Note-Taking on Smartphone: The Learner Experience

Maram S. Al-Zaidi, Mike Joy, Jane Sinclair
Department of Computer Science
University of Warwick
Coventry, UK
{M.S.Al-Zaidi, M.S.Joy, J.E.Sinclair}@warwick.ac.uk

Abstract—**Note-taking is considered as one of the main activities for students during lectures in the classroom. Indeed, many educators have suggested that note-taking can significantly improve students' educational performance. Therefore, there are many systems available to capture what the teacher presents or explains during the lectures. However, less attention has been paid to the great potential of integrating Web 2.0 technologies with the learning process at universities for note-taking purposes so as to make it more effective. As such, the purpose of this paper is to extend understanding of learners' experiences specifically when short text – the 140 characters, often used in social networks – was used for note-taking. The paper presents findings on learners' experiences of using such a "micro" note-taking approach involving just 140 characters and suggests a feature list for a future note-taking system. The qualitative approach focuses on learners from one university in the UK. The learners were at postgraduate level, and data were collected through focus groups with the learners. Findings indicate that the use of a short text feature leads to a positive learning experience.**

Keywords— ***micro note-taking; smartphone; social media; UK.***

I. Introduction

In recent years, there has been a considerable increase in the number of students carrying one or more mobile devices into lectures. These include laptops, smartphones and tablet devices. Sharples [1] highlighted the growth in using mobile phones amongst students as well as across all educational areas. New generations of smartphones support fast Internet connections through 3G and 4G wireless technologies in addition to faster Wi-Fi connections. Moreover, with new iPhone and Android phones providing millions of applications, there has been a dramatic increase in the interest level in using these devices for educational purposes [2]. Indeed, in the last decade, and due to these advances, researchers have shown an increased interest in using new technologies and computing devices for taking notes.

When it comes to capturing notes using traditional tools, many different forms of learners' behaviour can be observed. The majority of students intend to capture what the teacher presents or explains during the lecture, and these notes could either include specific details, or may simply record the most important points [3]. In line with this, some students attempt to capture everything presented by the teacher, while others attempt to select relevant points and a few indulge in a certain amount of doodling whilst they listen [4].

Note-taking is one of the common techniques used by learners during lectures [5], and, traditionally, this course of action is usually conducted either manually (i.e., pen and paper) or electronically, using electronic devices such as tablet PCs and PDAs. However, given the massive uptake in the use of information and communication technologies, there is great potential for integrating Web 2.0 technologies with the learning process at universities for the purposes of note-taking so as to make it more effective.

To give just a few examples of the value and benefits that can be delivered through the use of SMS features, and more specifically Twitter, in the practice of note-taking, it was found that one of the advantages of using Twitter in a classroom setting is that it offers students an additional channel for communication [6]. Scornavacca et al. [7] also found that, for the purposes of handling questions in a large classroom, using text messages is more practical and efficient than the traditional method of raising hands. However, a survey of faculty members, guests, and students on a pharmacy management course that was conducted by Fox and Varadarajan [8] showed that, although 80% of the sample found that Twitter facilitates class participation, 71% and 69% of the sample, however, indicated that Twitter was distracting, and prevented note taking, respectively. Hence, using Twitter during lectures to get involved in classroom activities may be annoying for instructors leading classes [9]. In line with this, Cherney [10] argued that students who use Twitter will lose the necessary space for thinking in depth compared to when they are taught by traditional teaching methods in classrooms. This research, therefore, contributes to the use of Web 2.0 technologies, and, more specifically, the features of Twitter, in the educational process so as to make it more effective than has been the case hitherto.

This paper reports the evaluation of a new approach which is mainly based on mobile and Web 2.0 technologies, and which relies primarily on the employment of *micro note-taking*, or so-called *micro-blogging*, a form of communication that allows people to generate content by posting short messages limited to 140 characters [11] [12]. To gain insight into the concerns of this paper, discussions with the learners who took part in the experiment were analyzed, in particular regarding their experience while using the micro note-taking approach.

The research presented in this paper aims at extending our understanding of what university-level learners' experiences are in terms of note-taking, when using just 140 characters on (Android) smartphones. Moreover, the nature of and reasons for the preferences of using this new format of notes in an educational environment was examined, as was how this prototype could be improved to support learners' note-taking practice in a classroom environment. In short, this paper describes experiences and lessons learned from a class activity that incorporated the micro note-taking approach which is mainly based on mobile and Web 2.0 technologies. It identifies the main positive and negative features of the proposed micro note-taking application and provides ideas and general design guidelines applicable to this approach.

The remainder of this paper is organized as follows: the second section describes the methodology used, the third section describes the experiment itself. In the fourth section IV findings and interpretations are covered. In the fifth and last section the conclusion closes the article.

II. METHODOLOGY

The goal in this section was to present learners' in-depth perspectives of their experiences with using a micro note-taking application. Specifically, this study aims to explore students' opinions about the main positive features and limitations of the proposed micro note-taking application, and of how the application could be improved to support their note-taking practices. Therefore, the decision was made to use a focus group due to the fact that it is a feasible way to represent the participants' feelings, beliefs and experiences [14]. The focus group is part of an evidence-based qualitative approach, which emerged as a distinctive approach, and which also involves in-depth interviewing, observation and projective methods among others [15]. This paper reports in depth the qualitative findings generated from two focus groups consisting of participants in an experiment aimed at enhancing the understanding of the user experience using the micro note-taking application. The two focus groups consisted of 14 users who participated in 45-minute discussions. The focus groups were audio recorded but only after all participants approved the recording. Data were then transcribed and subsequently analyzed using qualitative data analysis techniques as described by Guest et al. [16]. The main objective of the analysis was to transform data into findings but, more importantly, to make sense out of it. During the analysis, as a list of ideas emerged, those ideas were grouped based around significant headings to form the concepts. Next, related concepts were aggregated in categories to form the themes that constitute the results. The emerging themes were then examined based on their intensity, depth, and specificity with the research questions, with additional emphasis given to comments that were frequently repeated or refuted by the interviewees. NVIVO 11.0 software was used to analyse the qualitative focus group data. NVIVO is a computer assisted qualitative data analysis package (CAQDAP), settled by QSR International [21]. This software offers a set of functions that support the coding and recovery of text. Another remarkable privilege is that it assists researches to write down memos during the analysis process [22]. In an attempt to conquer reliable and informative data out of the interviews, each single focus group has skillfully created a transcript that was saved in a distinct word processor document (i.e. two documents). This has enabled sustaining fertility of the interviews data. Afterwards, the two documents were imported in NVIVO for reading, analysis and coding. The main objective of the analysis was to transform data into findings, but more importantly was to make a sense out of it. During the analysis, recurring ideas, patterns of beliefs, and salient themes were extracted with relevant quotations that demonstrated support for these themes. The emerging themes were then examined based on their intensity, depth, and specificity with the phenomenon of interest, with additional emphasis given to comments that were frequently repeated or refuted by the interviewees [23]. The results are then presented in a narrative form granting detailed insights into the main issues related to micro note-taking practice.

Since this micro note-taking is still at the evaluation stage, some background information was required, such as language, mobile experience and Twitter experience, to see whether or not these features could influence the generated results. The participants had different levels of experience in using mobile applications as follows: 25% had no experience, 63% had experience of less than 5 years and 13% had experience of more than 5 years. Furthermore, 38% of the total participants were not very familiar with Twitter in particular. The participants were from different backgrounds and English was not the first language of most of them.

III. EXPERIMENT

The main method of data collection for learners' perspectives was focus group interviews. The experiment was conducted at the University of Warwick with the help of 14 learners' studying courses entitled "Cyber security" and "Innovation". The learners' ages ranged between 20 years and 25 years. The only commonality among the participants was that they were part of a community of interest who were following postgraduate courses in the related fields just mentioned. They were expected to have enough experience and exposure to new IT-based note-taking tools to interactively take part and subsequently convey pertinent responses during the discussion. The learners volunteered to take part in the experiment, which was conducted within 45 minutes for each session. The participants in the focus group were divided into two groups, and were of mixed gender comprising 6 males and 8 females. The two sessions of the discussion were moderated by the main researcher.

During the experiment, an average of 14 participants were randomly assigned to one of the note-taking approaches defined as: traditional pen-paper, micro note-taking and electronic Microsoft word where requested to use the different approaches to take notes while viewing the video. The participants were exposed to the different approaches over the experiment time. The note-taking experiment was based on vide played like a lecture. The use of these approaches emphases on the effect of the proposed micro note-taking.

The focus group participants were approached after using a micro note-taking application in the experiment. An open ended approach, which was related to the use of the micro note-taking approach, was conducted. The discussion was kept focused around the proposed micro note-taking application. The research aimed to answer the following questions:

a) What are the positive features of the mobile micro note-taking approach?
b) What are the negative features of the mobile micro note-taking approach?
c) Would you prefer using 140 characters for writing your notes, and why?
d) What are the difficulties you faced when using the mobile micro note-taking application in lectures?
e) Do you think that other learners would find the application appealing, and why?
f) What other features would you recommend to add to the mobile micro note-taking application?

IV. FINDINGS AND INTERPRETATIONS

As mentioned earlier, data were gathered from the focus group interviews and analyzed using a thematic approach [16]. Each theme addresses an issue related to the use of the proposed micro note-taking application and reflects the experience of learners regarding their use of the application. Discussion was centered on these areas in order to ensure coverage of only key areas that were closely related or clearly relevant to the study.

A. Perceptions of positive features of the mobile micro note-taking application

Initially, participants were asked about the positive features they found using the prototype of the mobile micro note-taking application that is described in [11]. The results were consistent with those reported in the current state of the art as in [17], where learners reported as positive features the ease of use and that it is a "handy tool". For example, participant 1 described the proposed micro note-taking application by saying that "*it's simple, no previous experience required, affordable, easily accessible, all have a mobile in class*". Participant 4 also agreed with this by stating that "*there is no previous experience required*". Participant 7 mentioned "*it's an easy tool for note-taking*". Another positive point that emerged from the analysis is that the proposed tool is useful and handy, and participant 3 confirmed this point by stating "*you don't need a paper and pen also there is no need to carry the heavy laptop to start typing, really handy*". Participant 13 affirmed what his colleagues said "*it's simple to your eye, anyone can use it even people who don't have experience*".

Another positive feature is the applicability of using the micro note-taking application for quick revision. This capability has been explicitly expressed in the words of Participant 10, who stated: "*self-revision, jotting down important notes and bringing them before the examination, quick review, revision of any last minute study or some test*". Participant 2 affirmed what his colleagues said: "*I think it's good for revision for a quick review of any last minute study or some test, something like that is good*".

Most people use a mobile device such as a smartphone to support their personal and professional functions [17]. Technology is becoming a ubiquitous part of the academic environment generally and the process of note-taking in particular [18]. Mobile devices can be valuable in academic areas for higher education [17], and the results of a study by Ward and Tatsukawa [19] suggest that taking notes using such a system is feasible. Another study by Motiwalla [20] highlighted the fact that learners liked the ease-of-use and convenience of using mobile applications in learning. Consistently, in this paper, participants also revealed that the main positive feature of the micro note-taking application is that the application is affordable, convenient and accessible. Participant 9 said that: "*it's very affordable and is easily accessible because we all have mobiles, but nowadays mobiles are present everywhere. So like it's affordable; it's the best thing that I've had*". Participant 3 confirmed this point by saying "*mobile micro note-taking is affordable*". As for accessibility, participant 12 stated: "*... read the thing and you can do it anywhere even on the bus or when travelling*". Participant 6 also concurred: "*Because it's mobile, it can be easy to carry wherever you go*", as did participant 14: "*Because it's mobile, it can be easy to carry wherever you go. So I think it's appealing to the young generation because they only use or bring their mobiles everywhere*". These positive features of the micro note-taking application also have been explicitly expressed as Participant 1 stated: "*I think people feel comfortable using phones to take notes these days, and they are easy to carry around rather than the laptop or pen and paper and it's faster to take notes on. So it's easier to capture what you exactly want. I think it could be useful to have something like this. Definitely*".

B. Perceptions of negative features of the mobile micro note-taking application

When the participants were asked about what the limitations of the micro note-taking application are, they reported that, although the application includes many positive features, it does have a number of limitations. These include the small interface size and lack of a usable keypad on some actual smart phones, and also difficulties such as slow typing that can be connected to usability issues (although they had stated earlier that the application is easy to use). Moreover, they suggested that this tool may lead to students being distracted during a lecture and that there are usability issues due to lack of experience.. For example, Participant 7 stated: "*on the device itself, the keyboard is quite small to type actually*". Participant 11 also gave his opinion "*I think because we're not used to typing quickly, I'm speaking for myself, but otherwise it's okay especially I think with the new generation they are quicker in typing*". Similarly, Participant 8 said that: "*because when I concentrate on listening, and I just continue typing, I did not realize that actually the limit is already 140. So, when I look back, actually there's some missing words or sentences already*". Participant 6 found it might be a source of distraction during lectures and expressed these reservations by stating: "*make sure that they take it seriously and they are just not playing around with it*". Participant 13 concurred with this by saying: "*I found I was constantly having to look at what I'm doing so I lost a bit of concentration. That's because it was more distracting*". Only one student, Participant 8, mentioned that the lack of experience about how to use a micro note-taking application could lead to limited use of such application, she mentioned that: "*I think the difficulties I faced just because it's the first time to use it. So, I face a lot of problems and most of my notes wouldn't save because I've just done a mistake, so I didn't save or I just put back and then it's not saved. So I think just because we're not familiar with most of the difficulties*". To overcome this limitation, Participant 6 suggested: "*I think we need to do some kind of an introduction to the system before get to take notes*". Based on these results, we can conclude that unfamiliarity with using the micro note-taking application and Twitter is what leads to such negative outcomes.

C. Perceptions of using 140 characters for writing students' notes

Based on the analysis, two perspectives have emerged when the participants were asked about their preference for using 140 characters for writing their notes. The majority of participants explained that the limited notes of only 140 characters (i.e., similar to Twitter posts) could improve the ability to take short notes that can be easily managed and recalled later. For example, Participant 1 stated that: "*using just 140 characters helps us to think of what we want to write*". Participant 14 was also totally in agreement: "*I was not distracted as there was no option but to take only important points with limited words*". However, a few participants found that the restricted notes of only 140 characters might affect notes in terms of continuity. This concern has been explicitly expressed by Participant 10: "*For me it's the continuity of our notes because it's only 140 characters, so if we write something, you know, the sentence would be hanging*". Therefore, participant 5 suggested: "*... during a lecture I prefer more than 140 characters because during the lecture we just take any notes the lecturer speaks, so we don't have time to think about what is important and what is not – just take any notes*".

According to the findings of this study, it can be said that a 140 character note was a generally useful format for note-taking practice by learners, providing a positive note-taking experience but with some important reservations.

D. Suggestions to improve the mobile micro note-taking application

The participants were asked to share their experience about the micro note-taking application and suggest additional features so that it can be improved. Based on the analysis, Table 1 shows a list of the valuable features and functionalities that have been suggested by participants. All participants' suggestions were taken into consideration in the updated version of the micro note-taking application.

TABLE I. SUGGESTED FEATURES AND FUNCTIONALITIES

Feature	Suggested by
Use visual presentation that represents certain words. So each picture has correlated notes	Participant 5: "*Just make it a bit more appealing because it's very abstract from a point a view and you can use this drag-and-drop thing, like you can give them pictures and this can open up instead of just making it as simple and abstract as ....give them more options, more features and make them on icon thing so they just touch it and a note opens up or, for example, an annotation opens up, or a shape opens up.*"
Provide a feature to organize notes (e.g. folders or according to subjects)	Participant 3: "*I'm not sure if the pictures are already there or not but may be if it would be helpful if you could organize a note in folders or according to subjects because it seems if you have like different subjects, you could organize all the notes in one folders so it will be easy to access – I think this is one thing.*"
Annotate the content itself by providing different shapes based on the type of content. For example, for learner's notes, it is a rectangle, for lecture notes, it is a circle...	Participant 2: "*Basically we're talking about annotating the content itself, because sometimes you need to post somewhere and put a note there. So I think shapes make more sense. Beforehand you can divide the content into shapes and based on shapes we can take notes and annotate that directly on the shape or the subject or the idea within the class, just to making random notes and then putting*

Feature	Suggested by
	them altogether and you might not remember what it was related to. So it more like correlating what notes have been taken with the actual content. That would help a lot"
Provide options to have short notes and long notes	Participant 1: *"May be there should be an option to have short notes and long notes."*
Integrate Web 2.0 features (e.g. sharing, hashtags)	Participants 10 and 12: *"Maybe for sharing. Let's say we have three of us here...then we can share. So maybe it might be the notes that we take."* *"I think may be also having the feature of hashtag. So having hashtag would help you to organize notes so whenever you use this hashtags to retrieve all the notes which have this hashtag so that would maybe useful."*

Table 1 highlighted the features that should be considered to improve the note-taking system. These features are mainly related to the interface and functionalities.

V. CONCLUSION

The main aim of conducting the focus group was to extend the understanding of the learner's experience of using the proposed micro note-taking application, as an approach for note-taking practice in lectures. The findings of this study reflected the perspectives of students regarding their experiences of using such a tool. Positive features, limitations and suggestions for future improvement were identified. Based on the analysis, positive features of the micro note-taking application include: ease of use, the applicability of using the application for quick revision, improved access everywhere, any time (i.e., ubiquity) and affordability. However, as with all applications, the micro note-taking application is not free from limitations, which include: usability issues, learners' distraction during lectures, and lack of experience regarding how to use the application. The limitations of the current application provide opportunities for further improvements, and students suggested valuable functionalities that could be added to improve the proposed tool. These include: integrating Web 2.0 features such as sharing and hashtags, providing options to have short notes and long notes, providing a feature to organize notes into folders, and visually presenting notes in symbols. The proposed approach discussed qualitatively through the paper suggested an innovative approach for note-taking. The findings of this research add value to the current state of the art concerned with connecting mobile learning with the social feature of limiting the note taking to 140 characters using Twitter like states. This finding would have an impact on the academic areas to consider applying modern technologies for the current learners' age and facilitating their learning. However, as with all studies, this study is not free of limitations. The major limitation is derived from the sample size and the geographical location of the sample which is limited to only 14 participants located in the UK.

REFERENCES

[1] M. Sharples, "Big issues in mobile learning", Workshop by the Kaleidscope Network of Excellence Mobile Learning Initiative, 2006, pp.1-35.

[2] R. Godwin-Jones, "Emerging technologies mobile for apps language learning and technlogy", in Language Learning & Technology, vol. 15, 2011, pp. 2-11.

[3] J. Hartley and S. Marshall, "On notes and notetaking", Higher Education Quarterly, vol. 28, 1974, pp. 225-235, doi: 10.1111/j.1468-2273.1974.

[4] J. C. Moore, "Cueing for selective notetaking", Journal of Experimental Education, vol. 34, 1968, pp. 69-72, doi:10.1080/00220973.1968.11011076

[5] J. Hartley and I.K. Davies, " Note-taking: a critical review", Programmed Learning and Educational Technology, vol. 15, 1978, pp. 207-224, doi:10.1080/0033039780150305

[6] A. Tyma, "Connecting with what is out there!: using Twitter in the large lecture", Communication Teacher, vol. 52, 2011, pp. 175-181, doi: 10.1080/17404622.2011.579911

[7] E. Scornavacca, S. Huff and S. Marshall, "Mobile phones in the classroom: if you can't beat them, join them," Communication of the ACM, vol. 52, 2009, pp. 142-146, doi:10.1145/1498765.1498803.

[8] Fox, B. and Varadarajan, R., "Use of Twitter to encourage interaction in a multi-campus pharmacy management course," American Journal of Pharmaceutical Education, vol. 75, 2011, pp. 1-8.

[9] J.L. Hartman and J. McCambridge, "Optimizing millennials' communication styles," Business Communication Quarterly, vol. 74, 2011, pp. 22-44, 1080-5699

[10] I.D. Cherney, "The effects of active learning on studets' memories for course content," Active Learning in Higher Education,vol.9,2008,pp.152-171,doi: 10.1177/1469787408090841

[11] M.S. Al Zaidi, M.S. Joy and J.E. Sinclair, "Micro notes application for education: a proposed mobile micro note-taking architecture, in 13th European conference on e-learning (ECEL 2014), 2014, pp. 618-623.

[12] A.M. Kaplan and M. Haenlain, "Users of the world, unite! The challenges and opportunities of social media", Business Horizons, vol. 53, 2009, pp. 59-68, doi:10-1016/j.bushor.2009.09.003.

[13] M.S. Al-Zaidi, M.S. Joy and J.E. Sinclair, "Exploring the use of micro note-taking with social interaction features for Education," in International conference on Education and New Learning Technologies (EDULEARN 13),2013, pp. 6098-6106.

[14] A. Gibbs, "Focus groups,", Social Research Update, 1997, pp.1-8,[retrieved:Jan,2016], http://www.soc.surrey.ac.uk/sru/SRU19.html

[15] D.W. Stewart and P.N. Shamdasani, "Focus groups: theory and practice", 3rd ed., SAGE publication, 2015.

[16] G. Guest, K.M. MacQueen and E.E. Namey, "Applied thematic analysis", SAGE publications, 2011.

[17] A. Schepman, F. Rodway, C. Beattie and J. Lambert, "An observation study of undergraduate students' adoption of (mobile) note-taking software", Computers in Human Behavior, vol. 28, March 2012, pp. 308-317, doi: 10.1016/j.chb.2011.09.014.

[18] Y. Remier, E. Brimhall, C. Cao and K. O'Reilly, "Empirical user studies inform the design of an e-notetaking and information assimilation system for students in higher education", Computers and Education, vol. 52, May 2008, pp. 893-913. doi:10.1016/j.compedu.2008.12.013.

[19] N. Ward and H. Tatsukawa, " Software for taking notes in class", IEEE Frontiers in Education, vol. 3, pp. 2-8, 2003 [33rd Annual conf.] doi: 10.1109/FIE.2003.1265956.

[20] F. Motiwalla, "Mobile learning: a framework and evaluation," Computers and Education, vol. 49, Nov. 2007, pp. 581-596,doi: 10.1016/j.compedu.2005. 10.011.

[21] P. Bazeley, P. and L. Richards, " The Nvivo Qualitative Project Book", London: Sage Publications, 2000, pp.1-195.

[22] G. Gibbs," Qualitative Data Analysis: Explorations with Nvivo", London: Open University Press, 2002,pp.83-218.

[23] C. Marshall and G. Rossman, "Designing Qualitative Research ",5th Eds. London: Sage Publications, 2010, pp.205-227.

Assessing eLearning for Taking up Social Challenges

A Fitness Online Course for Senior Citizens

Agathe Merceron, Ilona Buchem, Jörn Kreutel
Department Computer Science and Media
Beuth University of Applied Sciences
Berlin, Germany
e-mail:{merceron,buchen,kreutel}@beuth-hochschule.de

Marten Haesner, Anika Steinert
Geriatrics research group, Charité
Universitätsmedizin Berlin
Berlin, Germany
e-mail:{marten.haesner,anika.steinert}@charité.de

Abstract—**In this paper, we investigate whether a novel kind of online course on fitness designed to take into account specificities of elderly people and integrating wearable trackers can motivate senior citizens to exercise more in a sound way and help improve their physical condition. The design principles of the online course including content, gamification elements and wearable fitness trackers are described, as well as a first evaluation with 20 participants. The results of the analysis of the users' interactions are promising.**

Keywords- healthy ageing; senior citizens; online course; wearable activity tracker; gamification.

I. INTRODUCTION

In many western countries, the population is ageing. This fact poses several challenges to the society. One of these challenges is to keep senior citizens in good health as long as possible. It is known that social interaction and sufficient physical activity have a positive influence on health. For example, the longitudinal creativity and ageing study by Cohen et al. [1] revealed positive effect of community-based interventions on improved ratings of physical health, reduced medication use, improved social interactions and less loneliness, and even fewer health problems compared to the control group. Further research [2][3] shows that even 30 minutes of daily moderate-intensity physical activity may significantly reduce the risk of chronic diseases. Recent research also suggests that digital technologies can be used with benefits with elderly people when they are properly designed, as shown by Ijsselsteijn et al. [4]. The work by Assad et al. [5] reports that well-designed games have a positive influence on Parkinson's disease patients. Furthermore, the proportion of senior citizens who use digital technologies has been growing worldwide. Duplàa et al. [6] report that from 1208 persons aged 55 or more declaring playing games in Canada about half of them answered that they also play digital games. The study by Ledger and McCaffrey [7] shows that the percentage of persons tracking fitness data through a smartphone has grown rapidly during the last two years.

The aim of the fMOOC (fitness Massive Open Online Course) project is to assess the use of e-learning and mobile devices to take up the social challenge of healthy ageing. More specifically, its aim is to develop an online course on fitness that integrates wearable activity trackers for senior citizens in such a way that these two aspects, social interaction and enhanced physical activity, are addressed. This kind of approach is novel; an online-course targeting senior citizens and integrating wearable activity trackers has not been realized so far. The targeted learners are older citizens who have some familiarity with information technology and are in relatively good health, though they might have some minor impairment, but who could improve their physical condition by doing more exercises and moving more daily. As exposed in Buchem et al. [8], the conceptual design of the fMOOC course includes digital content on weekly physical exercises and the integration of wearable activity trackers connected to the course to help seniors engage in physical activities. The conceptual design includes also forums for sharing and commenting, and for community-based exercises to enhance social engagement and a sense of belonging together of senior participants. Community-based exercises should allow for various learning and physical training scenarios, such as a group-walk for participants living in the same neighbourhood. After the walk, participants should be able to synchronize their wearable devices, so as to store the number of steps recorded by the system. Therefore, the course has to be accessible from mobile devices, such as smartphones. Furthermore, inspired by the work of Ijsselsteijn et al. [4] gamification elements are also part of the conceptual design to support and foster user engagement, as argued by Buchem et al. [9]. Gamification is the use of elements normally found in games like rewards or badges in another context like here in a learning context. In the spirit of agile development and following principles exposed Martinez-Maldonado et al. [10] to support learners better, specific user requirements were designed with potential senior users aged 65+ and tested iteratively. The online course has been tested with 20 senior participants.

This contribution presents the online course and its implementation in section II. The context of the evaluation is given in section III, which is followed by the analysis of the users' digital interactions in section IV. Section V concludes with discussion and future works.

II. THE ONLINE COURSE

Essentially, the online course provides to participants physical training for four weeks, communication forums,

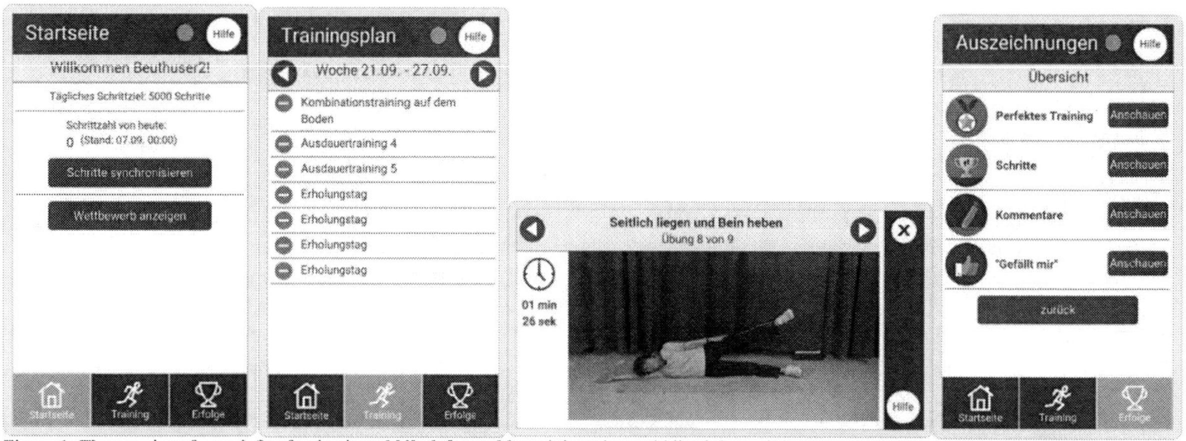

Figure 1. The user interface – left: after log in; middle-left: weekly training plan; middle-right: training-exercise; right: badges.

as well as an overview of their achievements. Participants are expected to wear an activity tracker that counts the steps they walk, presently the tracker Vivofit from Garmin [11].

The instructional design of fMOOC combines elements of Online learning with elements of gamification and principles of seamless learning. The fMOOC architecture integrates wearables, mobile and learning technologies to capture and share fitness data and learning/training content with other senior learners. The fMOOC can be accessed via the "fMOOC App" using a laptop, a tablet or a mobile phone phone phone. The fMOOC software includes a gamification service to incorporate rewards and playful elements in the course, including badges and battles, as argued by Buchem et al. [8][9]. The user interface has been designed to take into account specificities of older people, which includes among others simple vocabulary, short texts, big buttons and fonts, as exposed by Kurniawan and Zaphiris[12]. We first explain the course as a learner sees it, and then describe how the system has been implemented

A. Learner View

Fig. 1 left shows the screen that a learner sees right after logging in. At the top right of the screen, the help button (Hilfe) gives a hotline number where to call in case of problems. Below, the number of steps a learner is expected to walk daily is reminded, 5000 steps (5000 Schritte) and the number of steps already walked in the current day (Schrittzahl von heute:) is shown. The button synchronize your steps (Schritte synchronisieren) reminds participants to synchronize their tracker, so that the fMOOC system pulls their data from the Garmin host. For synchronization, a mobile application of the provider of the wearable activity tracker has to be installed on the smartphone and needs to run in the background. A user has to hold his/her tracker near enough to his/her smartphone and press the "synchronize" button. The transmission is automatic, but can last a few seconds. When the transmission is successful, the number of steps walked in the current day is almost immediately updated in the fMOOC system and displayed on the start view. The button show battle (Wettbewerb anzeigen) is to show the current status of the battle; this gamification element will be explained below. The three buttons at the bottom are always visible except when a user is in the process of completing a training day. The home button (Startseite) allows the user to come back to this view anytime. The button Training gives access to the training plans, while the button Achievements (Erfolge) allows the user to check her/his achievements.

The physical training has been developed according to medical recommendations as exposed in [13]. In particular, training begins with a warming up exercise and finishes with a cool down exercise. Further, endurance, strength and flexibility exercises are mixed properly. Each week is made up of three training days and four rest days (Erholungstag), as participants should not over-exercise; the interface shows a "–" in front of each day which is not completed. Fig. 1 middle-left shows an overview of the training plan at the beginning of a week. A learner can complete the training days in the order he/she wants. The intensity of the exercises vary as to fit 3 levels of fitness. Each exercise is explained with a sequence of 2-3 photos or a video of 1-2 minutes, and 1-2 lines of instructions. The user interface follows known principles of web navigation, see for instance [14], to guide users through the different exercises till the training is finished, then to make users rate the training and finally comment it. Participants can complete the training at their own pace. After completing the last exercise, they touch the finish button. At that point, the system records that this training has been performed with a timestamp. The next screen invites participants to rate how s/he feels and how s/he liked the training. The next screen invites participants to write a feedback on the training, to read / answer messages of others and to give "likes" to feedbacks of others.

To support engagement and motivation, the instructional design integrates gamification elements in the form of badges and battles. Participants can earn four kinds of badges, and in each category they can earn four badges:

A *"training" badge* can be earned at the end of each week if participants have accomplished a perfect training, doing every single training day of the week and leaving a rest day between two consecutive training days. Contrasting with the "step" badge below, there is no partial reward. A *"step" badge*, to encourage movement every day, can be earned at the end of each week as well. A step badge comes in three colors: bronze, silver and gold. A bronze badge is earned if the learner has walked at least 5000 steps 5 days of the week, a silver badge for at least 5000 steps 6 days and the gold badge for at least 5000 steps each single day of the week. The four *"comment" badges* can be earned any time as soon as a learner has written enough messages in some discussion thread (each training day has its own thread). The first badge goes with 2 messages written, the second with 4, the third with 6 and the last badge with 8 messages written. Similarly, four *"like" badges* can be earned anytime as soon as a participant has received enough likes from others on his/her messages. The first badge goes with 3 likes, the second with 6, the third with 9 and the last with 12.

Battles have been designed as a group competition, presently between female and male users, based on the number of steps walked by the whole group. As soon as some user has synchronized her/his tracker, the status of the battle is updated too. Participants can check their achievements anytime. The design follows the principle "overview first, details on demand" of Schneiderman [15]. With the show steps button (Schritte anzeigen) a user can see how many steps s/he has walked during the current day, or during the current week or since the beginning of the course by touching the corresponding button for these details. With the show battle button (Wettbewerb anzeigen) users can check which group currently leads. Fig. 1 right shows 4 badges: perfect training (Perfektes Training), steps (Schritte), posts (Kommentare) and like (Gefällt mir). By pressing the corresponding look (Anschauen) button, the four badges of that category are shown. The background colour indicates for each badge whether the user has already earned it or not, or whether the badge is in progress. By pressing an individual badge, learners can get details: how much they still need to do to earn that badge.

B. *Implementation*

The fMOOC course has been implemented as a Web application in responsive design using the platform Moodle as backend to store the content (training days) and to provide the forums, see Fig. 2 for the overall architecture.

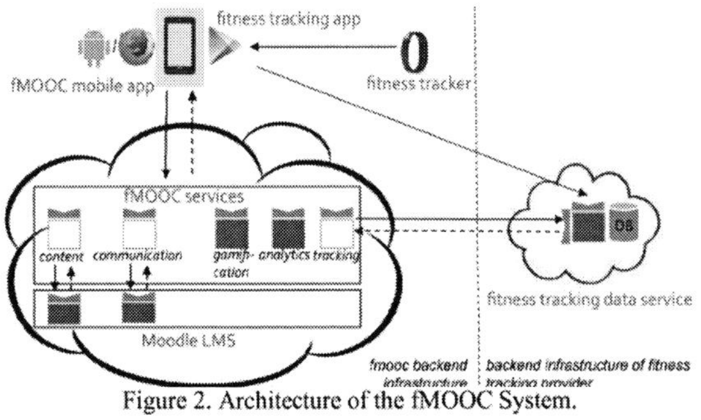

Figure 2. Architecture of the fMOOC System.

As already mentioned, the design of the user interface has adopted an agile methodology, testing most of the elements with senior users before implementation. In order to allow for a potentially "massive" opening of the fMOOC system beyond the scope of the user group envisaged in the pilot study, the user interface was developed as a mobile web application based on recent HTML5 standards [16]. It can be run on any browser installed on a reasonably modern smartphone regardless of whether it uses Android, iOS or Windows as an operating system. As for the backend components of the system, the application is currently deployed on a single server, but the overall architecture was designed according to the stateless paradigm of a RESTful architecture [17], which provides a solid basis for scalability.

As for the tracking service provider, the current version of the fMOOC system has only been integrated with the service of Garmin so far, which had been selected at the beginning of the project given the usability requirements of the user group. An agreement with Garmin allowed access to its backend service infrastructure through a specific connector. As structure and access to data collected by fitness trackers has not been subject to industry standardisation so far, commercial activity trackers and services are relatively "closed" system infrastructures, and providers differ with respect to how access may be realised by third party systems like fMOOC. For this reason, the fMOOC system has been designed as independent of any particular tracking provider, where different providers can be integrated by implementing a backend-side connector to the particular tracking service. Hence, also with regard to the tracking service, openness of the fMOOC system has principally been foreseen.

III. Context of the Evaluation

The evaluation has been conducted in a blended learning approach consisting of two face-to-face meetings separated by the four weeks online course. Twenty volunteers not possessing any wearable activity tracker have been recruited, 10 men and 10 women aged 62 to 75.

During the first face-to-face meeting, participants were introduced to the whole course. They received a properly installed smartphone and an activity tracker each. Learners were introduced to smartphones, had a chance to try the course, the activity tracker and the synchronization procedure. Their fitness level was determined so that they would receive the proper level of exercises, and their physical condition recorded. This included, among others, measuring balance ability, strength, the distance they can walk in 6 minutes and the percentage of body fat. During the second face-to-face meeting, the physical condition of the users has been recorded again. Further, participants filled anonymously a questionnaire regarding their overall experience with the course.

IV. Analysis of the Digital User Interactions

The usage of the interface has been analyzed using the piwik web analytics tool [18]. First, we analyse logging in the App and synchronisation, then the physical activities through training and steps badges and the rating of the trainings, then the social activity through the comment and like badges and finally how often users have consulted their achievements.

A. Logging in the Web App and Synchronisation

A learner eager to complete all physical activities of the course should log in at least once every day to synchronize the activity tracker, and possibly more on a training day. Table I shows how often users have logged in the App and how often they have touched the synchronize button during the 4 weeks. The large standard deviations indicate that users differ greatly; a closer look at the data gives two outliers: one with 90 log in and one with 702 synchronisation actions. An inspection of the weekly data shows that two users out of the 20 gave up after two weeks, which means nobody gave up right at the beginning of the course. The high number of synchronize interactions compared with log in might indicate some problem when synchronizing the activity tracker. This is confirmed when inspecting the sequential actions of individual visitors' log files: quite often the synchronize button is pressed twice in a row, or alternate with the help button.

TABLE I. LOGGING IN THE WEBAPP AND SYNCHRONISATION

	average	std
Log in	44	21
Synchronization	129	152.12

The help button has been pressed 100 times during the 4 weeks, 40 times during the first 3 days and 62 times during the first week. The hotline has been called 32 times by 16 users, including the numerous calls by one user for whom some setting needed to be redone. These interactions indicate some usability issues with the synchronisation of the activity tracker, which made users feel insecure in the first week of the course.

B. Physical Activity

The badges earned in the category "training" and "steps" assess whether participants have accomplished the training properly and included enough movement in their daily life.

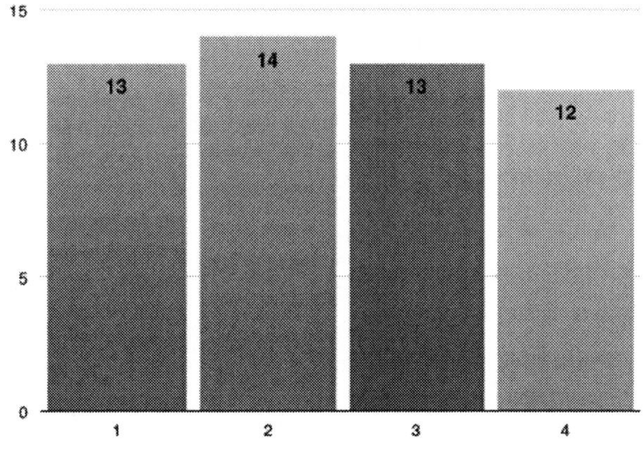

Figure 3. Number of learners who earned a "training" badge; the x-axis shows the weeks.

The histogram Fig. 3 shows that the majority of the users have earned a "training" badge each week. Taking into account that 2 users abandoned after 2 weeks, 68.4% of the "training" badges have been earned. Most of the users rated the training after completing it, thus following the design adopted for the interface. In total, 201 ratings were given for each of the two questions: "how do you feel after training" and "how did you like the training?". Ratings were mostly positive: 69.15% of the wellbeing-ratings was "great" and 64.7% of the liking-ratings was 3 or 4, see Fig. 4.

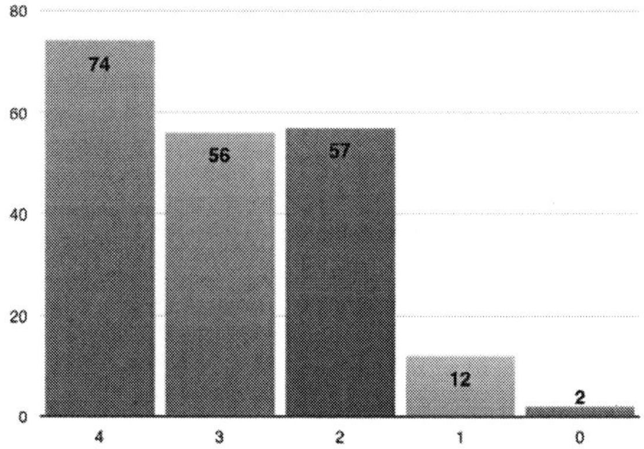

Figure 4. Liking rating given: 4 is the best, 0 the worst.

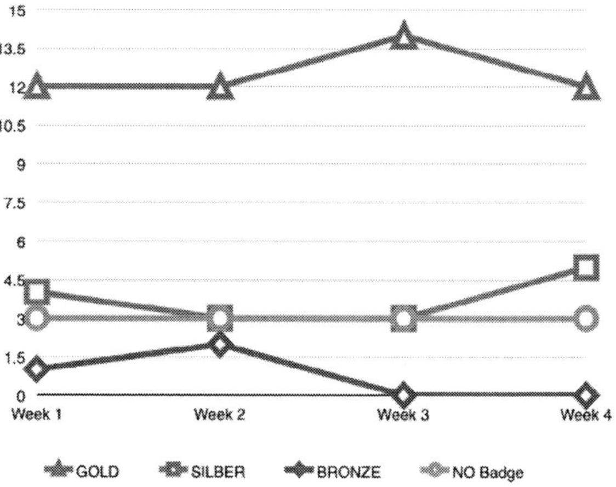

Figure 5. Number of learners who earned "step" badges.

Taking the training days perspective and counting how many stars each training has received, one cannot notice any training that stands out as particularly excellent or bad: the average goes from 2.44 till 3.4 for the liking-rating, and from 1.64 to 1.72 for the wellbeing-rating (scale 2, best, to 0, worst).

The majority of the users have earned a "step" badge each week, which results in 89.5% of the badges earned, when taking into account that two users abandoned after week 2 and aggregating all colors. The flat curve of Fig. 5 shows that each week three participants did not achieve 5000 steps on at least five days. These figures include the two participants who abandoned. Aggregating training and step badges shows that 19 participants earned a training badge or a step badge or both in the first week.

C. Social Interactions

The course has been designed to encourage social interactions by prompting feedback in the form of comments and likes after the completion of each training.

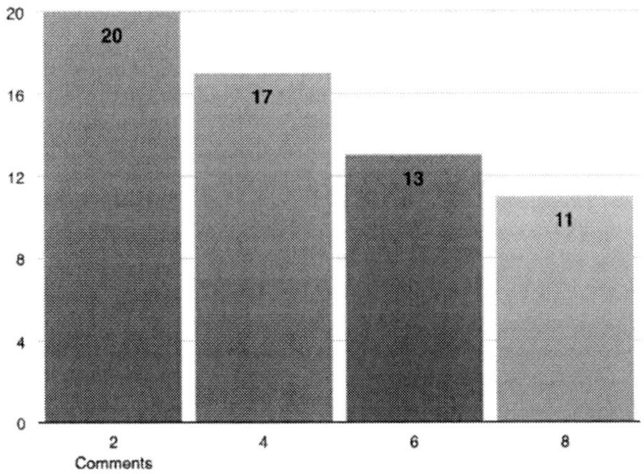

Figure 6. Number of learners who earned "comment" badges.

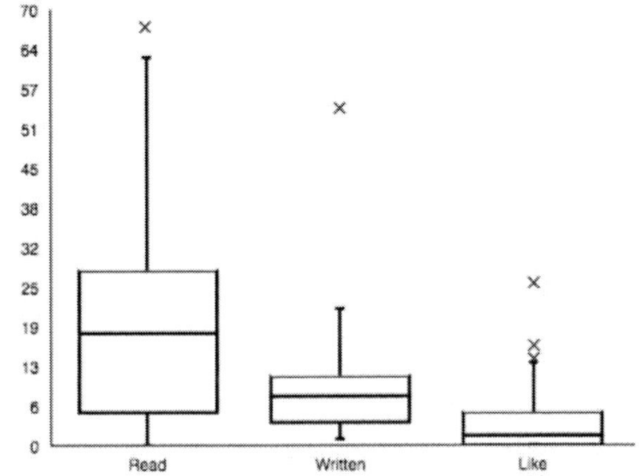

Figure 7. From left: number of read and written messages and number of likes given.

Fig. 6 shows that every user has written in some discussion thread, as 20 badges for writing at least two comments have been earned; the numbers on the horizontal axis: 2, 4, 6 and 8, are the numbers of comments a learner has to write to earn the corresponding badge. All together 76.25% of the "comment" badges have been earned. Fig. 6 shows also that only 11 participants have written 8 comments or more, which suggests that participants differ in their social interactions. This is confirmed by the box plots of Fig. 7 that show the number of times users have touched the read button to read a message, the write button to send a message, and the number of times they have given a like to a message. One finds again well known behaviors also observed Cobo et al. [19] or Merceron [20] in online courses: participants read more than they write, and a few outliers write more than the majority. Users have not given many "likes". As a consequence, less learners have earned "like" badges resulting in only 21.25% of the "like" badges being earned.

D. Consulting Achievements

The systemic gamification design has been implemented through two main elements: badges and a battle. How often have users looked at the current state of the battle or at their badges? Here too, behaviors vary greatly. With a median of 60, battle is the gamification element which has been the most consulted. These high figures are confirmed when analyzing the views that are accessed right after the start view of the app: the battle view has the highest proportion of moves, followed by the training view, where users can start their training, followed by the achievement view, where users can look at the badges they have earned, see Fig. 1 left. Remarkably, this pattern stays stable in each of the four training weeks.

The medians for consulting the badges lie around 10 with a peak of 17 (Training) and a depression of 6 (Steps). This indicates that 50% of the users have consulted their badges about 2 times a week on average. These figures suggest that participants have been interested in playing the game of the battle. They have appreciated the other badges, but might not have been eager to collect them.

V. Discussion and Conclusion

The analysis of the digital interactions has shown that users could log in, synchronize and use the fMOOC App during the four weeks. The two users who abandoned gave the following explanation: one found the training exercises too laborious, and the other lost interest. Therefore, one can conclude that the online course on a smartphone is easy to use. This has been confirmed by the interview of the second face-to-face meeting: the majority rated the App as easy to use. The synchronization procedure has posed some problems, as the analysis of the interaction data has shown. It has been confirmed by the calls received on the hot line: the worries mainly concerned synchronization. A better feedback in the App in case of an unsuccessful pulling of the data is necessary. However, one should also notice that after the first week users have learned to adjust.

Most of the users have learned to train properly and to include a minimum of 5000 steps in their daily life, as they have earned the corresponding badges. Inspecting the daily number of steps, one notices big differences between learners. This suggests replacing the common goal of 5000 steps by a personalized goal to be adapted each week.

The training proposed in the course is effective. Indeed, the physical condition check during the two face-to-face meetings has shown that all users who completed the course improved their physical condition and the improvement was statistically significant as shown by Steinert et al. [21]. Further, users reported that they felt fitter after the course.

The gamification elements have been introduced to support motivation and engagement of users. Users have consulted their achievements regularly, though they have consulted the battle most. During the second face-to-face meeting, participants confirmed that the battle was exciting, and indicated a moderate interest in the other badges, their main interest being to complete the physical activities.

Summarizing, the analysis of the interaction data enriched with the answers of the users during the second face-to-face meeting and the pre- and posttests concerning physical condition shows that the fitness online course provides an enjoyable user experience, that participants have learned how to exercise more in a sound manner and that the health-related goal is met, as participants who completed the course have an improved physical condition.

A future work is to run this course massively and openly. This slightly changes the targeted population, as participants will be expected to have their own activity tracker but not necessarily a smartphone, as the course can run on a personal computer. A digital introduction and physical condition check will be needed, to replace the two face-to-face meetings of the evaluation. An enhancement that is highly desirable is to develop connectors for other tracking providers, in order not to be limited to wearable activity trackers from Garmin. Though there is no technical difficulty to implement this enhancement, since the present system architecture has been designed to allow for it, the realization might be tedious because there is no standard. Further, with an increased number of learners, the conditions to earn comments and like badges need to be revised.

ACKNOWLEDGMENT

We thank F. Dubois, E. Manthey, C. Guder, J. Fuhrmann, A. Lebedeva for their contribution to the realization of the fMOOC system, and the participants of the evaluation. The German Federal Ministry of Education and Research supports the fMOOC project (16SV7100).

REFERENCES

[1] G. D. Cohen et al. "The impact of professionally conducted cultural programs on the physical health, mental health, and social functioning of older adults", Gerontologist, 46, pp. 726–734, 2006.

[2] C. Lister, J. West, B. Cannon, T. Sax and D. Brodegard, "Just a fad? Gamification in health and fitness apps." Journal of Medical Internet Research Serious Games, vol. 2 (2):e9 Aug. 2014, doi: 10.2196/games.3413.

[3] EU Physical Activity Guidelines, "Recommended Policy Actions in Support of Health-Enhancing Physical Activity", EU Working Group Sport & Health, 2008. URL: http://ec.europa.eu/sport/library/policy documents/eu-physical-activity-guidelines-2008_en.pdf retrieved: 03, 2016.

[4] W. Ijsselsteijn, HH. Nap, Y. de Kort and K. Poels, "Digital Game design for Elderly Users", Proceedings of the 2007 Conference of Future Play, Future Play'07. ACM, Nov. 2007, pp. 17-22, doi:10.1145/1328202.1328206.

[5] O. Assad et al. "Motion-Based Games for Parkinson's Disease Patients", Proceedings oft he 10th International Conference on Entertainment Computing ICEC 2011 (Vancouver, Canada, October 5-8) LNCS 6972, Springer Verlag, Oct. 2011, pp. 47-58.

[6] E. Duplàa, E. Taiwo, D. Kaufman, L. Sauvé and L. Renaud, "digital games as TEL Systems for Canadian seniors: what uses, what benefits?" ("Des jeux numériques comme EIAH pour les ainés canadiens : quels usages et quels bénéfices ?"), Proceedings of the 7th Conference sur les environnements Informatiques pour l'Apprentissage Humain, EIAH'2015, June 2015, pp. 246-257. ISBN: **978-2-9552774-0-9**

[7] D. Ledger and D. McCaffrey, "Inside Wearables How the Science of Human Behavior Change Offers the Secret to Long-Term Engagement", Endeavour Partners LLC, 2014, http://endeavourpartners.net/assets/Endeavour-Partners-Wearables-White-Paper-20141.pdf retrieved: 03, 2016.

[8] I. Buchem, A. Merceron, J. Kreutel, M. Haesner and A. Steinert, "Designing for User Engagement in Wearable Enhanced Learning for Health Ageing", Proceedings of the iLRN (immersive Learning Research Network) Conference 2015, IOS Press, July 2015, pp. 314-324.

[9] I. Buchem, A. Merceron, J. Kreutel, M. Haesner and A. Steinert, "Gamification Designs in Wearable Enhanced Learning for Health Ageing", Proceedings of the IMLC (immersive Learning Research Network) Conference 2015, IEEE, Nov. 2015, pp. 9-15, doi: 10.1109/IMCTL.2015.7359545

[10] R. Martinez-Maldonado et al. "The LATUX Workflow: Designing and Deploying Awareness Tools in Technology-Enabled Learning", Proceedings of the 5th International Conference on Learning Analytics and Knowledge (LAK15), ACM, March 2015, pp. 1-10. http://dx.doi.org/10.1145/2723576.2723583

[11] Garmin Vivofit http://sites.garmin.com/en-US/vivo/vivofit retrieved: 03, 2016.

[12] S. Kurniawan and P. Zaphiris, „Research-Derived Web Design Guidelines for Older People", Proceedings of Seventh International ACM SIGACCESS Conference on Computers and Accessibility 2005 (ASSETS' 05), pp.129–135.

[13] K. Hottenrott and G. Neumann, „Science of training: a guide in 14 lessons" („Trainingswissenschaft: Ein Lehrbuch in 14 Lektionen"), Auflage: 1., Auflage. Ed. Meyer & Meyer Sport, Germany, 2010.

[14] M. Pearrow, "Web Site Usability Handbook", Internet Series, Thomson, 2006.

[15] B. Scheiderman, "The Eyes Have It: A Task by Data Type Taxonomy for Information Visualizations", Proceedings of the 1996 Symposium on Visual Languages VL'96, IEEE Press, Sept. 1996, pp. 336 – 343.

[16] World Wide Web Consortium, "HTML5 – A vocabulary and associated APIs for HTML and XHTML", W3C Recommendation, 2014, http://www.w3.org/TR/html5/ retrieved: 03, 2016.

[17] R. T. Fielding, "Architectural styles and the design of network-based software architectures", Doctoral dissertation, University of California, Irvine, 2000.

[18] Piwik. http://piwik.org/ retrieved: 03, 2016.

[19] G. Cobo et al. "Using agglomerative hierarchical clustering to model learner participation profiles in online discussion forums", Proceedings of the 2nd International Conference on Learning Analytics and Knowledge. (LAK12), ACM, May 2012, pp. 248-251. DOI=http://doi.acm.org/10.1145/2330601.2330660.

[20] A. Merceron, "Connecting Analysis of Speech Acts and Performance Analysis – An Initial Study", Proceedings of the Workshops at the LAK14 Conference, Workshop 3: Computational Approaches to Connecting Levels of Analysis in Networked Learning Communities, co-located with 4th International Conference on Learning Analytics and Knowledge (LAK14), March 2014, pp. 24-28. ISSN 1613-00

[21] A. Steinert, I. Buchem, A. Merceron, J. Kreutel and M. Haesner "A novel fitness system for older adults, combining a fitness tracker with gamification elements – the pilot study fMOOC@Home. Submitted. 2016.

The Smart Learning Approach

A mobile Learning Companion Application

Christopher Krauss[1], Agathe Merceron[2], Truong-Sinh An[2], Miggi Zwicklbauer[1], Stefan Arbanowski[1]

[1] Fraunhofer FOKUS
Kaiserin-Augusta-Allee 31, 10589 Berlin, Germany
email: {forename}.{lastname}@fokus.fraunhofer.de

[2] Beuth Hochschule für Technik Berlin
Luxemburger Str. 10, 13353 Berlin, Germany
email: {lastname}@beuth-hochschule.de

Abstract— **The aim of the ongoing research project "Smart Learning in Vocational Training" is to introduce a novel mobile Learning Companion App in order to support a blended-learning approach in the energy consultant training. Thereby, students can keep track of their individual predicted knowledge level on different learning objects at every point in time and get personalized learning recommendations based on the determined learning need value. Moreover, teachers make use of Learning Analytics in order to get an overview of students' progress and so, be aware of possible weaknesses. This work in progress paper introduces the main ideas of the overall architecture and technical concepts in that project.**

Keywords-Smart Learning; Learning Companion; Recommendation Engine; Learning Analytics.

I. INTRODUCTION

Career advancement requires employees to continuously update their skills and, in many cases, to document their up-to-date knowledge with a certificate. In Germany, the Chamber of Crafts provides numerous vocational trainings that lead to the obtainment of a certificate. Trainees are full-time working professionals. Till now most of the trainings are fully face-to-face. The aim of the project "Smart Learning in Vocational Training" [1] is to introduce a blended-learning approach in the energy consultant training. Learning material is being currently structured and developed using different digital media: texts, animations, screencasts, videos, etc. During face-to-face phases trainees learn hands-on with a professional. To prepare and to review face-to-face learning, they can access online what they need when they need it with the help of a novel mobile web application called the Learning Companion App (LCA).

LCA provides trainees with access to learning materials and stores user interactions according to an opt-in procedure. In that respect, it is similar to a learning management system (LMS) that can also run on desktops or mobile devices. However, LCA makes use of a set of server-side software components. The full system integrates a recommendation engine and a learning analytics module. Based on the stored interactions and making use of the recommendation engine, LCA shows trainees their progress and recommends them learning material after calculating their current learning need. This feature of actively guiding learners in their learning through the learning material by means of recommendations distinguishes LCA from common LMS. A learning analytics module is being developed for instructors/ instructional designers. As LMS do, LCA differentiates between users according to their role. Instructors can use LCA to access dashboards that provide them with an overview of learners' progress. Thus, before face-to-face meetings for example, instructors can review the advancement of trainees and adapt their teaching. Other dashboards show the progress of learners when completing self-estimation of learning objectives before and after completing a learning unit. These dashboards, also accessible through LCA, are useful for instructional designers to judge and, possibly, review the quality of learning objects (LO).

This paper is organized as follows: Section II introduces related work on recommendation techniques and analytics for education. Section III explains the overall architecture of the currently implemented components and Section IV focuses especially on the Learning Companion App and the underlying techniques, recommendation and learning analytics modules. The paper concludes with a short summary and an outlook on the planned evaluations.

II. RELATED WORK

Many modern web services, such as movie portals and e-commerce services, but also online learning courses, offer a vast amount of items. So, users quite often lose the overview and get buried in information. A recommendation engine aims at identifying the most relevant items for a specific user that fit his/ her individual needs and thus, makes his/ her interaction on that web service more efficient.

Manouselis et al. describe learning and recommending learning objects in a digital environment, such as in Mobile, Hybrid and On-line Learning, as "an effort that takes more time and interactions compared to a commercial transaction. Learners rarely achieve a final end state after a fixed time. Instead of buying a product and then owning it, learners achieve different levels of competences that have various levels in different domains" [2]. The learner shall find appropriate content for the preparation of a lesson in order to: 1) Be motivated, 2) Recall existing knowledge and 3) Illustrate, visualize and represent new concepts and information [2]. Moreover, recommender systems in On-line Learning can also be used for actual teaching as well as knowledge evaluation and assessment. In a closed corpus, such as a course, students have to learn all relevant objects in order to pass the final exam, no matter if they are interested in it or not.

Therefore, recommendation engines shall also respect the intrinsic and extrinsic motivation of students. The "Moodle Recommender System" [3] showed the significant role of learning paths and completion rates of learning objects that are of interest for recommender systems to assist other learners. In [4], Pelanek et al. evaluated the closed correlation between multidimensional student skills and the timing of problem solving in intelligent tutoring systems that is "useful for automatic problem selection and recommendation in intelligent tutoring systems and for providing feedback to students, teachers, or authors of educational materials" [4]. Manouselis et al. listed an existing set of learning recommenders, but more than half of these systems were still at a concept or prototyping level [2]. Only 10 of the listed systems have been evaluated with real participants and most of the systems focus on past user behavior or on preferences and interests in order to predict new learning content. Unfortunately, it seems that in the area of mobile and online learning, no recommender system covers the time aspect of changing knowledge levels - even though it seems to have great impact. LCA will continuously track the learning behavior of individual users over the whole course period, forecast there learning need on specific LOs at every point in time and recommend appropriate learning objects.

Learning dashboards to support teachers in different teaching contexts have been proposed by different authors. All dashboards provide some form of visual summary of the use of learning materials by learners [5][6]. The visual summary proposed in [6] is particularly interesting: All interactive exercises and questions in the course have been tagged with learning objectives. Based on students' performance the Learning Dashboard provides instructors with an overview of all learning objectives represented by a bar each. The proportion of green, yellow and red in the bar reflects the proportion in the class; the grey portion of the bar shows students with too little activity to enable a classification of their performance. As argued in [8] it is essential to establish a dialogue with future users of dashboards while designing them. Adopting such a user-centered approach and re-using analyses developed in the LeMo tool [6] dashboards are being developed that adapt elements of the overview proposed in [6] to the bigger variety of learning objects present in LCA.

III. ARCHITECTURE

One focus of the Smart Learning project is to provide a reusable generic infrastructure for various users with different client devices, for different courses covering several topics - not restricted to institutions like chamber of crafts, but also usable by universities and adult education centers. While users are still managed in the LMS, learning objects are stored only once and can be shared by and accessed from various learning management systems.

Figure 1 illustrates the architecture and interworking of the core components. Each component is encapsulated and only connected to the so-called middleware, which, in turn, exchanges contents and metadata in standardized formats via standardized interfaces. Components are described in turn.

The Learning Companion App plays a key role. It is the entry point for students to access courses, learning objects and lecture dates as well as to get recommendations for the next best contents to be learnt and triggers the tracking of all relevant user interactions. It is a responsive web application to be displayed on regular modern desktop web environments, but especially on smartphones and tablets to enable mobile learning. The application gives everywhere-and-everytime-access to all learning objects. Students can optimize their free time by filtering the most important items that fit in the available time period - for instance when waiting for the bus or going to class. Moreover, teachers use the LCA to get access to the Learning Analytics module.

The LMS is used to register and manage all users and offers discussion forums. In order to allow a consistent interaction with all components, the students (and teachers) credentials of the existing Learning Management Systems are required to authenticate at the Learning Companion App. This kind of single-sign-on approach is implemented in the

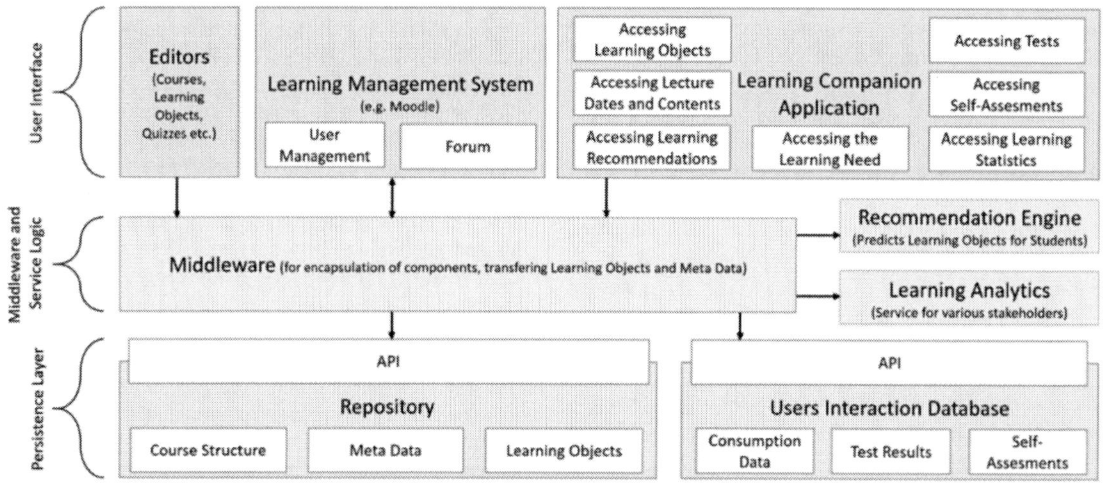

Figure 1. Architecture of the Smart Learning Project

middleware and transparent to users.

The repository acts as a digital asset store, which essentially holds course structures, learning objects and their metadata. At the lowest level, a learning object is a simple document (technically in HTML), a video, a screencast, a test and so on, all with at least one learning objective. Low-level LOs are stored as LTI-Tools [9] as to integrate them with different LMS. Moreover, questions and tests are specified according to the IMS QTI specification [10]. Low level learning objects can be bundled into bigger learning objects, and this iteration can be repeated. In the current energy consultant course, low-level LOs are combined in learning units, learning units in sections and a few sections make up the course. That way low level LOs can be reused in several courses. A so-called manifest file is created to bundle the LOs together. A player that is presently stored in the repository renders the learning units and QTI specified tests. Further, the player generates automatically self-assessments questions using the learning objectives contained of a learning unit. The metadata associated to a low level LO contains among others its learning objectives, at least one as mentioned above, average study time defined by instructors and prerequisite LOs. These data are stored using the LOM specification [11]. When LOs are combined, the metadata of the whole are generated automatically from the parts. A course structure is stored following the IMS Common Cartridge standard [12].

Different editors have been implemented as easy to use web applications for instructional designers. A LOM-Editor allows to specify the metadata of any existing LO and to store the corresponding file in the repository. A QTI-editor allows creating questions, to bundle them into tests following the QTI specification and to store them in the repository too; presently seven types of questions are available: choice, choice multiple, extended text, text entry, numeric, matrix and order. Finally, a LO-Editor allows bundling LOs into bigger ones and generating automatically the metadata file as written above.

Users' interactions with any LO are stored according to the opt-in procedure chosen by the user. Interactions are persisted using the xAPI specification [13] in the free

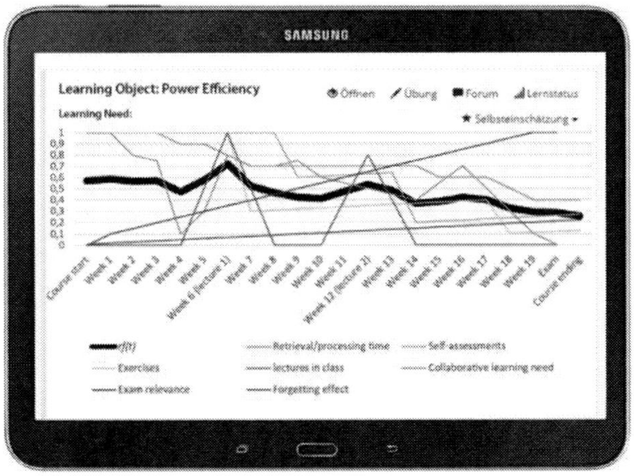

Figure 2. The mobile Learning Companion App

learning record store called learning locker[1].

The recommendation engine and the learning analytics service load the needed interaction data in regular intervals in order to determine students' performance. The Smart Learning Recommender aims at identifying the next best, most suitable learning object for the requesting student based on the calculated knowledge level and learning need for that item. The learning analytics service, in contrast, is designed for other stakeholders. So, teachers can observe the overall progress and performance of students and figure out weaknesses in learning and understanding.

IV. Recommendations and Learning Analytics in the Learning Companion App

A key role in connecting the users' interaction in LCA with the learning analytics service or recommendations engine is attributed to the formal and informal activity statements reflecting the collected user data. In recent years, the Experience API [13] with its xAPI statements continuously moves in the academic focus supporting long-term data mining. A typical statement consists of the three properties: "Actor", "Verb" and "Object". An xAPI statement can also carry the optional properties "Context" and "Results" containing more information for new insights like in the following statements:

- "StudentA (Actor) completed (Verb) Question1 (Object) in the *context* of Quiz1 in Course1 and the *result* of success with 2 attempts based on the raw score of 80 with a max score of 100 and a scale of 0.8" or
- "StudentB stopped VideoY started at position 00:01:30 in the *context* of LearningUnit2 of Course1 *resulting* in duration of 00:01:42".

The player mentioned in the preceding section as well as the app trigger the xAPI statements.

A. *Learning Need and Recommendations for Students*

In the Smart Learning Recommender [14], we relate each student with each available learning object in the taken course and aggregate all xAPI statements with time information into a relationship, called user-item-time-triplet. This triplet consists of various factors supported by different statements, and represents the personal knowledge level on a LO on a range from [0,1], where 0 is the lowest possible knowledge and 1 the highest. This triplet determines the learning need, which is inverse proportional to the knowledge level - the lower the knowledge level, the higher the learning need and so relevance of the current item for a student at the given time and vice versa. Presently, we consider the following factors that influence the learning need and so implicitly the recommendations:

- **Interaction** with a learning object: How much of the LO has been consumed?
- **Processing time** of a learning object compared with the pre-defined duration of the metadata and average consumption time of others.
- **Self-assessments** for this learning object.

[1] http://www.learninglocker.net/

- Performance in related **exercises**.
- The **forgetting effect;** the knowledge level decreases over time until learning has to be repeated.
- **Pre-requisites** of the underlying learning objects.
- Timely relevance for **face-to-face lectures**.
- **Exam relevance** in contrast to optional contents.
- **Collaborative learning needs** to offset under-estimations of the current student.

At the end, all single-factor values (each in range of [0,1], as well) are weighted. The weighted average of all factors describes the total learning need of the learning object for that user. A learner can see at any time the factors calculated by the system as well as her learning need, see Figure 2. The recommendation engine predicts the most relevant items by comparing the single learning need values and retrieves an ordered list of Top-N learning objects for a student.

B. Learning Analytics as Feedback for Teachers

As mentioned in the introduction, the main dashboard should allow instructors to obtain an overview of learners' progress and recieve details on demand [15]. In our context, several instructors teach in the same training program, each being responsible for specific training units. Thus, inside a course, the overview has to be at the learning unit level. It offers details on the selected learning object. We follow the approach of [6] in associating a bar to each object with the colors green, yellow and red. Taking the example of a test made of several questions green represents how often the test has been completely solved, yellow how often it has been partially solved and red how many students have not solved it at all. Details on each question of the test show the number of correct answers, partially correct and wrong answers following a similar scheme and adapting it to the question's type. Filters allow to chose particular time periods for the dashboard.

V. CONCLUSION & FUTURE WORK

We introduced a novel Learning Companion App, which allows learners to access standardized learning objects everywhere and any time. Thereby, each user interaction will be persisted and processed in order to predict the individual knowledge level of students, recommend the most important learning contents for a user and allows to analyze the overall performance in the course with the learning analytics service.

As a next step, studies with trainees enrolled in this 5 months training at the chamber of crafts will be conducted with two consecutive courses in order to improve the system iteratively; the first one begins in April 2016 and the second in September 2016. These studies evaluate real world learning behavior: how LCA performs and how users accept digital learning media and individual learning recommendations. Moreover, teachers will adapt their traditional courses to a LCA supported blended-learning approach with the help of the information provided by the learning analytics module. This component will be developed further to include analyses appropriate for instructional designers.

ACKNOWLEDGMENT

The authors would like to thank the whole Smart Learning team for their great work and many constructive ideas. This project is sponsored by the German Federal Ministry of Education and Research.

REFERENCES

[1] M. Zwicklbauer, C. Krauß, A. Merceron, M. Scharp, and J. Kania, "Smart learning: the digital learning companion for vocational training," [Smart Learning: Der digitale Lernbegleiter für die berufliche Bildung], Proceedings of DeLFI 2015, Gesellschaft für Informatik Publisher, Munich, 2015, pp. 227-232.

[2] N. Manouselis, H. Drachsler, R. Vuorikari, H. Hummel, and R. Koper, "Recommender systems in technology enhanced learning," Recommender systems handbook, Springer, 2011, pp. 387-415.

[3] J. Janssen et al., "Self-organising navigational support in lifelong learning: how predecessors can lead the way," Computers & Education, Elsevier, vol. 49, pp. 781-793, 2007.

[4] R. Pelanek and P. Jarusek, "Student modeling based on problem solving times," International Journal of Artificial Intelligence in Education, Springer, New York, vol. 25, 2015, pp. 493-519.

[5] K. Verbert et al., "Learning dashboards: an overview and future research opportunities," Personal and Ubiquitous Computing, vol. 18(6), 2013, pp. 1-16.

[6] M. Elkina, A. Fortenbacher, and A. Merceron, "The learning analytics application LEMO - rationals and first results," International Journal of Computing, vol. 12(3), 2013, pp. 226-234.

[7] A. Dollár and P. Steif, "Web-based statics course with learning dashboard for instructors," Proceedings of Computers and Advanced Technology in Education (CATE 2012), Napoli, 2012.

[8] R. Martinez-Maldonado, A. Pardo, N. Mirriahi, K. Yacef, J. Kay, and A. Clayphan, "The LATUX workflow: designing and deploying awareness tools in technology-enabled learning settings," Proceedings of the 5th International Conference on Learning Analytics and Knowledge, ACM, New York, 2015, pp. 1-10.

[9] IMS LTI, "Learning Tools Interoperability Specification," IMS Global Learning Consortium, 2015.

[10] IMS QTI, "IMS Question & Test Interoperability Specification," IMS Global Learning Consortium, 2005.

[11] IMS LOM, "Learning Resource Meta-data Specification," IMS Global Learning Consortium, 2006.

[12] IMS CC, "IMS Common Cartridge Specification," IMS Global Learning Consortium, 2015.

[13] J. Kevan and P. Ryan, "Experience API: flexible, decentralized and activity-centric data collection in technology," Knowledge and Learning, Springer Science Business Media Dordrecht, 2015, pp. 2211-1662.

[14] C. Krauss, "Smart learning: time-dependent context-aware learning object recommendations," Proceedings of the 29th International Florida AI Research Society Conference (FLAIRS-29), AAAI, Key Largo, 2016, in press.

[15] B. Scheiderman, "The eyes have it: a task by data type taxonomy for information visualizations," Proceedings of the 1996 Symposium on Visual Languages (VL'96), IEEE, 1996, pp. 336 – 34.

Development and Evaluation of a Blended Learning Course

Jan M. Nauta[a,b], Jo Platenkamp[b], Marike Hettinga[a]
[a] ICT-Innovations in Healthcare, Windesheim University of Applied Sciences, Zwolle, The Netherlands
[b] Computer Science Department (HBO-ICT), Windesheim University of Applied Sciences, Zwolle, The Netherlands
e-mail: {jm.nauta, jm.platenkamp, m.hettinga}@windesheim.nl

Abstract—**In a pilot project, a blended-learning course "Research and Development" was developed. This course is taught according to the flipped classroom principle. To develop the course, the ADDIE-model (Analysis, Design, Development, Implementation, and Evaluation) was used. During the evaluation phase, we wanted to learn how satisfied students were with the newly developed course. More specifically, student satisfaction regarding the digital material, the lessons in the classroom, and the course as a whole, was studied. During the penultimate lecture, twelve students completed a questionnaire. During the last lecture a focus group meeting was conducted. In the case of the questionnaire, the respondents agreed, on average, mostly with the positive statements or they answered neutrally. We can conclude that the respondents were reasonably positive about the course. The teaching method was not unfamiliar to the students. However, they felt a need for a better digital infrastructure, more variety in teaching methods and a more directive teaching style.**

Keywords-blended learning; hybrid learning; flipped classroom; research and development

I. INTRODUCTION

Over the last decade, the educational concept of Blended Learning has drawn considerable attention in the educational literature [1][2]. In 2015, a number of pilot projects were carried out at Windesheim University of Applied Sciences in the Netherlands, to integrate this concept into Windesheim's curricula and to gain further experience with it. In one of the pilot projects, a blended-learning course "Research and Development" was developed. This course is taught according to the flipped classroom principle [3][4].

Due to the fact that both concepts, blended learning and flipping the classroom, are relatively new at Windesheim, the teaching staff involved wished to gain insight in the learner's satisfaction with the newly developed course. As part of this course, a survey was carried out and a focus group meeting was conducted to learn more about the students' experiences. The work presented here is therefore initially intended as an effort by the faculty to evaluate its work in order to improve its educational skills, as well as the developed learning material. However, the lessons learned may be more widely applicable.

In Section II this paper first goes into the development of the course. After that, the evaluation method and results are presented in Sections III and IV, respectively. Finally, in Section V, conclusions are drawn, along with a number of lessons learned.

II. DEVELOPMENT OF THE COURSE RESEARCH AND DEVELOPMENT

To develop the course Research and Development, the ADDIE-model was used [5]. This well-known model comprises five phases: Analysis, Design, Development, Implementation and Evaluation, hence its name.

In the first phase, a needs analysis, a target audience analysis as well as a task and topic analysis was carried out. This elective course aims at third and fourth year students who have already followed one of Windesheim's Computer Science programs. During the course, they train the necessary skills by carrying out a small project of their own choice. The course takes approximately 84 hours of study.

The students are expected to carry out their research projects outside the classroom. Moreover, they are supposed to acquire the necessary knowledge by studying the e-learning material, prepared for this course, independently. This creates an opportunity to talk in class about the progress and results of the student's projects including specific topics such as an evaluation of the (Internet) sources found by the student groups. Based on these ideas, the design phase yielded an overview of the assignments which should be carried out outside the classroom and an overview of the necessary e-learning content to support these assignments. Moreover, a detailed plan was made for the lessons.

During the development phase, the online educational resources and face-to-face lessons were prepared, including 17 instructional videos (1.5 hours in total) to which existing material, such as YouTube videos, were added. The e-learning component, available through the institution's virtual learning environment, was developed using eXeLearning [6]. The virtual learning environment contained a forum to exchange ideas and information.

The first employment of the course took place in Autumn 2015, with 20 students attending, working together in teams of between two and five students.

III. EVALUATION METHOD

During the evaluation phase, we wanted to learn how satisfied students were with the newly developed course and to gain further insight in the advantages and disadvantages of the applied concepts. More specifically, student satisfaction regarding the digital material, the lessons in the classroom, and the course as a whole, was studied [7][8][9].

During the penultimate lecture, twelve students completed a questionnaire with 39 Likert items, using a 5-point scale, and one open question. Each Likert item contained a (positive) statement, the response options were: disagree much / disagree / neutral / agree / agree much.

To gain insight in the first point of interest, student satisfaction regarding the digital material, nine questions were asked about the form of the digital learning material such as the instructional videos and the assignments. Moreover, two questions were asked about the user friendliness of the realized e-learning component and the forum. Finally, six questions were added concerning the clarity of the digital material.

To learn more about the second point of interest, the students' opinions about the lessons in class, ten questions were asked about the form of the meetings in class. For instance, the opinion of the respondents about student presentations and receiving feedback in class was asked together with their opinion about organizational matters such as the timeliness of course information. Lastly, three questions were added concerning the interaction in class between students and lecturers and between students and their fellow students.

Finally, the students were asked to answer questions about the course as a whole. Three questions concerned the organization of the student teams. The teams had a certain freedom of choice regarding the way they presented their results (e.g., with a report, a paper, or a presentation). The questionnaire contained two questions about this subject. Three questions were added about the relationship between the sessions in the classroom and homework assignments. Lastly, students were asked whether they would prefer this way of teaching for other courses as well. They could also add comments if desired.

During the final lecture a focus group meeting was conducted in which notable results from the questionnaire were discussed in depth. Observations noted by faculty members during the lectures completed the collected results.

IV. EVALUATION RESULTS

The results of the questionnaire are collected in Table I. Twelve students filled in the questionnaire but not every student answered each question. On average, 89% of the questions were answered. The percentages in the table may not always sum up to 100% due to rounding off errors.

Table I shows that students often agreed with the statements, or they chose the neutral option. Mostly they did not disagree much, with three exceptions. The focus group meeting further clarified the results of the questionnaire.

Apart from comments on the overlap between the available videos, students were satisfied with the available learning content. Nevertheless remarks were made about the digital infrastructure. For example, students regretted the fact that videos could not be downloaded from the institute's media portal. A number of websites was embedded in the digital material. However, students preferred links to these websites. The percentages for user friendliness in Table 1 reflect these results. Moreover, the available forum was considered superfluous. Some students preferred alternatives, such as Dropbox.

TABLE I. QUESTIONNAIRE RESULTS

Respondents are satisfied with:	Disagree much (%)	Disagree (%)	Neutral (%)	Agree (%)	Agree much (%)
Form of study material	0	6	36	52	6
User friendliness of digital material	5	14	38	38	5
Clarity of digital material	0	0	36	53	11
Form of meetings in class	1	10	13	65	12
Interaction in class	0	6	18	73	3
Organization of student teams	8	6	33	47	6
Freedom regarding products	0	8	13	50	29
Relation work in class / assignments	0	3	21	76	0
Preferred for other courses	0	18	45	36	0

Students welcomed the opportunity to present their work and to receive feedback in class. They considered attending presentations of their fellow students as less meaningful because the discussions in class were not always beneficial for their own work. Assignments in class were also not favorable because of lack of depth due to the short time available in class. Students would prefer to discuss more examples of excellent or poor research projects.

Sometimes it appeared to be difficult for students to organize necessary team meetings due to scheduling problems. A number of students, for instance, had internships at the same time as they were following the course Research and Development. Generally, they were reasonably satisfied with the course, but they would appreciate suggestions and instructions regarding planning and papers. The students would rather favour a mix of the flipped-classroom model with a more traditional teaching style. In contrast to our expectation they appeared to be rather familiar with the applied teaching methods.

V. CONCLUSIONS AND LESSONS LEARNED

In this paper we treated the development of a blended course together with an evaluation in which the teaching staff studied student satisfaction regarding the digital material, the lessons in the classroom, and the course as a whole.

From the results, we may conclude that the respondents were reasonably positive about the course. However, they felt a need for a better digital infrastructure, more variety in teaching methods and a more directive teaching style. The teaching method was not unfamiliar to the students.

The evaluation presented in this paper has its limitations. Although all the students who took part in the first deployment of the course were invited to fill in the questionnaire, eventually only 12 of the 20 students took part in the evaluation. This number is too limited to draw general conclusions. Moreover, the staff developing the course also taught and evaluated the course. Therefore, some biases may have influenced the results.

Despite these limitations a number of lessons learned may be identified. We acquired experience in developing a blended-learning course. We experienced the value of a model such as the ADDIE-model for creating instructional materials. We also benefitted from Richard Mayer's guidelines for developing e-learning materials [10]. Finally, we experienced the (extra) amount of time necessary to develop these materials, which can be substantial.

Teaching the course, we learned that the quality of the digital infrastructure is a key factor for students. User friendliness, reliability and the possibility to download materials (for use off line, for instance in public transport) are important factors. The flipped classroom principle was applied strictly: students were expected to acquire all the necessary knowledge outside the classroom. During discussions in class and while grading the student products the impression arose that not every student was sufficiently acquainted with the theory. Therefore, a mix of the traditional knowledge transfer together with training, exchanging experiences and providing feedback in class may prove beneficial.

In our evaluation we focused on learner's satisfaction, which corresponds to the first level (Reaction) of Kirkpatrick's Four-Level Model [11]. An obvious next step would be to evaluate the increase in knowledge and skills, corresponding to the second level (Learning) of Kirkpatrick's model. Future work may therefore focus on the role blended learning plays in acquiring knowledge and skills which are relevant in the course Research and Development.

ACKNOWLEDGMENT

We thank Elles Gyaltsen-Lohuis who advised us on the design of the questionnaire, and Judith Wright for valuable comments on a draft of this paper.

REFERENCES

[1] G. Motteram, "'Blended' education and the transformation of teachers: a long - term case study in postgraduate UK Higher Education," British Journal of Educational Technology, vol. 37, 2006, pp. 17-30.

[2] A. Alammary, J. Sheard, and A. Carbone, "Blended learning in higher education: Three different design approaches," Australasian Journal of Educational Technology, vol. 30, 2014, pp. 440-454.

[3] S. C. Kong, "Developing information literacy and critical thinking skills through domain knowledge learning in digital classrooms: An experience of practicing flipped classroom strategy," Computers & Education, vol. 78, 2014, pp. 160-173.

[4] P. Desai and M. Vijayalakshmi, "Flipped Classroom: An Efficient Pedagogical Tool to Teach a Course for Final Year Computer Science and Engineering Graduate Students," Journal of Engineering Education Transformations, 2015, pp. 306-310.

[5] M. Molenda, "In search of the elusive ADDIE model," Performance improvement, vol. 42, 2003, pp. 34-37.

[6] "The new eXeLearning," Available: http://exelearning.net [17 March 2016].

[7] Y.-S. Wang, "Assessment of learner satisfaction with asynchronous electronic learning systems," Information & Management, vol. 41, 2003, pp. 75-86.

[8] M. T. Cole, D. J. Shelley, and L. B. Swartz, "Online instruction, e-learning, and student satisfaction: A three year study," The International Review of Research in Open and Distributed Learning, vol. 15, 2014, pp. 111-131.

[9] E. Anagnostopoulou, I. Mavroidis, Y. Giossos, and M. Koutsouba, "Student satisfaction in the context of a postgraduate programme of the Hellenic Open University," Turkish Online Journal of Distance Education, vol. 16, 2015, pp. 40-55.

[10] R. C. Clark and R. E. Mayer, E-learning and the science of instruction: Proven guidelines for consumers and designers of multimedia learning: John Wiley & Sons, 2011.

[11] D. L. Galloway, "Evaluating distance delivery and e - learning; is Kirkpatrick's model relevant?," Performance Improvement, vol. 44, 2005, pp. 21-27.

Follow-Up on a Numerical Methods Course Using m-learning and Proposal for an Evolution to Research Based Learning

Francisco Delgado
Physics and Mathematics Department
Tecnológico de Monterrey, campus Estado de México
Atizapán, Estado de México, México
e-mail: fdelgado@itesm.mx

***Abstract*— Education is changing deeper than at any other time with the constant improvement of information and communication technologies. Particularly, the last five years have brought a fast inclusion of mobile technologies in education at all educational levels. This work presents a modern vision for a numerical methods course for engineers integrating mobile applications into a blended learning strategy. It currently combines class, Web and mobile activities to reinforce and to develop the basic knowledge proposed in the curricula. A five years follow-up is developed to evaluate its performance. Outcomes suggest moving the design into pure online learning to introduce new improvements in the course goals. The improvements are realized by the inclusion of a research-based learning component. The proposed approach could become a differentiated and flexible scheme of instruction powered by mobile applications, but introducing a new version based on project-oriented learning.**

Keywords-m-learning; b-learning; math; course design; assessment.

I. INTRODUCTION

Nowadays, several educative tendencies are identified with the acquisition of technological skills as part of a successful professional life. Today, new generations have based their learning expectative on some kind of technology. Prensky [1] states that today's students are native speakers of the digital language of computers, video games and the Internet. Instead, people born before, digital immigrants, have a limited dominion of these technologies. It sets a natural division among these generations. Technology is related to a more accessible and cheaper education. Today, the low quality perception of education based on technology is decreasing, while increasingly it is being considered more engaged and personalized [2].

Currently, mobile technology is the real option to be connected with the world and the information. In 2013, mobile technologies became the main media to reach the Internet [3]. Consequently, it is evolving into a creative medium where education can reach effectively the people. In terms of sensory stimulation and learning styles being privileged [7], several authors have stated deep relations between the general history of distance learning and the chronology of the generations involved [4][5][6]. Johnson et al. [8] described the impressive short time of adoption of mobile technologies, including in education. Today, many apps and tools allow the development of educational products directly; the perspective is open to educative innovation based on technology. Members of university faculty have been reluctant to adopt educational technology, but this situation is changing very fast.

Numerical methods course is mandatory in engineering programs. This discipline has evolved in the last decades, together with information technologies. It has changed its traditional teaching with the spread of computer systems and their implementation in the universities. Therefore, the specific course presented in this paper has transitioned from a numerical analysis course into a computer simulation course in only ten years. It includes the computer visualization of technical and scientific problems to boost the research abilities [9]: curriculum integration, use of technology, and development of higher level skills. In this evolution, several technologies have been used to state its mobile management and to carry out a mobile learning approach [10].

The aim of this paper is to report the advancement of technology in the numerical methods course in the last five years while the mobile revolution was developed. A detailed analysis of the online evaluation is given together with the usage analytics of the current resources included. The results suggest alternative and flexible instruction schemes for the basic skills acquisition. This flexibility proposes the next step in the evolution course as an open online course still combined with face-to-face sessions to conduct challenge integrated problems under an open research scheme. Section II describes the mobile learning strategy using activities delivered through several media and tools. Section III analyses the efficiency of online evaluation predicting the basic skill development based on the usage of these activities. Section IV discusses the potential design to evolve the course into a Small Private Online Research (SPOR) supported by mobile learning and a series of research problems to be solved in class. Finally, Section V includes the conclusions and the future work.

II. COURSE DESIGN AND MOBILE DEVELOPMENT

A. *Historical course description*

Requirements for engineering education are based on the technological advancement, imposing the adoption of new technologies. The numerical methods course depicted here has evolved this way. Ten years ago, it sparsely contained a limited use of Fortran or C^{++} as a programming language, a limited time of programming practice, and applied problems were rarely included. Since then, the use of technology has increased significantly: Mathematica [11], Python [12] for programming and visualization, as well as Blackboard [13] to deliver digital course materials and online activities. Those technologies boosted the Problem Based Learning (PBL) and Project Oriented Learning (POL) [14][15] strategies in the course, reducing the gap between academic and professional engineering [9]. It was the course stage in 2008, before mobile and blended learning were introduced.

B. M-learning transitions and current design

In 2011, the author was involved in an institutional effort to develop and promote the use of mobile technologies in all higher education faculties [16]. Then, after Blackboard, leaner technologies were used to replace this tool with tailor-made tools such as Winksite [17], Weebly [18], Googledrive [19], Jotform [20], Wolfram Alpha [21], Socrative [22] and Classmarker [23]. Another key element was a public You Tube channel for the course, including screencasts for each topic in the course. Digital programming codes were included and then followed by the students at their own pace. Surprisingly, most of the users became informal users in other universities and countries, gathering almost one hundred thousand accesses in three years. These technologies allow to deliver the media resources and the online activities directly on mobile devices dealing with some weaknesses in the curricula and carrying out periodic computer quizzes in class or online. In 2008, an e-book was prepared for the course. It began to be distributed on Amazon and i-store as a new mobile version in 2014. Finally, in the newest version of the site, the programming component of the whole course can be followed online, theme by theme, through sixty screencasts.

Despite some of last developments required necessarily the use of laptops in the beginning (in particular for PDF documents and Mathematica files involving homework, resources, etc.), in the current time, the technology evolution has generated PDF mobile viewers and the development of Wolfram Cloud (deployed in the version 10.0 of Mathematica), allowing a complete transition into mobile management using cellular phones or tablets, the final target for which began to be prepared some years ago.

Figure 1 depicts the course evolution into m-learning in terms of the technology added, spaces and management. All of them were deployed to set the schedule of online activities, delivery, and feedback. It includes evaluation with online quizzes and exams, which substitute some of the in-class evaluations. Other elements and activities give the assessment in programing and numerical implementations.

Despite the fact that these activities were primarily introduced to provide support in some weak learning areas, they grew to become naturally integrated on an official mobile site (Figure 2). Inclusively, some of them, as assessment or evaluation have replaced some face-to-face practices with good performance [10]. Under this blended scenario, the impact of the online activities should be evaluated in order to determine if they are a strong replacement of some traditional elements in the learning process.

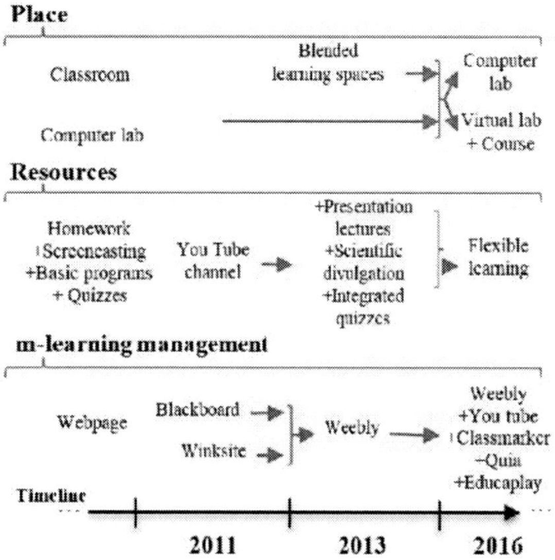

Figure 1. Five years of m-learning implementations in the numerical methods course in terms of tools, activities and resources.

III. EFFECTIVENESS OF MOBILE RESOURCES

The numerical methods course evolution in the last ten years introduced technology in the classroom as a mandatory policy [10]. Due to this improvement, students are expected to be more skilled. It has required additional support to face-to-face instruction to scaffold the programming practice. In addition, several years ago, the inclusion of integrated scenarios in PBL and activities based on POL promoted the curriculum integration, seeking a more professional practice to develop engineering competencies [24]. Unfortunately, two last improvements have a time conflict in the course with respect to the necessary coverage of the contents. For these reasons, the mobile revolution began providing resources to address such conflict [9]. Today, the course is fully reached and covered by mobile devices (an achievement of the last five years), so a concrete assessment about their increasing intervention in terms of basic knowledge assurance is in order. This evaluation could suggest moving the basic coverage of theory into online instruction, the centre of attention of this work. This action could free time in the face-to-face sessions to solve integrated and complex problems related to the basic contents, in particular, short engineering and science research problems requiring analysis and visualization.

A. Research objectives

When the online activities were gaining terrain, including evaluation, the following question arose: could m-learning materials replace parts of the face-to-face instruction? There are sufficient structured materials for that: repositories, class videos, programs, theoretical class lessons in slides, mobile management, and continuous online evaluation. Most of them are open to the students to improve their performance in the course. But, what is the interest to substitute the face-to-face instruction by a mobile one?

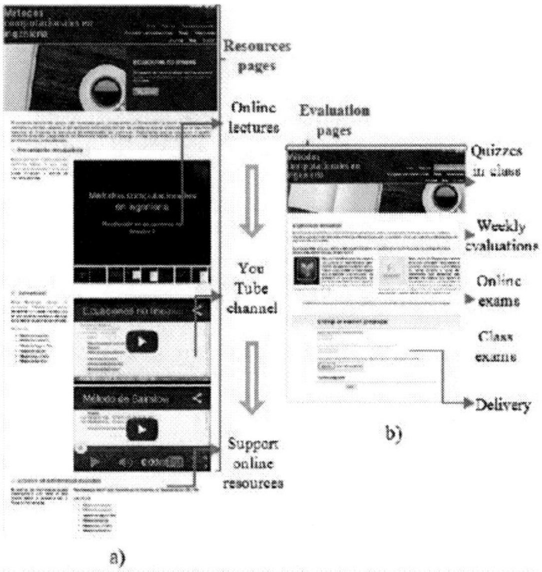

Figure 2. Views of numerical methods course site: (a) Section resource site, and (b) Evaluation section.

In numerical methods, the application of knowledge to challenge open problems is a more valuable educative task than just to learn the basics. Despite this, the first stage is normally reached when the second one is effectively done. Not all the numerical methods in the course are significant for all disciplines (and normally in the current professional practice some specialized software is used to solve attained problems). Thus, a combined structure including knowledge of numerical methods, programming and applications is finally more representative in terms of skill development. The main research question in this work is about the current mobile elements showing effectiveness in the teaching task of basic knowledge to address the face-to-face sessions into challenge problems solving.

A mobile implementation requires a deeper analysis of elements included and, in particular, from the evaluation conducted there. Currently, there are not sufficient criteria and specific analytics introduced in the mobile site to evaluate that. Despite this, there are historical usage analytics and quantitative information about for the online evaluation to get an introspective evaluation of those resources. Thus, the research objectives in this work have been settled as: a) to compare the effectiveness of online evaluation versus in-class evaluation, and b) to analyse the actual usage data to inquire the assigned value to the resources.

B. Effectiveness of online evaluation

On the course site, formative and summative evaluations are carried out with Socrative and Classmarker tools. It includes the access and the delivery of those evaluations through the forms developed in Jotform and integrated with Googledrive to submit the associated Mathematica files. In the last two years of the period considered in this work, partial evaluations have substituted the in-class evaluation. The final evaluation continues to be an in-class exam. This aspect is linked to the first research objective.

To address the corresponding analysis, the grades for the students in the last two years (2014-2015) will be considered. The results are presented in Figure 3 and the methodology is as follows. The ratio I/T between the averages of individual online work and online teamwork is considered for each student (it helps to discriminate the case when bad performance students obtain good teamwork grades). Then, I/T is related to the average of online evaluations in Socrative and/or Classmarker, but grouping students in three classes as a function of their final total grade (on a 100 point scale) and then deployed in Figure 3: a) less than 70, the students failing the course (black), b) between 70 and 85, the average students (red), and c) more than 85, the good performance students (green). Figure 3 includes three elliptic shades showing the mean and standard deviation for each axis parameter in each group. The horizontal dotted line marks the institutional limit to fail the evaluation. For the students with good performance, this graph exhibits a deep consistency between online individual work and teamwork together with a clear consistency in the online evaluations and the final grade.

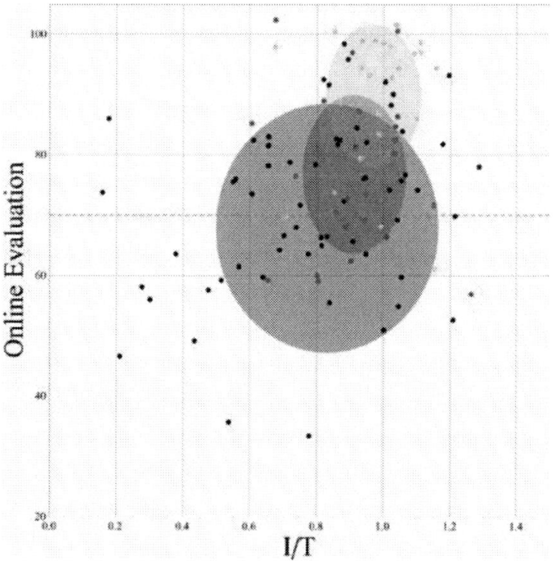

Figure 3. Analysis of effectiveness in the online evaluation.

For the students who failed, the dispersion is wider and the promotion is only barely predicted by the online evaluation, suggesting to keep the final in-class exam as a differentiating element.

C. *Analysis of usage statistics*

As was stated by [10], the mobile technology was first used to scaffold the potential learning weaknesses in the course. The repositories (simulations, programming codes, projects and applied complex problems) are constructed to follow the face-to-face sessions and the e-book content. Particularly, screencasts in the YouTube channel are integrated on the site as part of a three stages based learning methodology: a) online notes and lectures (in slides), b) screencasts, and c) downloadable Mathematica materials (as support to each screencast). They were primarily used to replace the face-to-face instruction for the students missing the session with a minimum of teacher tutoring. In addition, the daily class notes are downloadable files in another section. Finally, individual work and teamwork normally are online activities where a Mathematica file should be submitted. Class announcements and scheduled activities are published on the site. The blog contains questions, answers, and discussions about the course topics. The second research question can be addressed through the access analytics introduced in the last resources. They record the formal and informal students accesses (identified as the overseas students in the analytics) to each site section, revealing the demand on the open access resources.

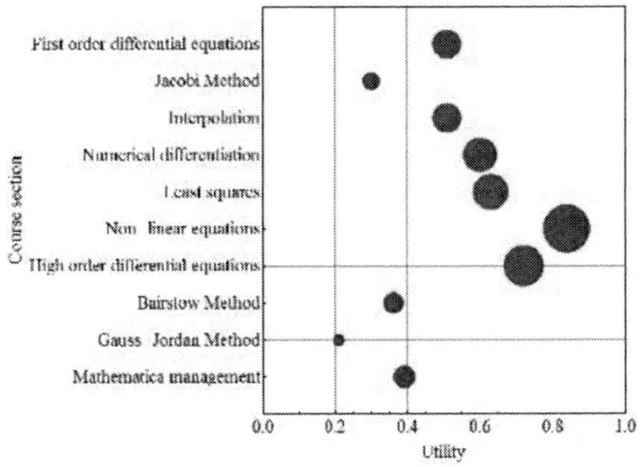

Figure 4. A utility index based on the percentage of visualization time versus Demand for each screencast on the mobile site.

The methodology to analyse this question was split into two parts. The first one is represented in Figure 4, where the average fraction of visualization (the part of the screencast effectively viewed) for all accesses is represented on the horizontal axis as a measure of the resource utility (1 means the best utility and 0 the worst), while the radius of each dot represents the relative percentage average with respect to the total accesses. Thus, the non-linear equations screencast is highly useful and strongly reviewed by a great number of students. While, for instance, the Jacobi method screencast is a resource highly reached by the students, it appears it is of little use because only a small part is effectively reviewed. The second part of the analysis is based on the usage of the different sections on the mobile site as a blended support to the face-to-face instruction for the formal students, as well as online resources for the informal ones. Data are shown in Table I for the 2014 users (near of 2000 accesses), where percentages were calculated for their own group. It reflects that the resources are valuable for both groups, as expected. Statistics for formal users show the Resources section as the most requested, while Resources and Daily notes sections are the most requested by informal students.

TABLE I. ACCESS STATISTICS FOR FORMAL AND INFORMAL STUDENTS BASED ON THEIR OWN GROUP

Sections	**Access percentage analytics for numerical methods site (2014)**	
	Formal students	***Informal students***
Resources	51%	53%
Evaluation	13%	1%
Homework	18%	2%
Daily notes	9%	37%
Announcements	6%	0%
Blog	3%	4%

D. *Discussion*

Summarizing the previous analysis, it suggests the online evaluations can substitute the whole basic knowledge evaluation, opening a wider horizon of flexibility based on a selective substitution of the traditional face-to-face sessions by the mobile learning resources (notes, screencasts and support files). The methodology discriminates which screencasts are being effectively used and which should be improved. Statistics suggest the importance given to these resources; nevertheless a deeper monitoring is still needed with more precise and linked analytics. Comparison between the two current communities (formal and informal) measures how the resources are valuable inclusively for the non-enrolled students.

Last outcomes are pretended to be taken as a support to use the mobile resources as a genuine space of online instruction to make room for a different learning approach oriented to solve open research and curriculum integrated projects. The new approach should address the course goals, taking care of the effectiveness of online learning strategy for the basic contents, still in the course basements.

IV. SMALL PRIVATE ONLINE RESEARCH APPROACH

Some years ago, the inclusion of complex integrated problems began in the course. Then, the development of the ability to solve applied and contextual problems (settled on engineering sciences) was shown in terms of deepness and knowledge usability (more than in grades improvement) [9]. This experience has been barely included, due to the limited time. Currently, the mobile scaffolding for the basic knowledge acquisition (materialized in the last years as concrete resources) opens an approach based on short research projects. The current section depicts this briefly.

A. Curriculum integrated education

More than fifteen years ago, the author was involved as a teacher in a curriculum integrated educative program in engineering. There, students had developed lifetime skills in research [14]. This practice has been carried out in other scenarios as single courses applying curriculum integration. The numerical methods course has been settled as this kind of courses due to its position in the curricula (after math and sciences courses and together with the beginning of engineering sciences courses in all engineering programs) [9][10]. Philosophy of curriculum integration matches research problems as a central goal in a course or group of courses. They normally should be solved with a multi-approach discipline based on the past, current and future curricula. This approach requires being considered as the main guideline in the course while basic knowledge apprehension becomes a subsidiary activity. Thus, mobile scaffolding can work a subjacent learning support to this implementation, if the previous conditions are fulfilled. Some pitfalls should be prevented [14]: a) the absence of basic knowledge spaces being included to clarify contents; b) the omission of a modified evaluation to include this kind of new skill development; and c) the absence of flexibility to fulfil a basic knowledge evaluation agenda.

B. The SPOR approach

As was stated before, the explicit development of technical skills related to numerical methods could be based on the use of mobile technology as scaffolding to substitute the face-to-face instruction for the basic contents. It frees most of the class time to introduce the open scientific or engineering problems solving based on research. This approach is referred to as Small Private Online Research (SPOR) due to the fact that the main contents are covered online, but the emphasis is on the research conducted in the face-to-face sections in a controlled size group. In it, a curriculum integrated approach should conduct the learning goals (instead of the dominion of basic knowledge), warranting a personalized evaluation of performance.

Due to the diversity of engineering programs attended in the course (industrial, mechanical, electrical, chemical and biotechnological), SPOR approach will require several parallel contextual problems based on the interest area of the students. The learning of basic knowledge rests on the online activities, requiring a deep effectivity of the mobile resources, including the associated evaluation. This orientation requires to restructure the current mobile site into a more concrete modular scheme, including resources and evaluation on each main topic in the current syllabus. This structure prepares and evaluates each student at a minimum allowed performance. The evaluation should be completed considering the contextual problems assigned in the course (individually or in teams). Results in the present work suggest widely this new step in the course evolution is affordable, but it requires the inclusion of more precise analytics and an effective evaluation to measure the learning outcomes at the basic knowledge level. Clearly, if students work in teams on the contextual problems, a differentiated evaluation should be required.

Currently, a semester deployment of this approach is running. There, a repetitive evaluation of basic knowledge in the course is applied together with a skill evaluation through the net of research projects. A complete mobile coverage of contents is developed through detailed screencasts and maker-based activities. Online evaluation of the basic contents of each course unit is applied up to three times at the own pace of each student to let him/her improve. Most of the face-to-face sessions are oriented to present, develop and work on open research problems based on scientific visualization.

V. CONCLUSIONS AND FUTURE WORK

Numerical methods courses have been evolving in the last decades by their natural approach to technology. Currently, the numerical methods course presented here is being developed and improved by sharing and discussing initiatives with colleagues in the faculty (who already have adopted the use of the computer lab and developed similar mobile resources). Faculty is prepared with a stronger training in new technologies to introduce blended learning scenarios. The potential developers of SPOR approach shares the interest to adopt the online-based instruction for the basic knowledge to then adopt the open research scenarios to guide the covering of contents.

For the numerical methods course depicted, the proposed improvement means not only to design a set of contextual research problems, but also a directed group of activities through several tools and channels covering the proposed learning objectives and supporting the individual monitoring of each student. The outcomes in the current work present a preliminary design of a mobile site with five years of mobile development. It includes elements working in the online education arena, but now being used under a different blended strategy. The analysis has shown that they can work under a pure online orientation in a controlled scheme introducing more specific analytics to assess their performance in the learning process. This change will free the face-to-face sessions to set the SPOR approach, a course version aligned with STEM initiatives [25].

Future work in the last direction should prepare more robust blended strategies linked with a net of parallel research problems covering the different interests for engineering students enrolled in the course. For the faculty, it is an opportunity to move the learning impact into professional standards. The innovation proposed should change the teacher position into a more professional role. For the student, a self-directed performance is expected. In this trend, it shows an approximation to the new education trends supported by technology being required in the world.

ACKNOWLEDGMENT

Support given to conduct this project and research work through NOVUS initiative for innovations in education is acknowledged to Tecnológico de Monterrey.

REFERENCES

[1] M. Prensky, "Digital Natives, Digital Immigrants", On the horizont, 9 (5), 2001, pp. 1-6.

[2] L. Johnson, S. Adams, and K. Haywood, The NMC Horizon Report: 2011 K-12 Edition. Austin: The New Media Consortium, 2011.

[3] L. Johnson, R. Smith, H. Willis, A. Levine, and K. Haywood. The 2011 Horizon Report. Austin: The New Media Consortium, 2011.

[4] F. Jardines, "Historical development of distance education", Innovaciones de Negocios 6 (2), 2009, pp. 225 -236.

[5] L. Gray, N. Thomas, and L. Lewis, Teachers' Use of Educational Technology in U.S. Washington, U.S. Department of Education, 2010. Available from: http://nces. ed.gov/pubs2010/2010040.pdf 2016.01.01

[6] R. Hobbes, Hobbes' Internet Timeline, 2013. Available from: http://www.zakon.org/robert/internet/timeline/ 2016.01.01

[7] Internet World Stats, Usage and Population Statistics, Internet World Stats, 2014. Available from: http:// www.internet worldstats.com/stats.htm 2016.01.01

[8] L. Johnson, S. Adams and K. Haywood, The NMC Horizon Report: 2011 K-12 Edition. Austin: The New Media Consortium, 2011.

[9] F. Delgado, and S. Martínez, "Curricular changes generated by the use of technology in the numerical methods teaching", XXXVIII ANFEI Conference Proceedings. Querétaro: ANFEI, 2011.

[10] F. Delgado, "A numerical methods course based on b-learning: integrated learning design and follow up", International Journal of Mobile and Blended Learning, 5 (1), 2013.

[11] Wolfram Research, Mathematica site, 2016. Available from: http://www.wolfram.com/mathematica 2016.01.01

[12] Python, Python site, 2016. Available from: http://www.python.org 2016.01.01

[13] Blackboard, Blackboard site, 2016. Available from: http:// www.blackboard.com 2016.01.01

[14] F. Delgado, "Problem Based-Learning in Sophomore and Freshmen Engineering Students: A Six Year Follow-Up," 4th Conference of European Research in Mathematics Education electronic proceedings, Barcelona: CRM, 2005.

[15] F. Delgado, "Designing PBL scenarios for a course with integrated curriculum, teamwork environment and use of technology", 10th International Conference of Mathematical Education electronic proceedings, Monterrey: UANL, 2008.

[16] F. Delgado, "Teacher actualization in educative technologies and mobile learning: an institutional development program", Revista de Formación e Innovación Educativa Universitaria, 7 (4), 2004, pp. 211-226.

[17] Winksite, Winksite site, 2016. Available from: http:// winksite.com 2016.01.01

[18] Weebly, Weebly Webpage, 2016. Available from: http:// www.weebly.com 2016.01.01

[19] Google, Googledrive site, 2016. Available from: https:// www.google.com/drive/ 2016.01.01

[20] Jotform, Jotform site, 2016. Available from: http:// www.jotform.com/ 2016.01.01

[21] Wolfram Research, Wolfram Alpha site, 2016. Available from: http://m.wolframalpha.com 2016.01.01

[22] Socrative, Socrative site, 2016. Available from: http://www.socrative.com 2016.01.01

[23] Classmarker, Classmarker Webpage, 2016. Available from: http://www.classmarker.com 2016.01.01

[24] ETA, Engineering competences model, Employment and Training Administration of United States. Washington, Department of Labor, 2015.

[25] H. Gonzalez and J. Kuenzi, Science, Technology, Engineering, and Mathematics (STEM) Education: A Primer. Congressional Research Service Report, 2012. Available from: http://fas.org/sgp/crs/misc/R42642.pdf 2016.01.01

Use of Tablet in College Chemistry Experiment

- An approach to developing an electronic textbook -

Akira Ikuo, Yusuke Yoshinaga, and Haruo Ogawa
Department of Chemistry
Tokyo Gakugei University
Tokyo, Japan
email: {ikuo, yyoshi, ogawah}@u-gakugei.ac.jp

***Abstract*—We are developing an electronic textbook for a basic chemistry-experiment for university students in which reaction mechanisms are shown by Computer Graphics (CG). The CG of chemical reaction was made based on empirical molecular orbital calculations. The CG included following reactions as a model of Walden's inversion where drastic change in structure takes place; hydroxylation of methyl chloride, formation of 2-butyl alcohol and 1-butyl bromide. The CG can simultaneously demonstrate the nature of the reaction such as structural change by the space-filling and ball-and-stick models in addition to providing an image of energy change by the reaction profile. The electronic textbook also displays pictures of apparatus and flow-charts of small-scale experiments. Therefore, students are able to conduct experiments smoothly and safely while studying dynamical reaction mechanism shown by the CG. The electronic textbook on a tablet could be used to integrate the experimental observable level and the molecular world.**

Keywords-Computer graphics; Visualization; Reaction mechanism; Electronic textbook; Chemical experiment.

I. INTRODUCTION

In order to understand the observed phenomena, chemists imagine and explain observations in terms of molecules. Observed phenomena and molecular level models are then represented in terms of mathematics and chemical equations [1], [2]. Student's difficulties and misconceptions in chemistry are from inadequate or inaccurate models at the molecular level [3]. A molecular structure visualized by the computer graphics (CG) provides a deeper understanding of a molecule [4].

It is our aim to produce a CG teaching material based on quantum chemistry calculations, which provides realizable images of the nature of a chemical reaction [5], [6]. We have reported that the CG on tablet was effective to provide images of chemical reaction, such as, "Energy" change, "Structure" change and "Migration of Electron" [7]. If the CG is linked with textbook for college chemistry-experiment, students could observe the reaction from the three thinking levels [1], [2], namely, phenomena in the observable level, the CG in the molecular level, and chemical equation in the symbolic level. Our ultimate goal is to produce an electronic textbook of chemistry experiment, which integrates these three thinking levels.

An electronic textbook has several advantages over the paper textbook. For example, realistic images can be shown by photograph, movie and CG. These images may include experimental procedures, molecular structures and reaction mechanisms. In addition, programmable capability [8], hyper-link and networking features provide interactive operation. Many electronic textbooks of chemistry exist, but most of them are almost identical to the paper book, and very few are related to the chemical experiment [9]. Moreover, tablet applications, which include CG movie of reaction mechanism related to student laboratory experiments, are not available.

In Section II of the paper, an approach to developing an electronic textbook for college chemistry-experiment, which tries to integrate the observable level experiment and the molecular world, is described. In Section III, the features of the proposed textbook are described. We conclude in Section IV.

II. PROCEDURE

The flow chart used to develop the electronic textbook for chemical experiment is shown in Figure 1. The chemical reaction was selected based on its importance in fundamental chemistry. To exhibit phenomena (left side), the experimental condition was optimized for college level small-scale chemistry-experiment.

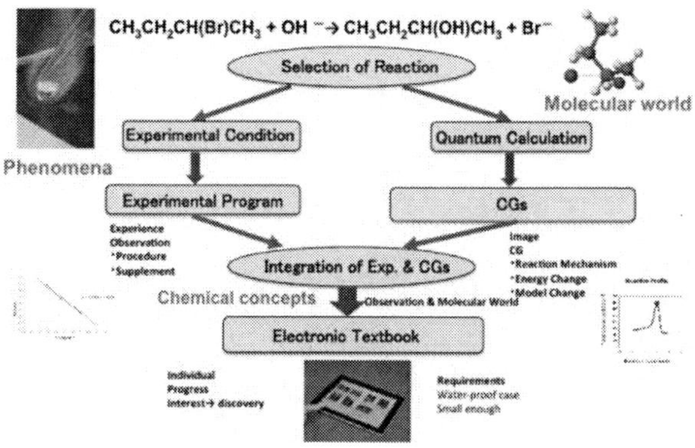

Figure 1. Flowchart of Developing Tablet for Chemistry-experiment

To provide the image of the molecular world (right side), CG images such as realistic shape of molecules and the CG movies of reaction mechanisms were made, based on the quantum chemistry calculation [5], [6]. A movie of the reaction path was produced by the software DIRECTOR (ver. 8.5.1J, Macromedia, Inc.) following the display of the bond order of the structures of the reactants in each reaction stage, which was drawn by SCIGRESS (Fujitsu). The obtained CG was combined with the reaction profile in the same reaction stage. It was confirmed that the drawn CGs of the molecular models of reactants moves smoothly. A ball, which indicates progress of the reaction, was arranged on the reaction profile and simultaneous movements of the ball and the reactants were confirmed. The created movie file was converted to the Quick Time movie for iPad by the Quick Time PRO (ver. 7.66, Apple, Inc.). After the combination of the experimental section and the CG section, the electronic textbook was produced with iBooks Author (ver. 2.1.1, Apple, Inc.) and was saved to tablet (iPad, Apple, Inc.) by using iTunes (ver. 11.2.1, Apple, Inc.). In order to use the electronic textbook on the lab bench, it needed to be covered with a waterproof, Zip-lock type, case.

III. Presentation On Tablet

In the experimental section, enlargeable-photos and flow charts were used for easier understanding of the procedure, in addition to regular text-base description. Supporting information, such as properties of reactants, was also included. The electronic textbook could acts as an individual electronic tutor.

The CG movie, shown in Figure 2, can simultaneously demonstrates the nature of the reaction, such as structural changes by the space-filling model and by the ball-and-stick model, in addition to providing an image of energy change by the reaction profile. Students are able to rotate the molecule freely and observe molecular geometry by touching 3D-CG on the right side of the text. Students are expected to obtain the image of an "umbrella reverse" like motion in the Walden's inversion while they are watching the actual reaction progress. This way, the experimental observable level and the molecular world could be integrated.

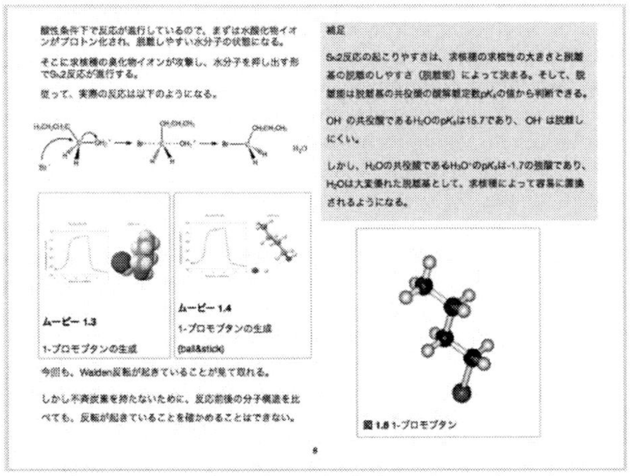

Figure 2. CG movies and 3D-CG of 1-bromobutane formation

IV. Conclusion

We developed computer graphics teaching material for university students, concerning chemical reactions with drastic change in the structure of reactants. The following chemical reaction was an example of Walden's inversion: hydroxylation of methyl chloride, formation of 2-butyl alcohol and 1-butyl bromide. The CG could demonstrate the drastic change of the structure and the reaction profile can provide an image of the energy change during the reaction. The textbook could display the picture of apparatus and a flow-chart of the experiment in addition to CG. From the preliminary study, students were able to obtain images of structural changes and conduct experiments smoothly and safely with the electronic textbook inserted in the Ziploc type plastic bag. The developed electronic textbook on the tablet could be used to integrate the experimental observable level and the molecular world.

Acknowledgment

This work was supported by JSPS KAKENHI Grant Numbers 25350188, 26350227.

References

[1] J. K. Gilbert and D. F. Treagust, in J. K. Gilbert, and D. Treagust, (eds.), "Models and Modelling in Science Education vol. 4 Multiple Representations in Chemical Education", Springer, pp. 333-350, 2009.

[2] R. Tasker and R. Dalton, in J. K. Gilbert, M. Reiner, and M. Nakhleh, (Eds.), "Models and Modelling in Science Education vol. 3 Visualization: Theory and Practice in Science Education", Springer, pp. 103-131, 2010.

[3] R. W. Kleinman, H. C. Griffin, and N. K. Kerner, J. Chem. Edu., vol. 64, pp. 766-770, 1987.

[4] I. Tuvi-Arad and R. Blonder, "Continuous symmetry and chemistry teachers: learning advanced chemistry content through novel visualization tools", Chem. Educ. Res. and Pract., vol. 11, no. 1, pp. 48-58, 2006.

[5] A. Ikuo, Y. Ikarashi, T. Shishido, and H. Ogawa, "User-friendly CG visualization with animation of chemical reaction: esterification of acetic acid and ethyl alcohol and survey of textbooks of high school chemistry", Journal of Science Education in Japan, vol. 30, no. 4, pp. 210-215, 2006.

[6] A. Ikuo, H. Nagashima, Y. Yoshinaga, and H. Ogawa, Calculation of potential energy in the reaction of "$I + H_2 \rightarrow HI + H$" and its visualization, The Chemical Education Journal (CEJ), Registration #13-2, 2009.

[7] A. Ikuo, H. Nagashima, Y. Yoshinaga, and H. Ogawa, "Development and practice of teaching material in tablet computer based on computer graphics by quantum chemistry calculation - Reaction of $I + H_2 \rightarrow HI + H$ –", Proc. 7th IEEE Intl. Conf. on Wireless, Mobile, and Ubiquitous Technologies in Educ., Mar. 2012, pp. 82-86.

[8] W. Singhose and J. Donnell, "Introductory Mechanical Design Tools", iBooks Store, 2013.

[9] C. M. Morvant and R. L. Halterman, "Organic Chemistry Laboratory Manual", iBooks Store, 2013.

GreedEx Tab: Tool for Learning Greedy Algorithms on Mobile Devices

Manuel Ortega Cordovilla, José David Patón Romero, Miguel Ángel Redondo Duque, Manuel Ortega Cantero, Ana Isabel Molina Díaz
College of Computer Science Engineering
University of Castilla-La Mancha (UCLM)
Ciudad Real, Spain
e-mail: Manuel.Ortega1@alu.uclm.es, JDavid.Paton@uclm.es, Miguel.Redondo@uclm.es, Manuel.Ortega@uclm.es, AnaIsabel.Molina@uclm.es

***Abstract*— This paper describes the process proposed in order to develop the *GreedEx Tab* mobile application for the Apple iPad. This application will handle the technology of this device to help the user learn greedy algorithms. This addresses the problems detected in the literature on the understanding of this programming schema by students and also the issues with the former desktop application *Greedex*. Thus, the application allows a student to perform the simulation with greedy algorithms for several problems related with knapsacks. After this simulation, the state of the knapsack will be shown in three dimensions and so will the data generated as a result. Preliminary results on the use of this tool show an improvement in the performance of the students using *Greedex Tab* over the results achieved with the previous development, named *Greedex*.**

Keywords- Greedy algorithms learning; m-Learning; Knapsack problem; iOS; iPad.

I. INTRODUCTION

A. Statement of the Problem

GreedEx [17] is a Java application developed by the University Rey Juan Carlos of Madrid (Spain) within the LITE (Laboratory of Information Technologies in Education) research group, whose objective is to facilitate the learning of greedy algorithms [2].

A greedy algorithm is a strategy that works well on optimization problems with the following characteristics:

1. Greedy-choice property: A global optimum can be obtained by selecting a local optimum.
2. Optimal substructure: An optimal solution to the problem contains an optimal solution to subproblems.

This kind of algorithms are difficult for students to understand [12].

This application has been evaluated by the CHICO (Computer Human Interaction and Collaboration) research group of the University of Castilla-La Mancha (Spain), in collaboration with the LITE research group of the University Rey Juan Carlos, using an eye tracking device available in the CHICO usability laboratory of the College of Computer Science Engineering of Ciudad Real.

The results of this evaluation [5] [6] have identified a number of shortcomings in the graphical user interface and in the learning methods that suggest that a more interactive tool could improve this learning. In [6] with the aim of improving the learning experience of students with the former Greedy system, we have carried out two experiments in order to assess the representations that this system supports. In these experiments, the information collected by means of subjective perception and motivation questionnaires was combined with the information obtained from an eye-tracker device.

For example, one of the conclusions reached was that the students preferred the tabular representations because the graphical representations were more complex and less representative, when it should be the other way around. In addition, the graphical representations lacked an interactive nature, which is an added difficulty.

Therefore, it is interesting to make an application where graphical representations take a greater role and actually help in learning greedy algorithms, improving, among other things, the interaction with the representation of the results.

B. Objectives of the Work

The main objective of this research is to implement a new version of the *GreedEx* application for iPad (*Greedex Tab* [14]), in order to improve and solve the problems encountered in the studies conducted on it.

This new version has to take advantage of the convenience of use and the ability of interaction, visualization, and animation of mobile devices, in order that users can learn the behavior of greedy algorithms. In this way, we intend to improve the learning of greedy algorithms as well as directly and objectively measure this improvement through eye tracking techniques.

Among the mobile devices currently available, we have opted for the iPad tablet, since the technology provides the necessary resources to develop this application. In addition, the *GreedEx* application is available only for conventional computers. Therefore, it is intended to extend the learning possibilities through this tool for other devices, such as mobile devices (in this case, the iPad).

C. Target of the Application

The developed application is targeted for use in university teaching in specialties and/or degrees of computing, in the field of learning of greedy algorithms. The subjects involved have different names at different universities, but the contents are framed in the typical algorithmic schemes that all computer engineering degrees have.

Furthermore, it is expected to be used by research groups in their work or part of it is based on the study and teaching of greedy algorithms, as is the case of the research groups of CHICO of the University of Castilla-La Mancha and LITE of the University Rey Juan Carlos.

Thus, this application is expected to have some impact on these areas and its use leads to the improvement of learning and research relating to greedy algorithms, as well as emergence of new applications related to this field and improvements/updates in the application in question.

In the present course 2015/2016 this application is used in several subjects of the Studies on Computer Science at the University of Castilla-La Mancha. Preliminary results show that the application fits the requirements needed in order to understand the complexity of the greedy algorithms and test over satisfaction and eye tracking studies will measure the improvement of this application in comparison with the former application *Greedex*. Some of these preliminary results could be shown at [15].

This article is structured into the following sections: first, in Section II we present the state of the art of this work. Section III focuses on presenting the working method used to develop the work. In Section IV we explain the Results obtained from our approach. Finally, in Section V, we discuss the conclusions arising from this work and the future work derived from it.

II. STATE OF THE ART

A. *Greedex*

The name of the *GreedEx* application is based on the acronym "GREEDy algorithms EXperimentation".

The *GreedEx* application is oriented to help in the learning of greedy algorithms. To this end, it gives support to interactive experimentation with different selection functions for a given problem, which is solved with a determined greedy algorithm.

The interactive experimentation on a particular problem allows the user to enter the data, execute greedy algorithm to reach a solution, and compare the obtained results.

In its current version, *Greedex* supports six optimization problems. One is the problem of selecting an activity, while the other five consist of exercises of the knapsack.

Among these exercises of the knapsack, the fractional knapsack, the 0/1 knapsack, and the variants of these exercises can be found. Each of these exercises has some selection functions with which the corresponding solution can be reached.

In Figure 1, the screen that shows *GreedEx* after solving a specific problem can be observed. In this case, it is the problem of the maximum number of objects, which is a variant of the exercise of 0/1 knapsack.

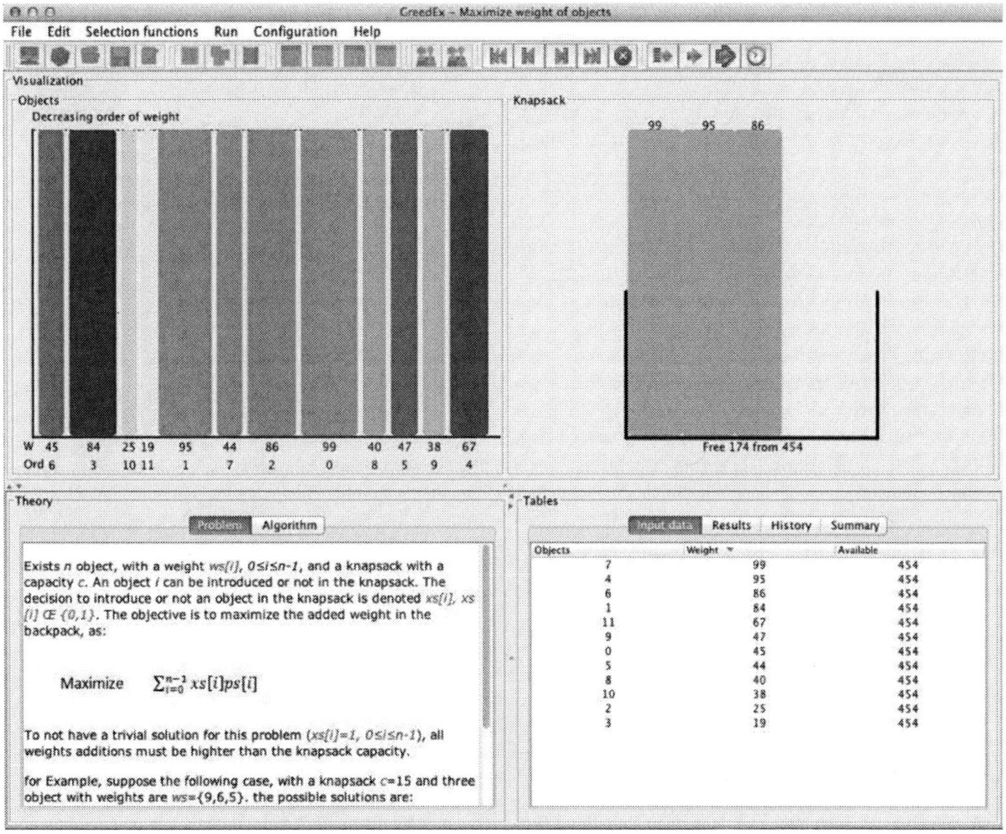

Figure 1. *GreedEx* screen after solving a specific problem with a greedy algorithm.

B. Development Technologies

Firstly, the device on which the development of the application in question has been carried out is the iPad, over iOS 9. The larger size of the device, which has a bigger screen, has been one of the motives for choosing this mobile device, since the representations to display will be seen much better and will be much more practical to orient the development, for example, for iPhone.

Secondly, to develop applications for iOS, it is necessary to use an integrated development environment (IDE). In this case, it is Xcode [18]. This is the integrated development environment of Apple, specific to developing applications for iOS and OS X.

Lastly, Objective-C as a programming language has been chosen. This is one of the major programming languages in Xcode to develop applications for iOS and OS X.

III. WORKING METHOD

A. SCRUM as Management Methodology

The research project development requires an agile management methodology, light, and, of course, flexible, due to the few people involved in it. We used a combination of OpenUp and SCRUM [10] methodologies and our methodology CIAM [4] [7] and CTTE [8] for task analysis, following a common schema in our CHICO Laboratory.

It is noteworthy to mention that SCRUM was conceived from the idea of following the *Manifesto for Agile Software Development* [1], and this has been one of the main reasons that motivated the choice of this methodology.

For our development users are teachers and students involved in the classes of subjects in Advanced Programming.

B. OpenUP as Development Methodology

As is the case with SCRUM, OpenUP [16] is also an agile methodology and was designed with the idea of following the *Manifesto for Agile Software Development* [1], and these are, again, the main reasons why OpenUP has been chosen as the development methodology.

Although sufficient and complete, OpenUP continues to be a variant of RUP (Rational Unified Process) [3]. That is why it retains some of their aspects, as is the structure of the life cycle divided into four phases (initiation, elaboration, construction and transition).

However, OpenUP refines the concepts inherited from RUP, to treat only basic aspects of project development, together with new concepts oriented toward facilitating the development of small projects.

All these reasons led us to choose OpenUP as the development methodology for the research.

C. Application of the Working Method

Based on the selected methodologies (SCRUM and OpenUP), the research was managed by *Sprints* with a duration of one week each, while the development was carried out by iterations according to a sequence of methods achieved through microincrements.

Although our aim is to do some research in order to facilitate the study of the greedy algorithms, in this paragraph we will use the term "Project" to refer to our research because these phases relate to the development of the application itself.

For the full development twelve *Sprints* were carried out, which are divided into four phases. The aspects that have been covered in each of these phases are initiation, elaboration, construction and transition.

In the transition phase, already having the final version of the application, the work was based on carrying out all necessary steps to finish the project and launch the final version of *GreedEx Tab*. Thus, a verification of the software quality was performed, performing black- and white-box testing, such as usability testing using the eye tracker with various students of the College of Computer Science Engineering of Ciudad Real, all in order to confirm if the expectations and objectives of the project had been met.

IV. RESULTS

In Table I, the features of *GreedEx Tab* can be observed.

TABLE I. FEATURES OF *GREEDEX TAB* APPLICATION

Functionalities	
1. Allow selection between different knapsack exercises. 2. Allow manual or random introduction of the necessary data for simulations. 3. Allow selection of different selection functions. 4. Allow making step by step, all steps at once, and intensive simulations. 5. Allow the state the state of the knapsack to be viewed in three dimensions after a simulation.	6. Allow access to historical simulations where the data and results thereof can be observed. 7. Having an "About" section, where information about the application is displayed, along with help about the function. 8. Allow a connection with iCloud, in order to store and load data from different simulations.
Graphical User Interface	
1. Allow navigation between the theoretical information of an exercise of the knapsack, the data used for simulation, the simulation of the exercise, and the historical data with the results. 2. Provide the necessary mechanisms to allow the introduction of the necessary data for the simulations. 3. Graphically and textually show the items in the knapsack (or knapsacks), as well as those who are still out.	4. When the knapsack is represented in three dimensions, display a legend about items by which it is formed. 5. Provide differentiation between elements of different kinds. 6. Provide feedback from those events that occur, that are in progress, or errors that may arise. 7. Follow the principles of Human-Computer Interaction, at no time using the application must become a tedious task.
Performance	
1. Perform simulations within reasonable limits of time and memory for this purpose.	

Different example views of the *GreedEx Tab* application are shown in Figures 2 to 13, and there how it is developed, how it works, its graphical interface, etc., can be observed.

A. Application Startup

At the startup of *GreedEx Tab*, the initial screen of the application is displayed, as shown in Figure 2, from which a user can start to interact with it.

From this view, we can see information about the version of the application ("Greedex Tab v1.3"), get access to the information and available help about the application (using the button "About Greedex Tab"), or select a specific knapsack exercise about which the simulation will be performed (among other features).

B. Theory of an Exercise View

Figure 3 shows the view displayed when a specific knapsack exercise is selected.

In that view, by default, the text and the code of the selected exercise, namely the theoretical part of the exercise, are displayed. The text and the code appear in different views with their own representation formats. The text appears on a laid paper, while the code is displayed in an OS X window. In this way, the essence of these parts is transmitted a little better to the user.

With this view of a knapsack exercise, in the bar at the bottom, a user can navigate to the different functionalities: "Theory", "Data", "Simulation", and "History". Each of these tabs has a symbol (in addition to the identification name in question), easily identified by the user.

Figure 2. *GreedEx Tab* initial screen.

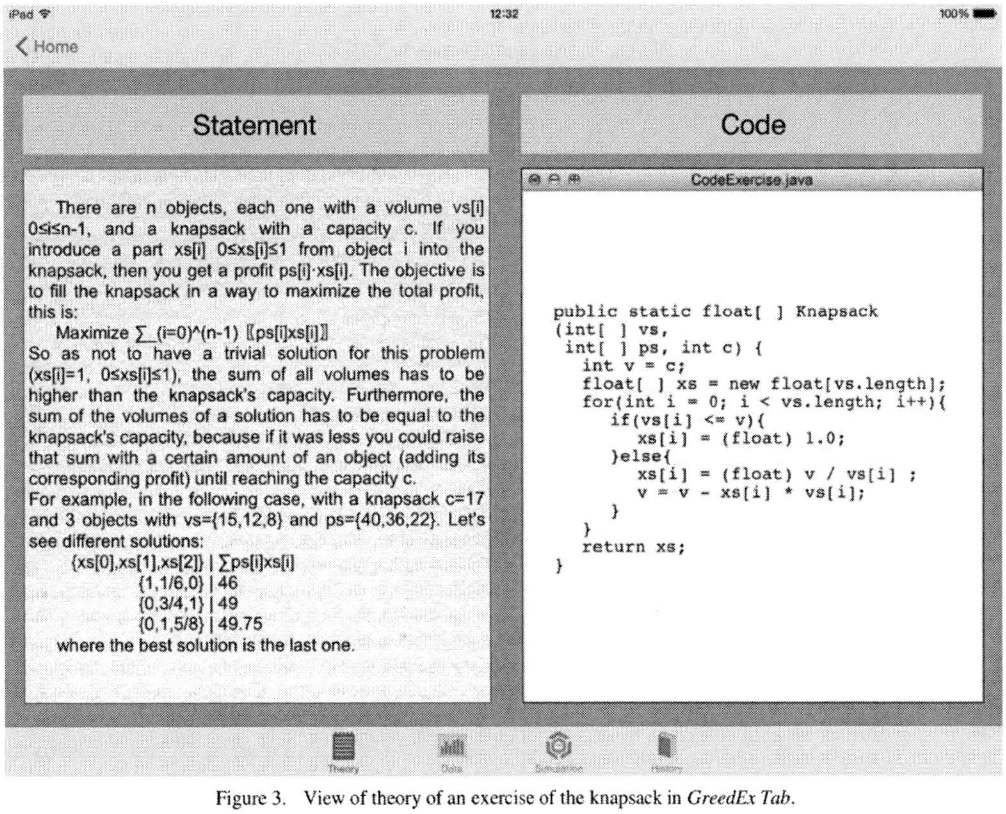

Figure 3. View of theory of an exercise of the knapsack in *GreedEx Tab*.

C. Data Creation View

Once the user has read and understood the corresponding theory of the exercise, to execute the simulation, the user must access the "Data" tab, where the data of the knapsack capacity, the maximum benefit by object, and the number of objects to create must be established, as shown in Figure 4.

In case of the exercise of two knapsacks, the view also includes a part to establish the capacity of the second knapsack.

Once the necessary data have been established, the result is the one shown in Figure 5.

Note that the data for the simulation can be entered manually or generated randomly by using the "Random data" button.

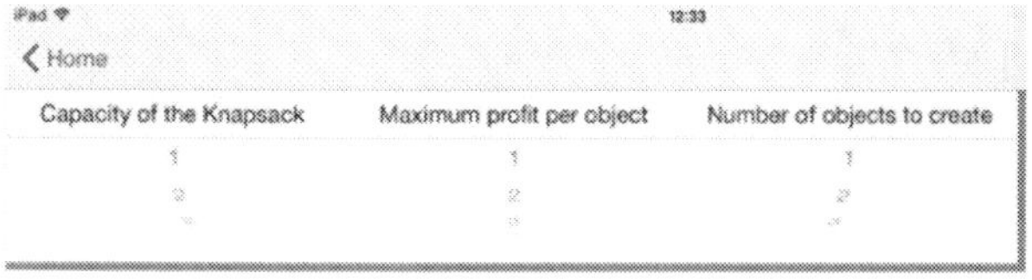

Figure 4. Part of the view dedicated to establishing the essential data for the simulation.

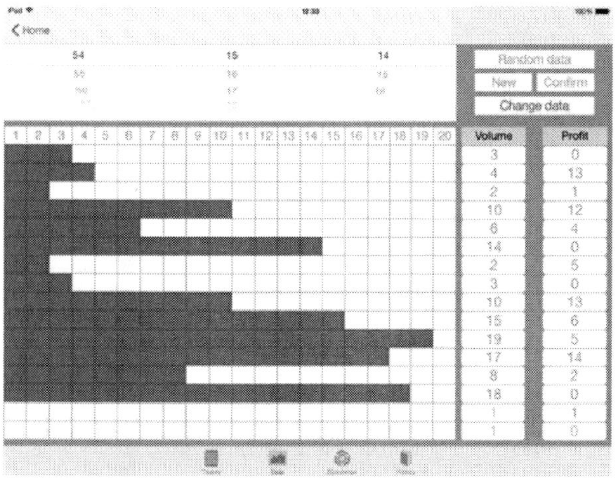

Figure 5. View with the data of the objects to create.

D. Simulation Objects View

Once the data of the objects established, these will appear created in the view of the "Simulation" tab, as shown in Figure 6.

In this view, when choosing a specific selection function, the objects created appear on the screen sorted by this selection function.

The selection functions are different depending on the knapsack exercise chosen. In Figure 7, the selection functions based on the available knapsack exercises are shown.

For example, in Figure 8, the objects created, ordered by the selection function "Increasing volume" are shown.

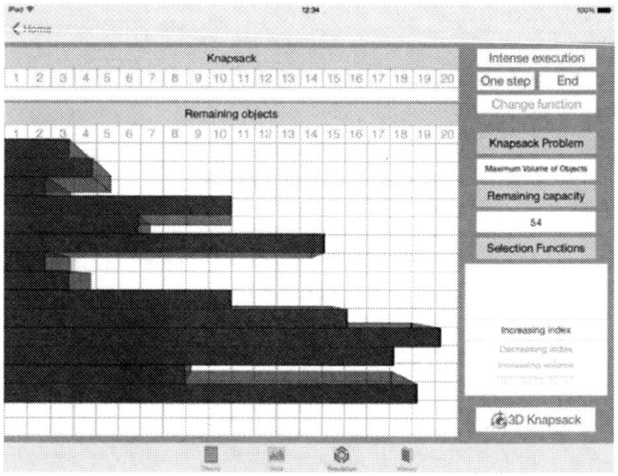

Figure 6. Simulation view with the created objects.

Figure 7. Selection functions according to the exercises of the knapsack.

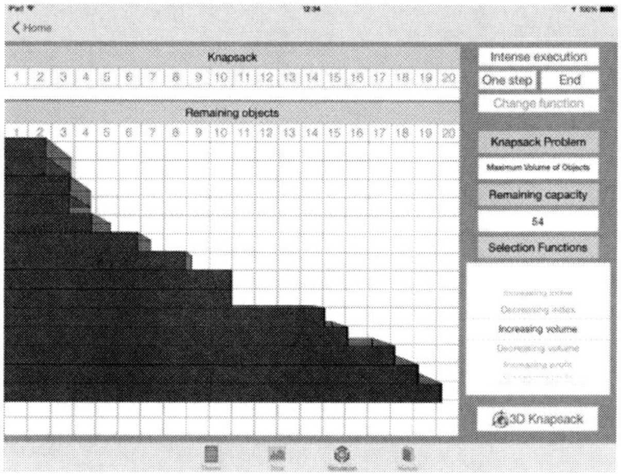

Figure 8. Sorting objects according to the selection function chosen.

To carry out the simulation that will introduce the objects in the knapsack and generate a series of results, there are three possibilities: step by step, all the steps at once, and intensive.

Firstly, using the example of sorting of the selection function chosen in Figure 8, when the step by step execution in the simulation (using the button "One step") is performed, the first object is inserted into the knapsack, which will reduce its remaining capacity, as can be seen in Figure 9.

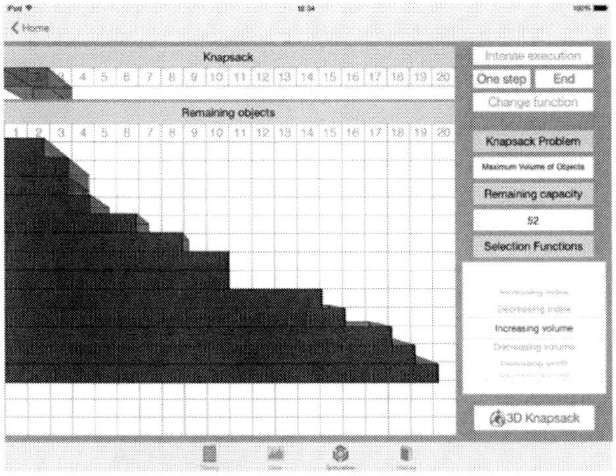

Figure 9. Introduction of an object in the knapsack when executing a step in the simulation.

Secondly, instead of carrying out the step by step execution, all the steps of a particular selection function can be performed at once, using the "Final" button, which will introduce all remaining objects following the order established, as shown in Figure 10.

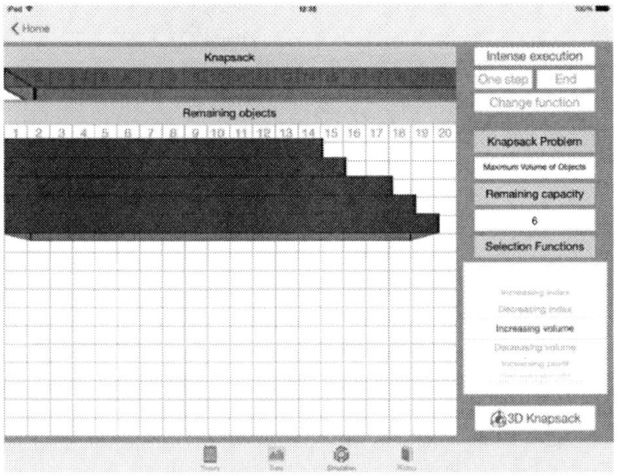

Figure 10. Final execution in the simulation that introduces all the objects in the knapsack.

Finally, the user also has the option to make an intensive execution (using the button with the same name). It is, therefore, not necessary to choose a selection function, since it is made with all the selection functions available in the exercise.

Note that the simulation view in the exercise of the two knapsacks differs from the rest because, logically, it contains two knapsacks to introduce objects and, therefore, two remaining capacities, as can be seen in Figure 11.

E. Three Dimensions Knapsack View

After carrying out the execution of "One Step" or "Final", the user can view the status of the knapsack in three dimensions by pressing the button "Knapsack in 3D" which can be found in the "Simulation" tab, which will display the view on the screen shown in Figure 12. The user can interact with this knapsack in three dimensions, being able to rotate it and view it in its entirety.

It is important to note that this representation of the knapsack in three dimensions has been implemented using the OpenGL graphics library [13].

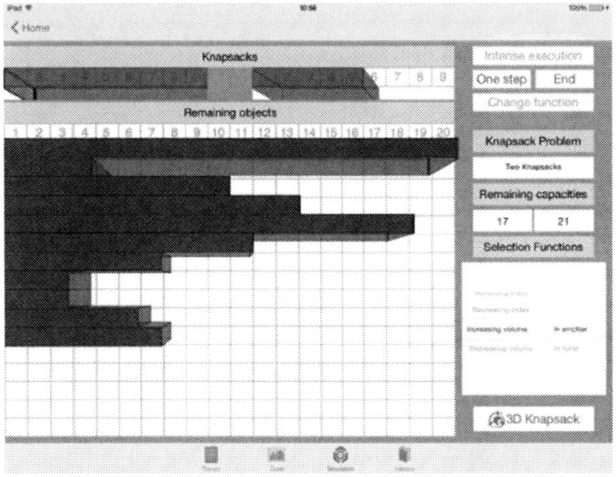

Figure 11. View of simulation with two knapsacks.

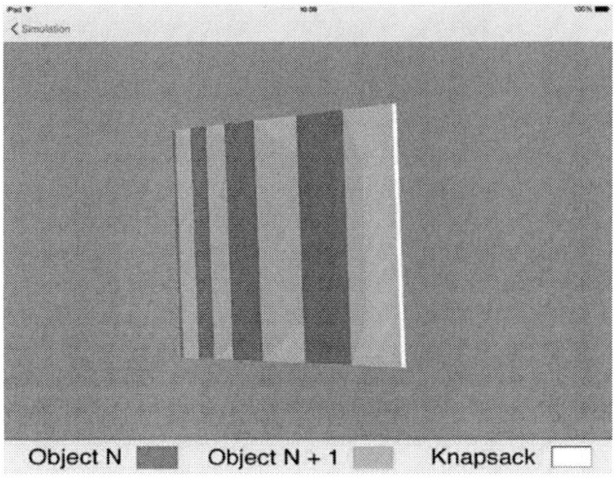

Figure 12. View of the knapsack in three dimensions.

F. Historical Data of Simulations View

All executions that are performed for a specific exercise in a session are recorded and appear in the "Table of execution" of the "History" tab along with the data and information relating to them, such as the selection function, the candidates and selected objects, the remaining capacity of the knapsack, and the result.

In this view of historical data of simulations, a functionality allows a user to store and load data from any simulation in iCloud.

Whether the data are from local executions during the current session, or loaded from iCloud, the success rates of selection functions and other affected results will be updated.

The user is notified of any access to iCloud, or whether there has been a change of data in the "Data" tab.

Figure 13 shows the view displayed in the "History" tab, in which, by way of example, the result of different executions with various selection functions is shown.

In this view, we can see the available buttons for the functionality that allows a user to upload and store the data of the executions on iCloud. These buttons, located in the upper right, are represented with their characteristic symbol and with the function that they perform.

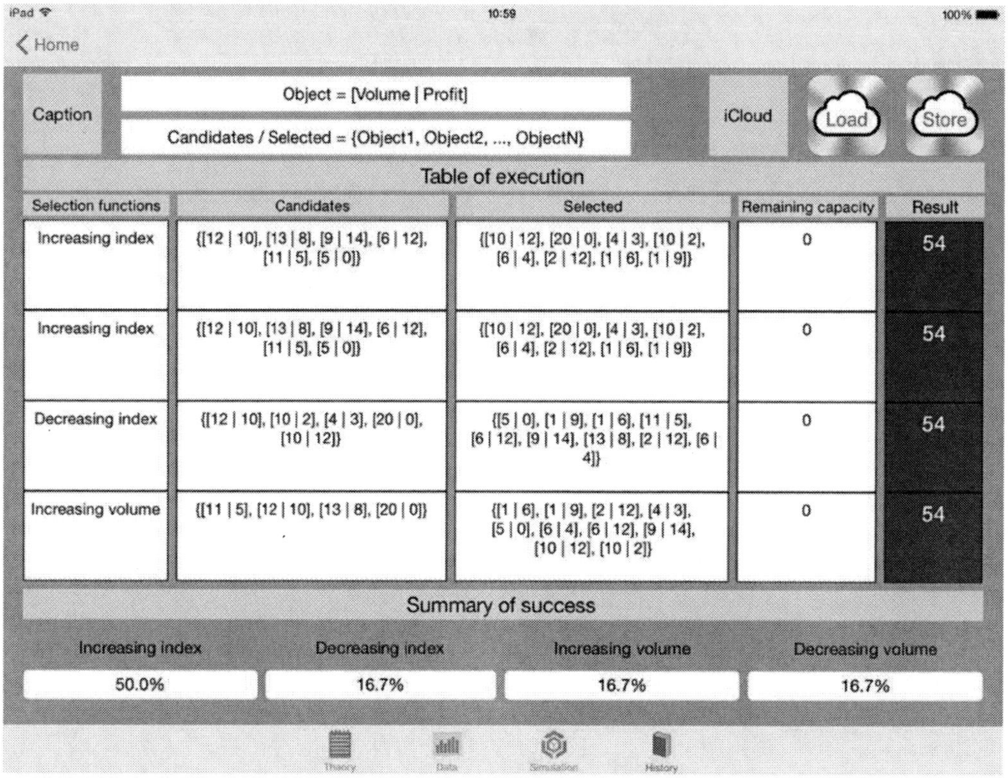

Figure 13. View of the historical data of the executions performed.

G. *Internationalization*

The application has full versions in English, Spanish and German, which will appear if these are the native languages installed on the iPad of the user.

H. *About the Application*

It is important to note that *GreedEx Tab* has been developed following the golden rules of Ben Shneiderman [11], which establishes the eight basic principles of usability in the interfaces design. In addition, the principles of designing applications for iOS established by Apple have also been followed, as well as the usability patterns for mobile devices defined by Jacob Nielsen [9].

V. CONCLUSIONS

The *GreedEx Tab* application is born with a strong didactic nature, as it is a very useful tool in learning greedy algorithms for users who are studying such algorithms.

Throughout the implementation, we have tried to make the *GreedEx Tab* an intuitive and a fast application that allows the user to interact in the simplest way possible, giving him the functionality that he needs so that learning does not become a complicated and tedious task.

An aesthetically elegant and attractive application has been created, allowing the user to focus on functionality, characteristics that define the lines of development that Apple follows nowadays in all their applications.

A. *Usability Tests*

To analyze the usability improvements added to the application and check the resolution of the problems found in preliminary studies about *GreedEx*, a series of tests was carried out [15].

These tests were performed with students of the College of Computer Science Engineering of Ciudad Real, and consisted of raising a series of activities to do in the *GreedEx Tab* application with the iPad device, while registering and recording all activity with the eye tracker.

Before and after performing the tests on the application, the participants had to fill out a questionnaire about their knowledge of greedy algorithms and their experience with the application. After collecting all the information, the comparison and the analysis of the data collected was carried out through the questionnaires and the eye tracker.

After analyzing all the information, it can be determined that the shortcomings in the graphical user interface and in the learning methods detected in preliminary studies of the *GreedEx* application [5] [6] have been resolved.

The tabular representations have taken a back seat and now the graphical representations are the most consulted and most representative. Furthermore, the interaction with knapsack in three dimensions has become an attraction at the time of learning the functioning of greedy algorithms with this application.

B. Future Work Lines

Firstly, the *GreedEx Tab* application has been limited to its implementation only for iPad, but it could also be implemented for other types of mobile devices, not necessarily of the Apple brand, or also for conventional computers. The more mobile devices or computers of different brands and operating systems that can run *GreedEx Tab*, the faster the application could expand.

Therefore, a version of *GreedEx Tab* for web could be developed, to be accessible from all types of mobile devices or computers of any kind and any operating system.

Secondly, the application could be improved by increasing the available knapsack exercises, allowing for the simulation of more types of exercises.

Thirdly, considering that users of the application will belong to the field of computer science, and more specifically, they will be teachers and students from an engineering college or a professional training center, the implementation of a cooperative environment would be a marked improvement. In this environment, students and teachers could simulate knapsack exercises together and access the simulation data, so that they could discuss what the best solution is.

Furthermore, instead of each user having an individualized space on iCloud, this space could be common for all students in a class, allowing each student to contribute their efforts to better understand greedy algorithms.

Fourth, following this line, the application could also perform knowledge tests to demonstrate to the teacher that the students understand the concepts of greedy algorithms. For example, verify that the student knows how to anticipate the corresponding simulation algorithm and knows which object will be inserted into the knapsack, or, given a particular exercise of the knapsack, the student knows how to estimate which selection function will fulfil its purpose better.

Finally, *GreedEx Tab* has been developed in Spanish, English and German. Additionally, they could be implemented in more languages, such as French, Italian, etc.

ACKNOWLEDGMENTS

This research has been partially funded by the Ministry of Science and Innovation through the project TIN2015-66731-C2-2-R, the Thematic Network of CYTED 513RT0481, and the JCCM Projects PPEII-2014-012A and PPII11-0013-1219.

REFERENCES

[1] K. Beck et al., Manifesto for Agile Software Development. Agile Alliance, Wasatch, UT, USA, 2001.

[2] E. Horowitz, S. Sahni, and S. Rajasekaran, Computer Algorithms / C++ (2nd Edition). Silicon Press, Summit, NJ, USA, 2007.

[3] P. Kroll, P. Kruchten, and G. Booch, The Rational Unified Process Made Easy: A Practitioner's Guide to the RUP. Addison-Wesley Longman Publishing Co. Inc., Boston, MA, USA, 2003.

[4] A. I. Molina et al., "CIAT-GUI: A MDE-compliant environment for developing Graphical User Interfaces of information systems," Advances in Engineering Software, Vol. 52, pp. 10-29, October 2012, doi:10.1016/j.advengsoft.2012.06.002.

[5] A. I. Molina, M. Paredes, M. A. Redondo, A. Velázquez, and M. Ortega, "Evaluación basada en eye tracking de las técnicas de visualización de programas soportadas por el Sistema GreedEx," SINTICE 2013, September 2013.

[6] A. I. Molina, M. Paredes, M. A. Redondo, and A. Velázquez, "Assessing representation techniques of programs supported by GreedEx," The Sixteenth International Symposium on Computers in Education (SIIE 2014), Vol. 56-58, November 2014, doi:10.1109/SIIE.2014.7017704.

[7] A. I. Molina, M. A. Redondo, and M. Ortega, "A methodological approach for user interface development of collaborative applications: A case study," Science of Computer Programming, Vol. 74, No. 9, pp. 754-776, July 2009, doi:10.1016/j.scico.2009.03.001.

[8] G. Mori, F. Paternò, and C. Santoro, "CTTE: support for developing and analyzing task models for interactive system design," IEEE Transactions on Software Engineering, Vol. 28, No. 8, pp. 797-813, August 2002, doi:10.1109/TSE.2002.1027801.

[9] J. Nielsen, and B. Raluca, Mobile Usability. New Riders, Berkeley, CA, USA, 2013.

[10] K. Schwaber, "SCRUM Development Process," OOPSLA Business Object Design and Implementation Workshop. Advanced Development Methods Inc., Burlington, MA, USA, 1997.

[11] B. Shneiderman and C. Plaisant, Designing the User Interface: Strategies for Effective Human-Computer Interaction (5th Edition). Addison-Wesley Publishing Co., Reading, MA, USA, 2010.

[12] J. Á. Velázquez-Iturbide and A. Pérez-Carrasco, "Active learning of greedy algorithms by means of interactive experimentation," ACM SIGCSE Bulletin – ITiCSE '09, Vol. 41, Issue 3, pp. 119-123, September 2009, doi:10.1145/1595496.1562917.

[13] Apple Inc., OpenGL ES Programming Guide for iOS. Retrieved March 01, 2016, from Apple Developer Website: https://developer.apple.com/library/ios/documentation/3DDrawing/Conceptual/OpenGLES_ProgrammingGuide

[14] M. Ortega, Wiki of GreedEx Tab. Retrieved March 01, 2016, from CHICO Wiki: http://chico.inf-cr.uclm.es/greedextab/wiki/index.php

[15] M. Ortega, Usability Tests of GreedEx Tab. Retrieved March 01, 2016, from CHICO Wiki: http://chico.inf-cr.uclm.es/greedextab/wiki/index.php/Pruebas_de_usabilidad

[16] The Eclipse Foundation, OpenUP. Retrieved March 01, 2016, from EPF Eclipse Wiki: http://epf.eclipse.org/wikis/openup/

[17] GreedEx Project Official Website. Available at: http://www.lite.etsii.urjc.es/greedex/

[18] Xcode Official Website. Available at: https://developer.apple.com/xcode/

Designing Questions to Teach Python with a Classroom Response System

Luis A. Álvarez-González, Gabriela González-Sáez, and Esteban Huenumán
Grupo de Investigación en Tecnología de Aprendizaje
Instituto de Informática, Universidad Austral de Chile
Valdivia, Chile
emails: {lalvarez@inf.uach.cl, gabriela.gonzalezsaez@gmail.com, esteban.huenuman@hotmail.cl}

Abstract— **To do an effective class using a Classroom Response System, two important questions appear: What questions to ask? and How to ask them? This paper tries to contribute with answers for these questions for an introductory course of Python language. For the first question, the Question Driven Instruction (QDI) methodology is introduced. For the second one, the questions are divided in content questions and process questions according to the content objectives and process objectives. Some examples questions are shown. The Classroom Response System (CRS) called "Mobile QTI" is used. "Mobile QTI" was designed for mobile devices (tablets and smartphones), supports eight types of questions, and is under IMS Question & Test Interoperability Specification (QTI). Finally, an experiment is presented in order to validate the methodology. The experiment shows a relationship between Grade Point Average (GPA) and the use of the QDI and the CRS Mobile QTI.**

Keywords-Mobile–learning; Classroom Response Systems; Question Driven Instruction; Python Language.

I. Introduction

As a way to improve learning, the research community in educational science has promoted the concept of Active Learning [5][11]. Learning-centered evaluation indicates that it must be continuous, and feedback essential to guide students in the learning process. In order to give response to learning-centered evaluation, the formative assessments contribute to know the learning of the students during the teaching process [3][6][10]. This is in contrast with the summative assessment, which is usually made at the end of a learning unit, and tries to measure how much the student learned. The main purpose of formative assessment is learning and the main purpose of summative assessment is the qualification. Formative assessment is probably one of the best "innovations" in education to improve learning. However, for that to happen there must be feedback as soon as possible. Using Classroom Response Systems (CRS) helps transform classroom dynamics, allowing learning focused assessment. In other words, a CRS, can be used to increase the frequency of questions and reduce response times in the formative assessment, so to have improved and faster feedback. The CRS can help the student-centered learning and active learning in general, but it depends on how the teacher uses it. The CRS is a tool and not "the solution". A CRS can be used in many different ways and many of them questionable, such as taking attendance in classes [8][12].

However, the most of the CRS only support multiple choice questions, true/false question and short texts [8] [17]. To support more types of questions it was necessary to develop a new CRS called Mobile QTI [1][18]. Mobile because use mobile devices, and QTI because is under IMS Question & Test Interoperability Specification [14] (IMS QTI Specifications).

The Agile Teaching/Learning Methodology (ATLM) is a systemic approach to teaching/learning that has taken place in several courses of Computer Science at the City University of Hong Kong [9]. As the name implies, ATLM is a methodology for both teaching and learning. Teachers have a well-defined way of educating, in the same way that students have a very clear path to learning. ATLM is a methodology that tries to balance a good teaching with good learning. This approach has been obtained from the software engineering field, where the development process can become complex and dynamic, which often require changes in order to minimize risks. The teaching process in many ways is similar to the software development process, which involves different objectives (sometimes conflicting), completion dates, limited resources and high expectations. Like software engineering, teaching requires detailed planning, monitoring and management of assessments and feedback from participants.

According to Bransford et al. [7] effective learning environments are:

1. Student-centered. Organises learning from prior knowledge of the student.
2. Knowledge-centered. Treat knowledge as an interconnected structure, that can be organised and improved in order to expanded.
3. Assessment-centered. Considers assessment as a continuous process, where education should be commented on while the teaching/learning process takes place. This is contrasted with summative assessment conducted after instruction. So, the first objective is formative assessment [3][4][6].
4. Community-centered. It recognizes that students belong to a community of students in a course of a degree, an institution, a society and promotes collaborative learning

Section II explains why Python as first programming language is recommended. In Section III, a brief explanation of the main functions of Mobile QTI as CRS is given. In Section IV, the relationship between the methodology Question Driven Instruction, formative assessment and the use of CRS is explained. In Section V, some questions used in an experiment are shown. In Section VI, a brief explanation of the experiment and the results are described. Finally, in Section VII, the conclusion and future work are presented.

II. PYTHON AS THE FIRST COMPUTER LANGUAGE

The training of engineers needs to develop logical thinking, which subsequently helps them to plan solutions, algorithms or procedures and also to create and solve problems in general. The development of logical thinking is achieved by learning a computer language, among other subjects. There are several computer languages, but few are recommended as the first language. In several universities, C++ or Java is used as a first language; however, Python is easier to use [16]. For example, the typical first program that every student takes is for screen display "Hello World!"

In C ++ corresponds to:

```
#include <iostream.h>
int main()
{
   cout << "Hello World!";
}
```

In Java to:

```
public class HelloWorld
{
   public static void main(String[]
args)
    {
      System.out.println("Hello
World!");
    }
}
```

While Python is simply

```
print("Hello World!")
```

In other words, while in C++ and Java, several statements and explanations are needed, Python uses only one sentence, easy to understand. Additionally, Python is interpreted and available in mobile devices, making it easy to use.

Figure 1 shows an exercise for learning Python lists using a mobile phone. A list of integers is filled and then several lines with asterisk ("*") according to the integer in the list is displayed. The number of asterisks on each line corresponds to the integer value of each item.

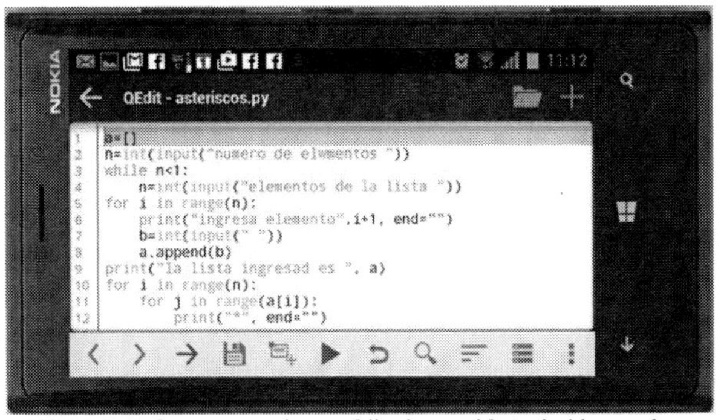

Figure 1. Python program in a mobile phone with Android operating system.

Its availability on mobile devices allows students to practice Python on their own devices, anytime, anywhere.

III. MOBILE QTI

The Mobile QTI is a web player for question under IMS-QTI Specification that can be used as a CRS. The question can be built with either the Web QTI or AquRate, both editors are under IMS QTI Specifications. The Web QTI is a web editor [19] and AquRate [20] need to be downloaded to use it. To develop Mobile QTI, Javacript, PHP and HTML5 were used. The users (teacher and students) need to be registered because they have different functions. After the teacher has launched the questions, the students answer and, in real-time, the answers are relayed to the teacher for inspection [18]. Figure 2 shows the main menu in a mobile device.

a) b)

Figure 2. The Mobile QTI, a) Teacher's view, b) Student's view

The main menu for teachers shows the following options:

- **Download Interaction** (*Cargar Interacción*): The teachers download questions from his/her laptop or repository.

- **Create a Test** (*Crear Test*): The teacher creates a test with the questions previously stored in Mobile QTI. The teachers can then select who participates in the test and who doesn't. In others words, a teacher can do several tests to different group of students.
- **Download Test** (*Cargar Test*): The teacher launches the test.
- **Results** (*Resultados*): Shows the results of each test per students and class.
- **List of Users** (*Lista Usuarios*): Shows all the users of Mobile QTI.
- **Administration** (*Administración*): For the management of questions, test and users.

Figure 3 shows a summary of the students' answers on a class with four questions and ten students. The tick is for a correct answer, the cross for an incorrect answer and dash for an incomplete question. In case the teacher needs to do a detailed analysis, the summary can be exported to an Excel File. Also, the answers of each student can be seen.

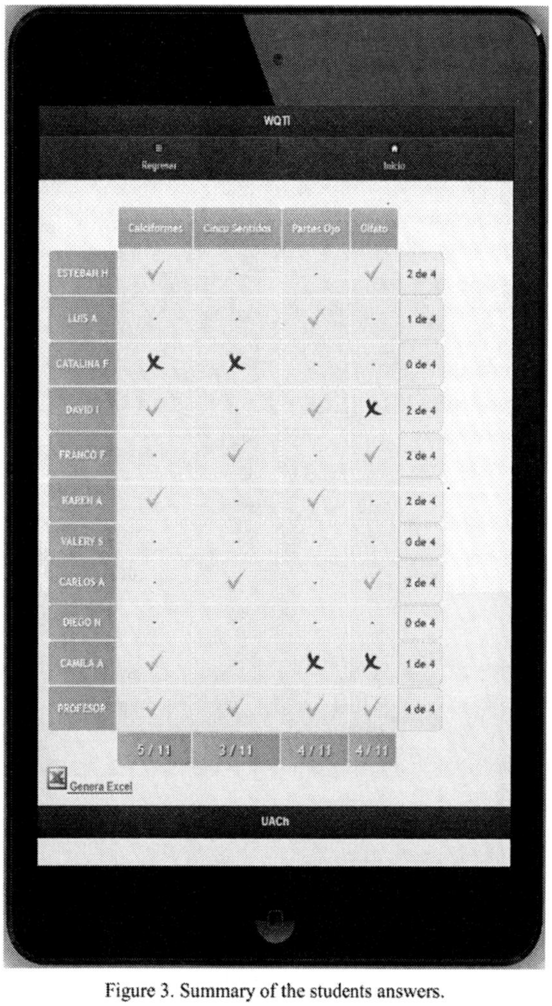

Figure 3. Summary of the students answers.

The teacher needs to download one or several questions and then launch them to the students. For example, a teacher can launch question by question to a class or launch several questions at the same time (test). The teacher can see this live table for each question to know the progress of each student; very useful when you are lunching question by question to a class to know the students understanding. This way, the teacher can see the progress of the students at any time.

Eight types of question are supported by Mobile QTI:

1. Choice: The student selects one of several alternatives.
2. Order: The student order concepts according to a criteria.
3. Associate: The students associated concepts.
4. Inline choice: The students need to fill blanks with a word.
5. Text entry: The students need to fill blanks with a sentence.
6. Hotspot: The students select one of several images.
7. Graphic order: The student sort several marks in an image.
8. Slider: The students need to move slider between two points bound to the answer.

The question type order is very useful in programming language. Typically in a question, several sentences are displayed and the student needs to order them correctly.

Most of the CRSs support only multiple choice, true/false, and text entry, and do not work under any specification. For this reason, Mobile QTI was developed [1].

IV. Question Driven Instruction

Active learning and the strengthening the four "centered learning" is possible with the help of Classroom Response System (CRS); however, this is only a technology and its effectiveness depends on the teacher and the methodology to be carried out.

The CRS, as any technology, can be used in many different ways, with varying degrees of impact on learning, for example with diagnostic tests, summative assessment class discussions, etc. However, the Question Driven Instruction (QDI) [2][13], tries to be an alternative to traditional "transmit and evaluate". In QDI the learning activity starts with a question and the periods between feedback should be very short, so that the teacher can monitor student's progress, identify difficulties in learning of each student, and take decisions in order to make an effective class. This methodology is under the notion of agile teaching/learning methodology [9] and personalized learning [15].

Formative assessment is the focus of the QDI methodology and provides quick feedback for the student to "drive" their learning activities and teacher to "drive" their teaching strategies.

A teacher using QDI requires experience and a good knowledge of the subjects that they teach, especially in environments with students of differing levels and speeds of learning. In other words, the teacher needs to be continuously adapting. Many teachers, unconsciously, develop this methodology for smaller classes, but for larger classes is very difficult without the use of technology.

A typical class using QDI begins with a question (a traditional class begins with an exposition). It takes a few minutes for students to respond. Students respond using CRS and the teacher shows a graph of the students' answers. Without disclosing the correct answer, the teacher asks for a volunteer looking to respond with their answer (whether correct or incorrect). The next step is to discuss each result without saying whether it is correct or incorrect. This way the teacher can analyses several related matters. Therefore, it is very important to design good questions in order to cover the learning objective. Also, it is possible to do more questions to explore the matter more profoundly. The teacher can finish with a summary of ideas from the different answers or present a slide to clarify the concepts discussed in the class. Figure 4 shows the different stages of the methodology.

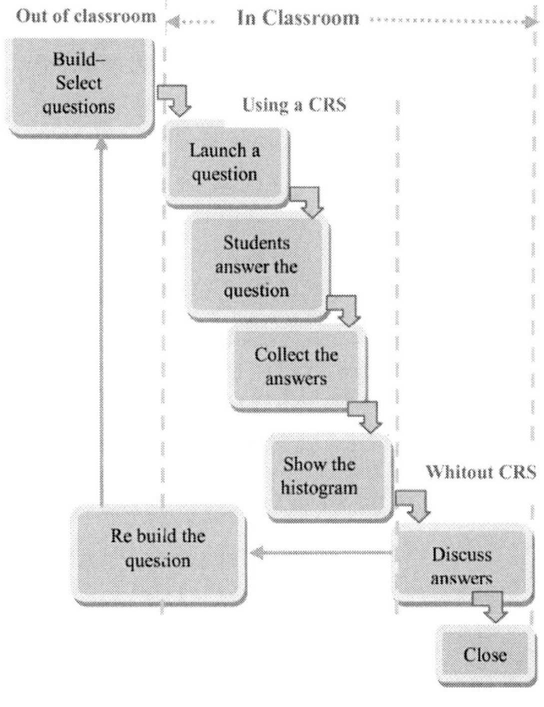

Figure 4. Cycle of the Question Driven Instruction methodology.

The cycle starts building and selecting questions according the learning objective, these questions are "launched" to students, the students answer by group or individually, according to the lesson plan, the answers are collected and a histogram with the answers of each student is displayed (the right answer is not shown) and the discussion starts. To have a profound discussion the questions must be very content rich. To start the discussion, the teacher asks for a volunteer (ideally with a wrong answer). The volunteer student then argues her/his answer, and then the rest of students discuss it, until the right answer is discovered. The cycle ends with a summary where all the possible answers are analysed.

The time must be sufficient so that most of the students can participate, and no so much as to lose the learning objective. Flexibility is very important. Some questions may be easily understood by some students whilst others may struggle. The teacher needs to adjust the teaching method according to time constraints and the learning objectives. This is the essence of the Agile Teaching. However, all learning material must be available for every student.

This methodology needs to be analysed according to the context, i.e., type of objectives and learning characteristics, for example if the objective is an individual skill, probably another methodology could be more appropriate.

A. *Type of questions*

Before building or selecting questions, the teacher needs to have declared the learning objective. In general the objectives can be classified into content objectives, process objectives, and metacognitive objectives.

Content objectives: with questions related to content, usually a brief discussion is enough. In programming languages, these types of question can be related to the syntax of a language. In this case, the cycle of QDI can be brief. However, they are very important in order to understand more advanced concepts.

Process objectives: the questions of contents are oriented towards basic knowledge; the process question is oriented about the relationship of this basic knowledge. How are they related? i.e., the answers require a small analysis. The cycle QDI could need more time.

Metacognitive Objectives: the metacognition, generally, relates to building knowledge based on the previous knowledge, e.g., solving news problems. These questions are usually reserved for summative assessments.

V. QUESTION FOR FORMATIVE ASSESSMENT IN PYTHON

To teach introduction to Python language, the contents are structured in four units of learning: a) simple statements, b) conditional statements, c) loop statements, and d) list. For each of these units of learning, the knowledge of syntaxes and semantics (content objectives), and how to use this statements (process objectives) are necessary. So, eight sets of questions were made: two learning objectives (contents and processes) by four units of learning. Each question was discussed with the teaching team, in order to have rich question.

A. Simple statements

The simple statements are related with the use of variables, data type, operators, and built-in function. Here, it is important to know the syntaxes, the semantic, and introduce the simple sequences, to solve small problems.

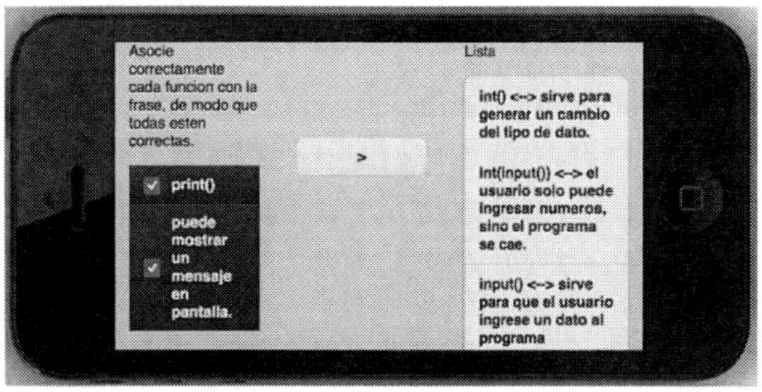

Figure 5a. Question of content for Python language. Associative question.

Figure 5a shows a content question and Figure 5b shows a process question for simple statements. Figure 5a, shows an associative question, where the students relate some function of Python (`int()`, `input()`, and `print()`) with their use.

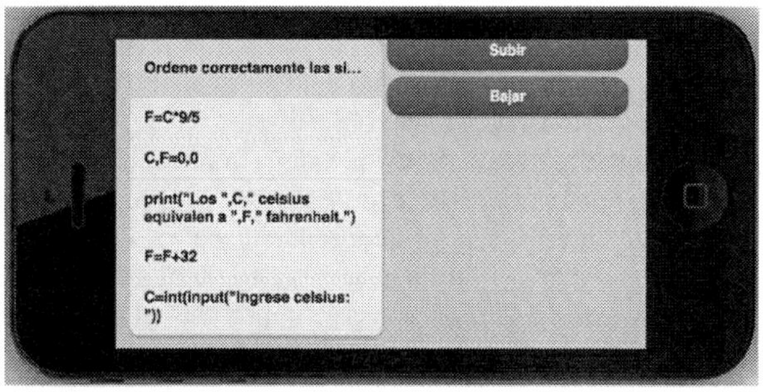

Figure 5b. Question of process. Order question.

After knowing the concepts of variables, data type, and basics built-in functions, the next step is how to build a program in Python. Figure 5b, shows an example, where the student needs to order, several sentences that convert degree Celsius to degrees Fahrenheit.

B. Conditional statements

The conditional statements in Python are `if`, `else` and `elif`, and also these statements can be nested. Figure 6a shows a content question to identify the right use of these statements.

Figure 6a shows typical errors when the `if` statements is used, and Figure 6b shows a program in Python to calculate if a quadratic equation has real roots or complex roots.

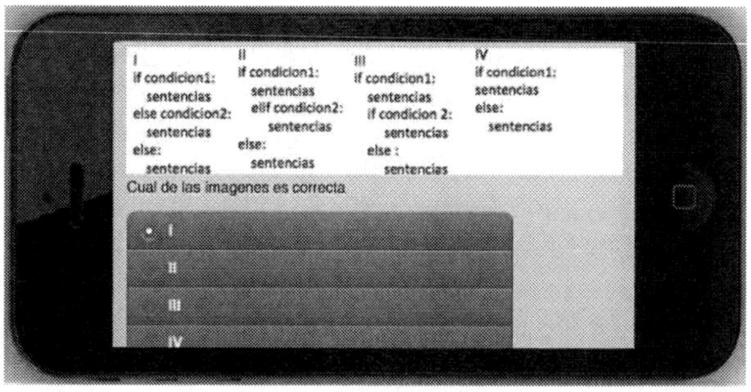

Figure 6a. Content question for statement `if`. Multiple choice question.

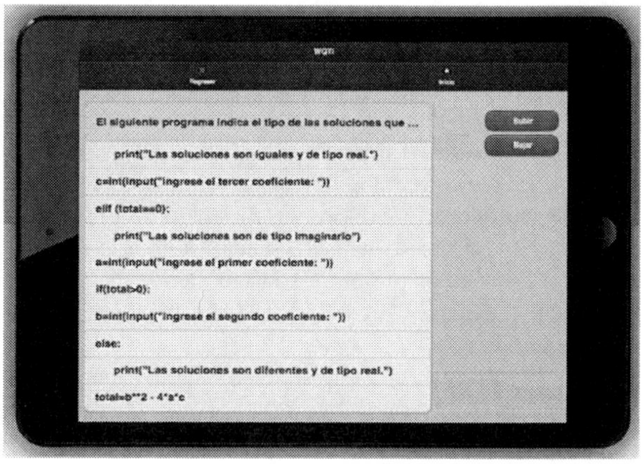

Figure 6b. Process question for `if` statement. Order question.

Here, the important point is that the student can recognise the right sequence, according to the data input and calculus.

C. Loop statements

The `while` and the `for` statements are studied. The first one needs a condition to repeat the loop, the second one needs an index in a range. Figure 7a shows an example of content question and Figure 7b an example of process question. The content questions are oriented to the syntaxes of the statements and the process questions oriented to the execution of the statements.

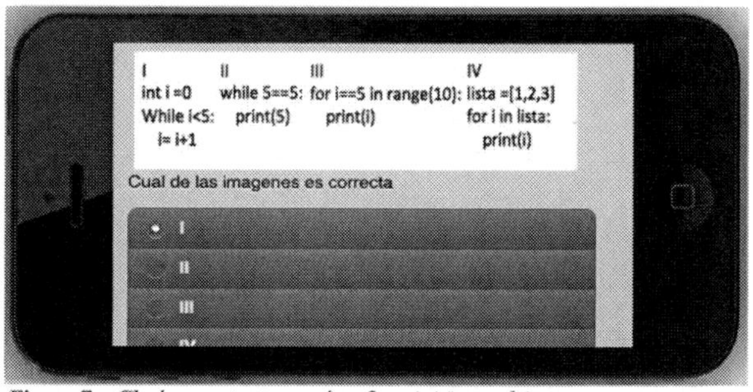

Figure 7a. Choice content question for `while` and `loop` statements.

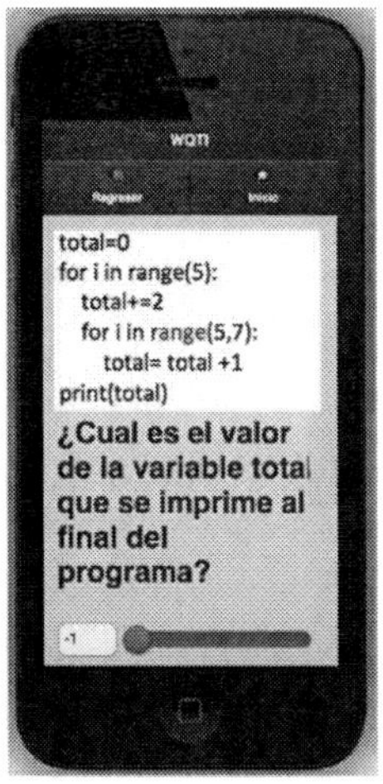

Figure 7b. Slider process question to `for` loop statement.

D. *Data Types: List*

The lists are necessary as an introduction to structured data in Python. To start with lists, the students need to know some methods as `append()` and some functions as `len()`, and identify the list elements. The content questions are oriented to learn this basic terminology. After this, is necessary to understand how to use a list, to do that, process questions are needed. Figure 8a shows a question oriented to learn the basic methods, functions and identify the elements.

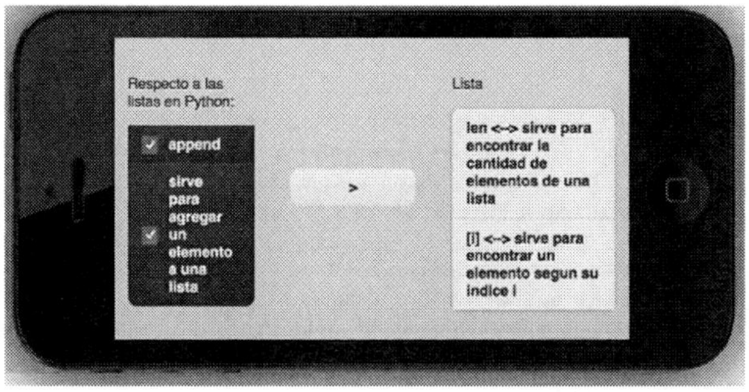

Figure 8a. Content question for lists. Associative question.

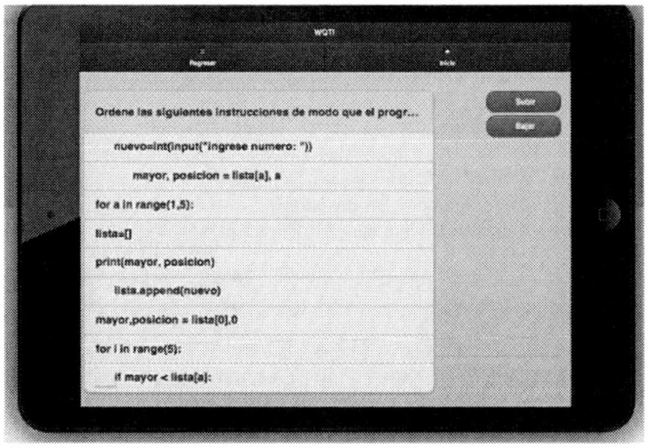

Figure 8b. Process question for list. Order question.

Figure 8b, shows the sentences of a program that the students need to order, to obtain the biggest number and the position in the list.

VI. An Experiment

The Mobile QTI and the QDI methodology were used with an experimental group to teach Python language in the Universidad Austral de Chile. In Chile, the Grade Point Average (GPA) ranges are from 1.0 up to 7.0 (with one decimal place). Table 1 shows the Chilean GPA.

TABLE I. CHILEAN GPA

GPA	% Achievement	Meaning	Honours
6.0 -7.0	83% - 100%	Outstanding (7.0)	Highest Honours
5.0 - 5.9	66% - 82%	Good	Honours
4.0 - 4.9	50% - 65%	Sufficient	Passed
3.0 - 3.9	33% - 49%	Less than Sufficient	Failed
2.0 - 2.9	16% - 32%	Deficient	Failed
1.0 - 1.9	0% - 15%	Very Deficient	Failed

https://en.wikipedia.org/wiki/Academic_grading_in_Chile

The contents are organised in three unit of learning, so, three summative assessments were considered (S1, S2, and S3). In the summative assessments, only problems to solve are presented (metacognitive objective). In S1 problems, simple and conditional statements are evaluated, in S2 problems loop statements are used. And S3 problems where the data type: list; including the loop, conditional and simple statements; are needed. Students write their solutions in pseudocode, Nassi–Shneiderman diagram (NSD) [21], and Python language. The assessments are at the same time in several classrooms. The answers made in paper and the lecturers review one by one.

The Mobile QTI and QDI were used only in the second unit of learning. So, the impact is possible to see in the second summative evaluation (S2). Table 2 shows the results in experimental group.

TABLE II. RESULTS OF THE EXPERIMENTAL GROUP

Number of students: 20	S1	S2	S3
GPA	3.5	4.0	3.6
Variance	2.0	2.1	6.1
Increase of GPA respect of S1		14.3%	2.9%
Number of students with grades over 4.0	8 (40%)	13 (65%)	10 (50%)
Increase number of students with grades over 4.0 respect to S1		62.5%	25%

The programming language is not easy to learn, especially for the beginners. For example, in the summative assessment (S1), only eight students had grades greater than or equal to 4.0. For the second unit of learning (S2); with Mobile QTI and QDI; the GPA increased from 3.5 to 4.0 (14.3%), and the students with grades greater than or equal to 4.0 increase from 8 to 13 (62.5%). However, the GPA for the last unit of learning (S3), decrease from 4.0 to 3.6

and the students with grades greater than or equal to 4.0, also decrease from 13 to 10.

VII. Conclusion and Future Work

The programming language is difficult to learn for engineering students, with a GPA of just "Sufficient" in S2, and "Failed" for S1 and S3.

To define questions for content objectives and process objectives, a procedure is needed in order to cover most of the related material. Motivation also needs to be included.

Using CRS and QDI in the second unit of learning allows an increase of the GPA of S2, but, more importantly, it also increases the number of students with grades greater than or equal to 4.0 (from 45% to 65%).

The variance in the last summative assessment is three times the variance in S1 and S2 (6.1), because several students left the course, and it is important to consider this variable.

Designing effective questions that cover more contents and more learning processes is a big challenge. In fact, it is always possible to improve the questions and their answers. Designing effective questions is a dynamic process, because every course is different from another.

The complete course has 156 students divided in several groups, according to grade, where the professors and programming examples are different. So, it is not possible to consider the rest of the course as control group. In the previous semesters, the course was different, thus, it is also not possible to compare with the previous courses.

An increase in the number of students in the experimental group is necessary to have better conclusions.

A redesign of the experiment with one or more control groups is necessary to obtain more conclusive evidence.

A qualitative evaluation is also necessary, that can consider the relationship between the methodology, mobile devices, and the active engagement of the student in learning. Also, the qualitative evaluation must consider to find out how the students are thinking and solving problems.

VIII. Acnowledgments

The authors wish to thank the Research and Development Office of the Universidad Austral de Chile through project DID S 2015-20 entitled SEI: Interactive Evaluation System under the IMS QTI Specification. Additional gratitude to the valuable comments from all members of the Research Group on Learning Technologies (www.gita.cl)

IX. References

[1] L. Alvarez González, A. Campos, M. E. De la Maza, and D.Ojeda, "Interactive assessment learning environment system under IMS-QTI specification," Education Technologies and Computers (ICETC), IEEE Press, Sept. 2014, pp. 7-11.

[2] I. D. Beatty, W. J. Leonard, W. J. Gerace, and R. J. Dufresne, "Question driven instruction: Teaching science", in Audience response systems in higher education: Applications and cases, 2006, p. 96.

[3] B. Bell and B. Cowie, "The Characteristics of Formative Assessment in Science Education", in Science Education, vol. 85, no. 5, 2001, pp. 536-553.

[4] P. Black and D. Wiliam, (1988). "Assessment and classroom learning", in Assessment in Education: Principles, Policy & Practice, vol. 5, no. 1, 1998, pp. 7-71.

[5] C. C. Bonwell and J. A. Eison, Active learning: Creating excitement in the classroom . ASHE-ERIC Higher Education Reports. ERIC Clearinghouse on Higher Education, The George Washington University, One Dupont Circle, Suite 630, Washington, 1991, DC 20036-1183.

[6] C. Boston, "The concept of formative assessment ERIC Clearinghouse on Assessment and Evaluation College Park MD", ED470206, 2002.

[7] J. D. Bransford, A. L. Brown, and R. R. Cocking, How People Learn: Brain, Mind, Experience, and School, Eds. Washington, D.C.: National Academy Press, 1999.

[8] Byrne Richard, "Seven Good Student Response Systems That Work On All Devices". Available from http://www.freetech4teachers.com/2014/03/seven-goodstudent-response-systems.html#.VWR8ikZlaVA. [retrieved: April, 2016].

[9] A. H. W. Chun, "The agile teaching/learning methodology and its e-learning platform", In Advances in Web-Based Learning–ICWL, 2004 [Springer Berlin Heidelberg. pp. 11-18,2004]

[10] E. H. Hobson, "Formative Assessment: An Annotated Bibliography", in Clearing House, vol. 71, no. 2, 1997, pp. 123-125.

[11] P. W. Laws, "Millikan Lecture 1996: Promoting active learning based on physics education research in introductory physics courses," American Journal of Physics, vol. 65, no. 1, 1997, pp. 14-21.

[12] C. H. Fies, "Classroom Response Systems: What Do They Add to an Active Learning Environment?," unpublished doctoral dissertation, University of Texas at Austin, Austin, TX. Available from: http://repositories.lib.utexas.edu/handle/2152/1859. [retrieved: April, 2016].

[13] G. González Sáez and L. A. Álvarez González, "Designing Question to Teach Python in a Interactive Assessment System" Conferencias Chilenas en Tecnologías de Aprendizaje. Universidad de Tarapacá, Ag. 2015. Available from: eudev.uta.cl/cclt2015/pdf/python.pdf. [retrieved: April, 2016].

[14] I. QTI, "IMS Question & Test Interoperability Specification" IMS Global Learning Consortium, 2005.

[15] E. Alepis and M. Virvou, Object-oriented user interfaces for personalized mobile learning, Springer, 2014.

[16] J. M. Zelle, "Python as a first language", in Proceedings of 13th Annual Midwest Computer Conference, vol. 2, March 1999,p. 145.

[17] D. A. Carrera Escobar and L. A. Álvarez González, "Free Classroom Response Systems to use with Mobile Devices". Conferencias Chilenas en Tecnologías de Aprendizaje, Universidad de Tarapacá, Arica, Ag. 2015. Available from: http://eudev.uta.cl/cclt2015/pdf/Carrera_Escobar.pdf. [retrieved: April, 2016].

[18] E. A. Huenumán Villarroel, L. A. Álvarez González, and R. Krause, "Mobile-QTI: An Interactive Mobile System under IMS-QTI Specification". Conferencias Chilenas en Tecnologías de Aprendizaje, Universidad de Tarapacá, Arica, Ag. 2015. Available from: http://eudev.uta.cl/cclt2015/pdf/mobileQTI.pdf. [retrieved: April, 2016].

[19] Web QTI, "Web editor under IMS QTI Specification", Available from: http://www.gita.cl/proyectos/web-qti/. [retrieved: April, 2016].

[20] G. Alsop, J. Annesley, Z. Cai, A. Campos, M. Colbert, and J. Orwell, "AQuRate Final Report". JISC Capital Programme. Univ. of. Kingston, London, AQuRate, Tech. Rep. 2008.

[21] I. Nassi, and B Shneiderman, "Flowchart techniques for structured programming". ACM Sigplan Notices, 8(8), 12-26. 1973.

PlayLearn: A Platform for the Development and Management of Learning Experiences in Location-Based Mobile Games

Dimitris Makris, Konstantinos Makris, Polyxeni Arapi, Stavros Christodoulakis
Laboratory of Distributed Multimedia Information Systems and Applications (TUC/MUSIC)
Technical University of Crete
Chania, Greece
e-mail: {dmakris, makris, xenia, stavros}@ced.tuc.gr

***Abstract*—Mobile location-based games, exploiting the unique capabilities of mobile devices, such as camera, GPS and compass, can have high learning potential. On one hand, they present a very attractive form of learning for modern students, even very young ones, who have already developed their skills in computer games and are very familiar with the use of mobile devices. On the other hand, location-based games provide a unique opportunity for education since they connect an area with a story, and their activities may result in social, experiential and situated learning. These characteristics can make them a powerful tool in a number of applications, including education, nature and museum exploration, city sightseeing, natural disasters awareness and prevention training. In this paper, we present the design and implementation of PlayLearn, a platform for the development and management of learning experiences in mobile location-based games, consisting of: (a) an authoring tool, supporting the creation and management of games, scenario editing, user interface customization and organization of gaming activities, and (b) a mobile application, compatible with most state-of-the-art mobile devices and platforms, supporting the play of games created by the authoring tool. Our implementation supports the Experience API, allowing the activities that happen as part of gaming (learning) experiences to be recorded, tracked and shared in a Learning Record Store.**

Keywords- mobile educational games; location-based games; learning experiences; experiential learning.

I. INTRODUCTION

Location-based services on mobile phones have become very popular in recent years. These services have been developed to provide location-based information and can be used to create games that exploit the geographical location of the user or other people. A -so called- mobile location-based game [1] is a type of pervasive game in which the game-play evolves and progresses via a player's location. Such games must provide some mechanism to allow the players report their location by some kind of localization technology like GPS. The difference between a video game and a location-based game focusing on the same story is that the later has a closer connection between game and reality.

In terms of the main objective, mobile location-based games may be categorized as games that are created for fun, for learning or for mixed objectives [2]. All these categories of games seem to have a higher learning potential. On one hand, they present a very attractive form of learning for modern students, even very young ones, who have already developed their skills in computer games and are very familiar with the use of mobile devices. On the other hand, location-based games provide a unique opportunity for education since they connect a geographic area or object with a story. The physical and cultural surroundings are an integral part of the game space, and the location of the gamers is a key aspect of the game-playing activity. By visiting the actual locations, the story becomes more authentic and leads to better educational results. Essentially, games of this kind allow the user to collect data from the real world and assign them to the game's map. De Souza et al. [3] observed that these activities produce learning that is social, experiential and situated. The combination of informal learning and mobile outdoor games can be seen as a relevant arena for conducting novel learning activities that involve learners in different tasks including physical motion, problem solving, inquiry and collaboration [4].

Learning experiences are those events and activities from which we learn by experience and can identify, to a certain extent, what we have learned [5]. Different learners have different characteristics and preferences (e.g., learning style, educational level, background knowledge) affecting how learning experiences might be organized in terms activities and learning material to achieve certain goals. Experiential learning, according to Kolb [6], can exist without a teacher and relates solely to the meaning-making process of the individual's direct experience. Knowledge is continuously gained through personal and environmental experiences.

The Experience API (xAPI) is an eLearning software specification that allows learning content and systems to interoperate in a manner that records and tracks all types of learning experiences [7]. Results of learning experiences are stored in a Learning Record Store (LRS), which may exist in a traditional Learning Management System (LMS), or on its own. xAPI does not require a learning experience to take place in any particular medium (mobile, desktop, tablet), offline or online, or in any particular system. By collecting and analyzing xAPI for a specific learner, a picture of the learner's activities, achievements, competencies and interests can be created, drawing on experiences using multiple devices and activities [8]. Exposing data through the xAPI provides a means for interoperability and enables innovation of learning content, experiences, and systems [9].

The use of xAPI with mobile devices can leverage learning by enabling the capturing of activities from diverse learning experiences that exploit the capabilities of the mobile platform. This may lead to new kinds of learning experiences and a much wider adoption of mobile-based performance support [9]. For instance, if a learning design was predicated on students taking pictures of examples of a particular phenomenon, and then sharing and discussing these with other students, the xAPI enables the various activities to be recorded and tracked in an LRS in the form of activity streams. Later, the teacher could retrieve this information, initiate a discussion with the students in class, or even improve the learning design of the game according to the results to fit better the needs of the learners. These are only some of the many uses and benefits of adopting xAPI.

In this paper, we present the design and implementation of PlayLearn, a platform for the management of learning experiences in mobile location-based games, consisting of: (a) an authoring tool, supporting creation and management of games, scenario editing, user interface customization and organization of gaming activities, and (b) a mobile application, compatible with most state-of-the-art mobile devices and platforms, supporting the play of games created by using the authoring tool. Our implementation supports the xAPI, allowing the activities that happen as part of gaming experiences to be recorded, tracked and shared.

The rest of this paper is structured as follows: Section II presents the related work. Section III specifies the model for describing educational games. Section IV presents the architecture that has been designed and implemented, while Section V provides some insight on the implementation of the platform. Finally, Section VI summarizes the presented work and sketches some perspectives for future extensions.

II. Related Work

Geocaching [10] is an outdoor treasure hunt activity where players try to find hidden caches using coordinates. Activities are supported by a desktop and mobile application, enabling the searching and previewing of geocaches, and providing basic navigational assistance. PlayLearn, on the other hand, supports a variety of gaming activities and allows the user to create and share his own game. Moreover, it provides the means to organize location-based events, offering an in depth gaming experience to the participants.

WHAIWHAI [11] is an interactive story based on a gaming platform and developed to offer a way of exploring the less touristic and unknown city places. Although games are customizable in terms of difficulty, time limit and number of players, WHAIWHAI is limited to exploration activities. On the contrary, PlayLearn provides tools for creating and playing various types of games, exploited under different contexts and targeting users of certain age groups.

Tourality [12] is a location-based game where the user's goal is to visit several spots of certain interest. In multiplayer mode, the game focuses on time, requiring the user to maintain a high score and compete either by participating in a team or alone. Although it enhances competitiveness and cooperation, it focuses strictly to these characteristics leaving aside any in depth educational activity that a game may provide. Using PlayLearn, on the other hand, a user is able to create games consisted of a variety of educational activities. The player apart from visiting places, is able to browse educational material, answer riddles, perform metadata annotation tasks and search for hidden treasures.

AnswerTree [13] is a collaborative mobile location-based educational game designed to teach 8-12 year old players about trees and wildlife. The game is designed around collecting virtual information cards about notable trees by answering questions. Collaboration is encouraged by the fact that solutions to these questions are obtainable through sharing knowledge with other cardholders. Apart from this, AnswerTree is a static game targeting users of specific profile, interests and goals.

ARIS [14] is a platform for creating and playing mobile games, tours and interactive stories. Its authoring tool provides the ability to specify the game location and create quests, but lacks of functionality for organizing gaming events. Unlike PlayLearn's authoring application, the game creator cannot customize the user interface of the game. Another important limitation is that ARIS game player application is designed as a mobile application available only for iPhones. On the contrary, we provide a native game player for the majority of mobile phone operating systems including iOS, Android and Windows. PlayLearn's game player application is also available through the browser.

III. Model

The model for the creation of location-based educational games has been designed with flexibility and extensibility in mind, to be able to describe a variety of game types. Figure 1 presents the core model entities of Playlearn.

The *Users* of the system are the game creators and the

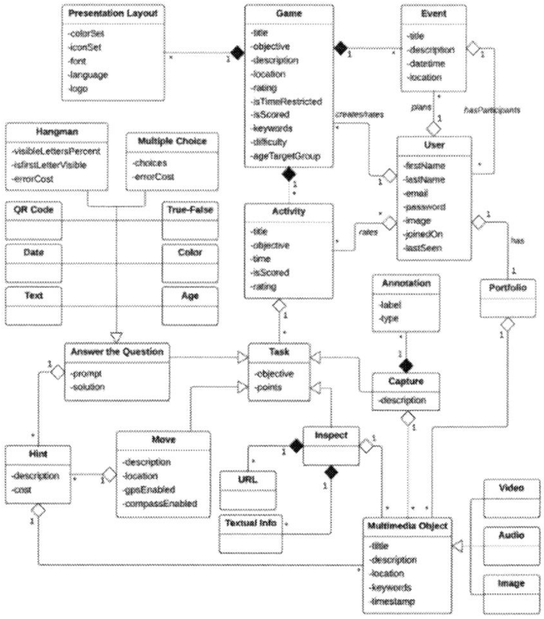

Figure 1. PlayLearn core model

players. The *Game* class represents the games which can be created, managed and played by *Users* using PlayLearn. A *Game* has a goal and consists of several descriptive and presentation metadata, while it is possible for the creator to adapt its *Presentation Layout* (color set, icon set, fonts, language, logo). A *Game* consists of a sequence of *Activities* with certain objectives that have to be tackled by the player to support the game goal. *Activities* consist of *Tasks* which are considered as the actions to be performed in order to achieve the respective activities' objectives. There are currently four types of *Tasks*:

- *Move:* the user needs to navigate in order to reach a specific destination.
- *Inspect:* the user has to read a document or any piece of *Textual Information*, view an image/video or listen to a sound (*Multimedia Object*).
- *Answer the Question:* the user should provide an answer for a given question. The type of question can be *Multiple Choice, True–False, Text* (the player should provide his answer in plain text), *Hangman* (the player needs to find a hidden word), and *QR Code* (the player should scan a pattern code, after searching for it in a specified location range).
- *Capture:* the user has to take a photo, or record a video/sound. The task may require the *Annotation* of the captured *Multimedia Object* with metadata.

The *Multimedia Object* class represents multimedia objects of type: video, image, text, and audio. Each type is depicted as a different class, holding its own descriptive attributes. The *Audio* class represents the multimedia objects of type sound. Optionally, it contains a GPS point specifying the location that has been recorded. The *Image* class represents the multimedia objects that are of type image. Optionally, it contains a GPS point with information about the location where it was captured, as well as other descriptive metadata. The *Video* class represents the multimedia objects that are of type video. Optionally, it contains a list of GPS points with information about the location where it was recorded, as well as any other information provided by the camera. The list of GPS points can be used to recreate the path that the user took for the duration of the capturing. Each User has a *Portfolio* that corresponds to a library with *Multimedia Objects*, which are used in games creation.

Games can be used for the organization of gaming *Events*, which can be created and shared by *Users* in order to promote gaming activities in certain locations. Each *Event* may refer to a specific game, location and date/time. Additionally, the list of the event participants can be either open or restricted to specific user groups. Since Games can be bounded to a specific place, such information along with game classification, target group, rating and difficulty can be used for game searching and filtering.

Figure 2 presents a simple game example for a visit of preliminary school pupils to a Botanical garden to explore olive trees, consisting of three activities corresponding to the pre-visit, visit and post-visit phases.

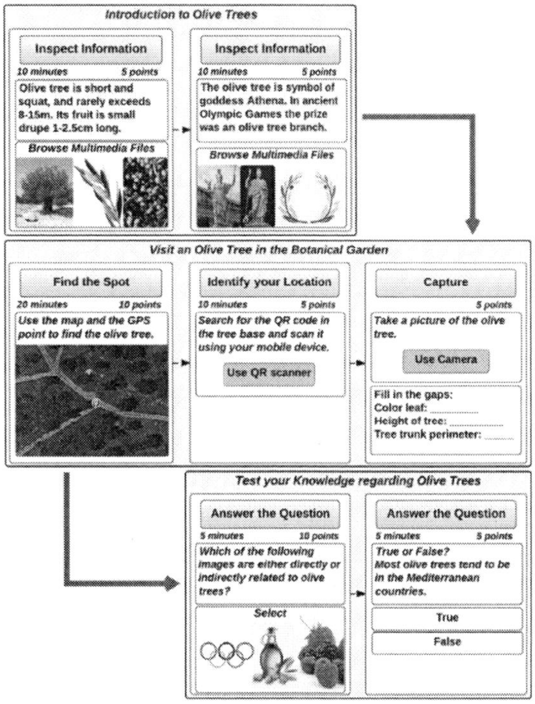

Figure 2. A simple game example for a visit to the Botanical garden

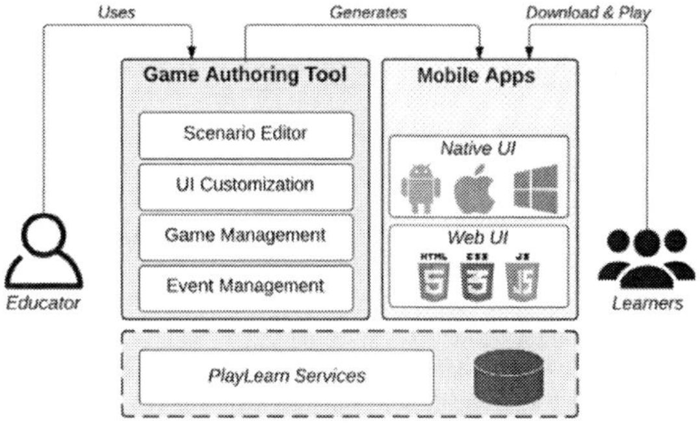

Figure 3. PlayLearn conceptual architecture

IV. ARCHITECTURE

Built as a web application, the system adopts the Rich Internet Application (RIA) principles, which promote the development of web applications as desktop applications, performing business logic operations both on the client and server side. The client side logic operates within the web browser running on a user's computer, while the server side logic operates on the web server hosting the application.

Figure 3 presents the conceptual architecture of the PlayLearn platform. The main parts of this architecture are: (a) The *Game Authoring Tool* used by the Educator for the creation of games, providing functionality for game scenario design, game and event management, and UI customization, and (b) the *Mobile Apps* providing both Native UI to support mobile devices with different OS (Android, iOS, Windows) and a Web UI, which are used by the Learners to download and play the games created by the Authoring Tool during events organized by the Educators. The *Game Authoring Tool* and the *Mobile Apps* are supported by a number of services and repositories that are described in detail in the following paragraphs.

The overall system architecture is presented in Figure 4. For the development of the application we adopted several design patterns [15]. The use of well-established and documented design patterns speeds up the development process, since they provide reusable solutions to the most common software design problems [16][17]. The Model-View-Controller (MVC) design pattern [18][19] and the Observer pattern were used on the client side, and a multi-tier architecture was implemented on the server side, which are described in the following sections.

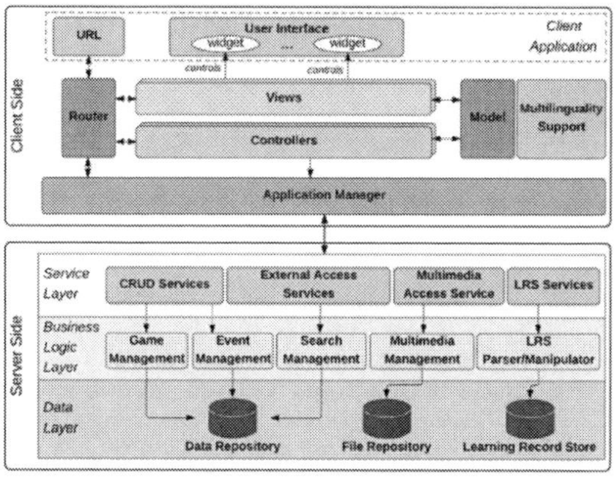

Figure 4. PlayLearn system architecture

A. Server Side

The Server Side part of our platform adopts a multi-layered architectural pattern consisting of three basic layers (Figure 4): *Service Layer*, *Business Logic Layer* and *Data Layer*. This increases system's maintainability, reusability of the components, scalability, robustness, and security.

The *Service Layer* controls the communication between the client-side logic and the server-side logic, by exposing a set of services (operations) to the client-side components [20]. These services comprise the middle-ware concealing the application business logic from the client and have been built as RESTful [21][22]. The basic system services are:

- *CRUD Services*, facilitating the creation, retrieval, update and deletion of games, events associated with games, and users.
- *External Access Services*, providing the means for the client side and external applications to use the data of the system.
- *Multimedia Access Services*, enabling access to the uploaded multimedia files and their thumbnails.
- *LRS Services*, facilitating the persistence of statements generated by the use of xAPI.

The *Business Logic Layer*, also known as *Domain Layer*, contains the business logic of the application and separates it from the Data Layer and the Service Layer. In more detail:

- The *Game Management Module* is responsible for the game management, as well as for the activity and task (de)composition in our system.
- The *Event Management Module* is responsible for the event management.
- The *Search Management Module* handles the search and filter queries posed on our dataset and delivers the obtained results to the appropriate component of the Service Layer.
- The *Multimedia Management Module* is responsible for managing the persistence and serving of multimedia files, as well as for performing basic metadata extraction and thumbnail generation.
- The *LRS Parser/Manipulator Module* is responsible for the persistence and accessing of gaming results that have been collected and obtained during a gaming activity.

The *Data Layer* accommodates external systems used to index and persist both data and multimedia files, such as:

- *Data Repository*, storing all the data of the system.
- *File Repository*, persisting multimedia files and thumbnails.
- *Learning Record Store*, archiving the collected results of gaming activities.

B. Client Side

The Client Side of PlayLearn application is responsible for the interaction with the user. It refers to both the authoring tool (web application) and the player application (mobile application). All the actions performed by an individual are handled by client side logic which undertakes the presentation of the information as well as the communication with the server. In order to achieve a high level of decoupling between the components forming the client logic, we adopted the Model View Controller (MVC) design pattern, as well as the Observer pattern. The use of MVC introduces the separation of the responsibilities for the visual display and the event handling behavior into different entities, named respectively, View and Controller.

The *Model* refers to the business objects which are being used by our system. When the system needs to present information about a business object, the client side requests the respective information from the server side using the services that the later exposes. Similarly, when an update on the Model needs to be persisted, the client side sends the updated Model to the server side, triggering the indexing and storage of the business objects by the appropriate modules and external systems.

The *Views* are responsible for the presentation of information in the user interface. Each view controls a number of widgets on the application's graphical user interface. It consists of several handlers that are responsible for listening user actions, as well as HTML templates that define the presentation of the widgets.

The *Controllers* are the modules that respond to the user input and interact with the Views in order to perform any change on the user interface. Furthermore, they maintain the Model and change it appropriately. Every View has a dedicated Controller managing, handling and propagating any changes that are to be performed or have already been performed to the user interface. Moreover, there are several cases where a "composite" Controller manages a number of other Controllers in order to create complex widgets.

The *Router* is used for deep-linking URLs to controllers and views. It manages the URL of the client browsers, providing a different path to each distinct interface, without raising a browser event that will force a reload on the whole page. When the URL changes the Router analyzes the new path and handles the transition to the new View. This is performed using mappings between the different URLs supported in the system, the Controllers and the Views.

The *Multilinguality Support* module manages the translation of the user interface elements through the use of certain configuration files. The process is easily adaptable and the system can be extended to support any language with minimum effort. Currently the graphical user interfaces of the system have been translated in English and Greek.

V. Implementation

PlayLearn has been successfully implemented as described in previous sections. Its server side is based on Java and makes extensive use of the Spring Framework in order to tackle certain backend aspects like data access. For persistency storage, MongoDB is used. One of the reasons that led us to choose MongoDB is that most of our data does not conform to a rigid relational schema. Hence, we cannot bind it in the structure of a relational database and we need flexibility. Due to the fact that MongoDB allows us to store parts of our data in different forms with minor effort, our back end is considered compatible with LRS and xAPI.

Regarding the client side, both the game authoring tool and the player application are based on the latest web-application standards, rely on the JavaScript programming language and make extensive use of the AngularJS framework. Moreover, they have been created in order to match different user requirements, and thus their user interfaces are implemented differently in order to match the goals of their stakeholders. Apart from JavaScript, the user interface layout has been built using HTML5 and CSS3. The player application has been packaged as a native mobile application with the use of Phonegap, making it compatible with all the major mobile platforms. This allows our application to run without the need of internet access, or loading its source each time that the user accesses it. Additionally, the use of Apache Cordova allowed us to provide more functionality by using various native platform features that are otherwise unavailable to web applications.

Figure 5 presents the graphical user interface of the game authoring tool. Specifically, it shows the use of the scenario editor while the user creates a new task of type "Capture" to populate an already existing activity of a game named "Explore Olive Trees". The left side of the user interface is used for presenting the game activity list, while the right side is used as the main working area for customizing activity tasks. The top bar is used for the main menu inspection, user interface customization (in terms of language and layout), and personal settings editing. Figure 6 presents the graphical user interface of the mobile application that was generated by the game authoring tool in Figure 5. The screenshot on the left side shows the preview presented to the user just before starting the game. It includes basic information such as the event, the game, the creator and the list of activities that need to be completed. On the other hand, the screenshot on the right has been taken during playing the game and shows an activity task of type "Move" requiring the user to use the map in order to navigate to a specific spot of interest.

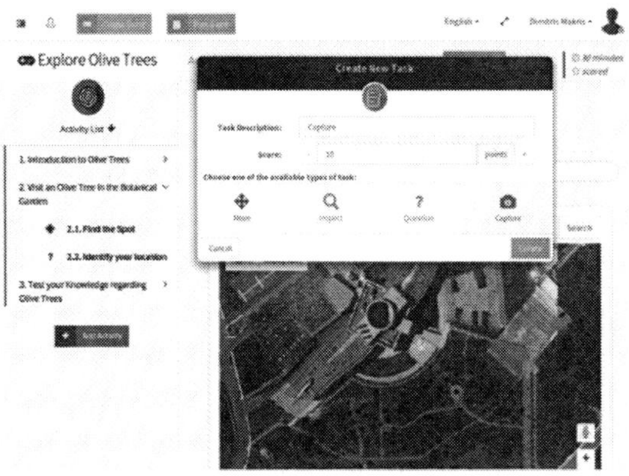

Figure 5. Game authoring tool (web application)

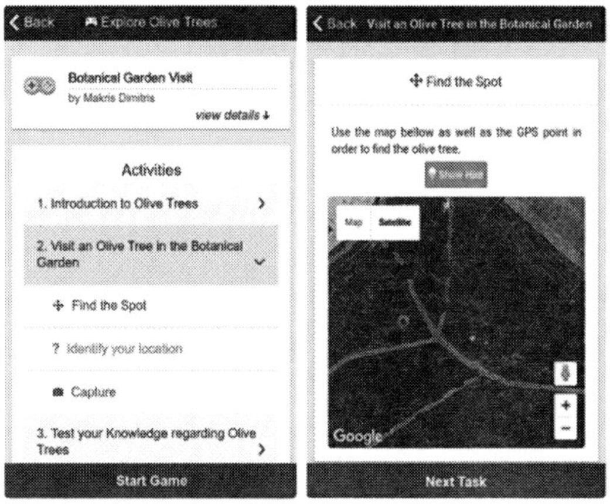

Figure 6. Player application (mobile application)

VI. Conclusions

In this paper, we presented the design and implementation of PlayLearn, a platform for the development and management of learning experiences in mobile location-based games. PlayLearn provides: (a) an authoring tool supporting the creation and management of games, scenario editing, user interface customization and organization of gaming activities, and (b) a mobile application supporting the play of games created using the authoring tool. The player application is compatible with most state-of-the-art mobile devices/platforms, while both tools have been designed with flexibility and extensibility in mind. The underlying model supports a great variety of basic building blocks that can be exploited by a user in order to create a great range of complex and structured location-based gaming experiences. The activities that happen as part of these gaming (learning) experiences are recorded, tracked and shared in a LRS by supporting xAPI. Both applications have been evaluated for their usability through the use of pluralistic walkthroughs and extensive paper prototyping.

The work presented in this paper is part of the EVANDE project learning infrastructure. EVANDE (Enhancing Volunteer Awareness and education against Natural Disasters through E-learning) [23] is a European project co-funded under the Union Civil Protection Mechanism. It aims to create a new learning tool to educate and train civil protection volunteers and local authorities' staff through identification of best practices and knowledge, develop a web platform and tools to host e-learning courses, games and training activities, as well as to organize and implement local-based dissemination and training actions. Promoting exploration with mobile location-based educational games is vital in teaching players about specific areas where a crisis can happen [24] and practicing on best practices to prevent and respond on the most effective manner benefiting the maximum from human and technical resources.

Our future work includes the following: (a) direct connection with repositories persisting observational data like GBIF, BioCASE and Natural Europe [25], in order to easily enrich the educational content of a game, (b) direct connection with well known cultural heritage repositories like Europeana [26], and (c) enabling the creation of observations during the play of a game [27], as well as their further dissemination to related repositories.

ACKNOWLEDGMENT

The work presented in this paper is partially funded in the scope of the EVANDE (Enhancing Volunteer Awareness and education against Natural Disasters through E-learning) project, co-funded under the Union Civil Protection Mechanism, Grant Agreement ECHO/SUB/2014/693261.

REFERENCES

[1] Location-based , game. [Online]. Available from: https//en.wikipedia.org/wiki/Location-based_game.

[2] N. Avouris and N. Yiannoutsou, "A review of mobile location-based games for learning across physical and virtual spaces," Journal of Universal Computer Science, 2012, vol 18,(15), pp. 2120-2142.

[3] De. Souza, E. Silva, and G. C Delacruz, "Hybrid Reality Games Reframed Potential Uses in Educational Contexts," Games and Culture, Sage Publications, 2006.

[4] D. Spikol and M. Milrad, "Physical activities and playful learning using mobile games," Research and Practice in Technology Enhanced Learning, 2008, vol. 3 (3), pp. 275–295, doi: 10.1142/S1793206808000562

[5] P. Arapi, N. Moumoutzis, M Mylonakis, and S. Christodoulakis, "A Framework and an Architecture for Supporting eLearning Applications on top of Multimedia Digital Libraries," DELOS Conference on Digital Libraries, 2007.

[6] D. A. Kolb, Experiential learning. [Online]. Available from: https://en.wikipedia.org/wiki/Experiential_learning.

[7] J. Delano and A. Shahrazad, "Using the Experience API to Track Learning," Infoline (Numbered), vol. 1304, American Society for Training & Development, 2013.

[8] P. Durlach, J. Poltrack, K. Murray, and D. Regan, "Modernizing Education," MT2, 2013, vol. 18(5).

[9] K. Murray, P. Berking, J. Haag, and N. Hruska, "Mobile Learning and ADL's Experience API," Connections 12(1), 2012, pp. 45–49.

[10] Geocaching. [Online]. Available from: https://www.geocaching.com/

[11] WHAIWHAI. [Online]. Available from: http://www.whaiwhai.com/en/

[12] Tourality. [Online]. Available from: http://www.tourality.com/

[13] A. Moore, J. Goulding, E. Brown, and J. Swan, "AnswerTree – a Hyperplace-based Game for Collaborative Mobile Learning," mLearn Conference, 2009.

[14] ARIS Games. [Online]. Available from: http://arisgames.org/

[15] E. Gamma, R. Helm, R. Johnson, and J. Vlissides, Design Patterns, Elements of Reusable Object-Oriented Software. Addison-Wesley, 1995.

[16] D. Alur, D. Malks, and J. Crupi, Core J2EE Patterns: Best Practices and Design Strategies (2nd Edition). Prentice Hall, 2 edition, 2003.

[17] M. Fowler, Patterns of Enterprise Application Architecture. Addison-Wesley, Boston, ersteauflage edition, 2003.

[18] T. Reenskaug, Models - Views - Controllers. Technical report, Technical Note, Xerox Parc, 1979.

[19] T. Reenskaug, The Model-View-Controller (MVC) Its Past and Present, 2003.

[20] G. Alonso, Web Services: Concepts, Architectures and Applications. Springer, 2004.

[21] C. Pautasso, O. Zimmermann, and F. Leymann, "RESTful Web Services vs. "Big" Web Services: Making the Right Architectural Decision," The 17th international conference on World Wide Web, ACM, New York, 2008, pp. 805–814.

[22] R. T. Fielding and R. N. Taylor, Principled Design of the Modern Web Architecture. ACM Transactions on Internet Technology (TOIT), 2002, 2(2):115–150.

[23] EVANDE . [Online]. Available from: http://www.evande.eu

[24] I. Di Loreto, S. Mora, and M. Divitini, "Collaborative Serious Games for Crisis Management: An Overview," The IEEE 21st International Workshop on Enabling Technologies: Infrastructure for Collaborative Enterprises (WETICE), 2012.

[25] G. Skevakis, K. Makris, V. Kalokyri, P. Arapi, and S. Christodoulakis, "Metadata Management, Interoperability and Linked Data Publishing Support for Natural History Museums," International Journal on Digital Libraries (IJDL), 2014.

[26] K. Makris et al., "Federating Natural History Museums in Natural Europe," The 7th Metadata and Semantics Research Conference (MTSR), Special track on Metadata & Semantics for Cultural Collections & Applications, Thessaloniki, 2013.

[27] C. Tsinaraki, G. Skevakis, I. Trochatou, and S. Christodoulakis, "MoM-NOCS: Management of Mobile Multimedia Nature Observations using Crowd Sourcing," The 11th International Conference on Advances in Mobile Computing & Multimedia (MoMM), Vienna, 2013.

SNA-Based Recommendation in Professional Learning Environments

Mohamed Amine Chatti, Peyman Toreini, Hendrik Thüs, Ulrik Schroeder

Informatik 9 (Learning Technologies)
RWTH Aachen University, Germany
Email: {chatti;schroeder;thues}@cs.rwth-aachen.de; peyman.toreini@rwth-aachen.de

Abstract—**Recommender systems can provide effective means to support self-organization and networking in professional learning environments. In this paper, we leverage social network analysis (SNA) methods to improve interest-based recommendation in professional learning networks. We discuss two approaches for interest-based recommendation using SNA and compare them with conventional collaborative filtering (CF)-based recommendation methods. The user evaluation results based on the ResQue framework confirm that SNA-based CF recommendation outperform traditional CF methods in terms of coverage and thus can provide an effective solution to the sparsity and cold start problems in recommender systems.**

Keywords–Professional Learning; Recommender Systems; Collaborative Filtering, Social Network Analysis

I. INTRODUCTION

Over the past years, companies and researchers are starting to recognize relationships and intersections between the professional learning and knowledge management fields and to explore the potential and benefits of their integration [1]. Professional learning is no longer regarded as an external online training activity separate from the work flow, but rather as a learner-controlled evolving activity embedded directly into work processes [2]. Professional learning environments are characterized by self-organization and networking. There is a wide agreemnt that effective professional learning environments need to follow a learner-centric model that supports the self-directed learning process by surrounding the professional learner with the environment that matches her needs best. Moreover, there is a crucial need to adopt a learning model that fosters continuous networking and collaborative knowledge creation by enabling professional learners to network, collaborate, and actively participate in a continuous learning process. One concern with a learner-centric model is information overload. Professional learners are lifelong learners who continuously try to create and update their own knowledge environments where they can pull knowledge that meets their particular needs from a wide range of knowledge sources. This is a highly challenging task, given the abundance of information and the complexity of the new knowledge-intensive working and learning environments. It thus becomes crucial to examine some mechanisms that would help professional learners to cope with the information overload problem. This is where recommender systems can play a crucial role to foster self-directed professional learning [3].

Recommender Systems (RS) is an effective solution to deal with the information overload problem. RS track user's actions and provide proper results by identifying information relevant to them, based on their individual interests and preferences. RS are important and successfully implemented in e-business applications. They assist people in different domains like bookshops, research papers, news and articles, web pages, movies, music, etc. In addition to the e-business applications, RS are increasingly being developed in the technology-enhanced learning (TEL) area. They offer a promising approach to facilitate both learning and teaching tasks, by identifying suitable learning resources from a potentially overwhelming variety of choices [4]. There is a large number of RS that have been deployed in TEL settings [5]. However, relatively little significant work around the application of RS in professional learning environments has been undertaken. Traditional RS need adaptation in order to meet the characteristics of professional learning environments. Professional learners rarely share the same or similar learning resources due to the fact that they follow their individual interests and preferences. Thus, recommendation in professional learning environments should rely on the interests of the professional learners and take into account the social networks in which they perform. In this paper, we explore the potentials of RS to support professional learning. We consider using the interest and network informations and incorporating them into traditional collaborative filtering recommendation methods in order to provide effective recommendation of collaborators in professional learning settings.

The remainder of the paper is organized as follows. Section 2 is a review of the related work. Section 3 provides the details of the conducted case study. We then present the study evaluation results in Section 4. And finally, we summarize our findings and outline perspectives for future work in Section 5.

II. FUNDAMENTALS AND RELATED WORK

RSs are used to solve the information overload problem and provide a personalized recommendation. They are software tools and techniques providing a suggestion for items that the user might like by identifying information relevant to users [6]. The relevant information of the users are collected by tracking their actions and follow user's profile in different environments. The first paper on collaborative filtering (CF), as one of the first recommendation techniques, published in the mid-1990s and since then this topic became popular for RS researchers in different fields [7]. One of the first implementation of RSs is Amazon's RS which is used to recommend relevant products to the users [8]. Another early application that focused on numerical scores and mathematical treatment was Movielens [9].

Technically, RS are classified into three main classes, based on how recommendations are made, namely collaborative filtering (CF), content-based recommendation (CB), and hybrid recommendation [7]. We will focus further only on the CF recommendation techniques as they are the main interest for this paper.

There exists different types and techniques to provide recommendation by means of RSs. In this article, we focus on investigating the performance of memory-based CF, Trust-based CF and two types of SNA-based RS. In the following sections, background of these techniques are discussed.

A. Collaborative Filtering RS

In Collaborative filtering (CF) RS, the user will be recommended items that people with similar tastes and preferences liked in the past. CF RS have two primary tasks, first rating prediction in which they predict the rating of the target user for the target item [10]. The second one is Top-N recommendation in which they predict the top-N highest-rated items among the items not yet rated by the target user [10].

CF RS can be classified in two categories: memory-based and model-based CF techniques. Memory-based CF is a RS method that makes a prediction about interests of a user by collecting information from many other users. This information includes the list of favorites and their ratings. In the memory-based version, similar users or similar items are detected and missing ratings are predicted based on those. If the similarity is computed based on users, it is called user-based CF and if it is based on items, it is called item-based CF. User-based methods predict the rating $r_{u,i}$ of a user u for an item i using the ratings given to i by other users who are most similar to u. These similar users are called nearest-neighbors and k-nearest-neighbors (k-NN) of u are k users with the highest similarity to u. There are different ways to calculate the correlation of users in memory-based CF such as Pearson, Cosine, Jaccard similarity. After computing the correlation between users and find k-NN neighbors of the user u, the prediction procedure starts. User-based CF algorithms can predict the rating of a user in an item that has not rated or recommend a list of items as top-N items.

Model-based CF is another type in CF RS. Algorithms based on this type learn a model by means of the collection of ratings and then make rating predictions. Memory-based CF algorithms are more popular than model-based versions as they are simple and do not have the complexity of the model-based algorithm. Furthermore, there are accurate when sufficient data is available. On the other hand, there are shortcomings for memory-based CF. These include [10]:

- Cold start: The cold-start problem refers to the problem of giving an accurate recommendation to a user who is new in the system. In user-based CF, it causes the problem with computing similarity between users, as some of them do not have any rating.
- Sparsity: The user-item matrix can be vast and sparse. The number of users who would have rated the same set of items would be quite less.
- Scalability: There can be millions of users in the database, memory-based CF system needs to compare the target user to all other users to find similar users. Doing recommendation is computationally expensive in this case.

To overcome the limitations of traditional CF recommendation, some research has been done recently in trying to generate recommendations by harnessing the user's social network information. Formally, these approaches introduced new type of RS, namely Trust-based CF and SNA-based RS.

B. Trust-Based RS

The trust has different meanings in different domains. In the field of RS, the trust-based approach assumes a trust network among users and makes recommendations based on the rating of the users that are directly or indirectly trusted by the active user. These approaches consider only the information provided by the user's trusted neighbors [11]–[14]. One of the conventional approaches of trust-based RSs is using trust over CF approach [15]. Traditional CF RS find neighbors by computing the similarity between users. By involving social relationships to the CF, the neighbors of the active user can be selected by trust relations instead of similarity [15]. The number of these neighbors is dynamic for different users as they have a different number of trust relationships. The recommendation results of these methods show that the performance of traditional RSs can be improved by utilizing trust relations [16]. Moreover, using trust-based CF will solve the problem of scalability in memory-based CF by means of clustering. However, the cold start and sparsity problems are not addressed by means of this method. In fact, it is still hard to recommend items to users without or with fewer ratings.

C. SNA-Based RS

One of the ways to improve the performance of CF RS is using social network analysis (SNA) [17]. SNA explores relationships among entities of networks and analyzes their features. There are several metrics available for SNA. These metrics help to identify the important node in a given social graph such as: Degree, Betweenness, Closeness, Eigenvector [18]. SNA-based RS algorithms apply the social influence of the users on the procedure of recommendation to improve its accuracy. This technique has the ability to provide the recommendation for cold start users as long as they are connected to the social network. Several SNA-based RS approaches have been proposed in the literature [19]–[30]. In general, these approaches use social networks as the source of information to generate recommendations. However, none of these approaches build social networks based on the user's interests.

III. STUDY

In this paper, we focus on leveraging network and interest information to generate effective recommendation of collaborators in professional learning environments. As a proof of concept, we addressed in this work academic networks for two reasons. First, academic researchers are lifelong professional learners who continuously network for research purposes. Second, interests can be easily gathered from researchers' publication activities. To note, however, that the concepts discussed in this paper are valid in other professional learning environments where it is possible to build interest-based social networks. We conducted a study to investigate SNA-based recommendation methods and compare their performance with both user-based CF and Trust-based CF.

A. PALM

This study was conducted based on a dataset generated within the PALM environment. PALM is a personal academic learner modeling service that combines the web, text, and interest mining techniques to create a learner model based on the collected publication information. It has three main tasks to do. First, mining interests of a researcher based on the researcher's published papers. Second, assigning a score to each stored interest of the researcher. This score is assigned based on the level of researcher's concern toward the subject. Third, storing publications of target researcher to identify co-authors in further steps. As a result, PALM provides a user-item matrix, where users are researchers around the world, items are research topics, and the scores show the levels of interest of the researchers in the topics. Additionally, since it finds publications of a researcher, co-authors of a particular researcher and information about them are also accessible [31].

The PALM dataset includes 754 researchers, 14.208 individual interests, and 40.674 publications. 169 of the stored researchers do not have any collected interests and can be seen as "cold start researchers". In this study, the minimum requirement to provide recommendations to the researchers is to have their co-authorship information.

B. Architecture and Implementation

The system architecture of the PALM recommender system is shown in Figure 1. As it can be seen, there are four primary components in this architecture. The first component is an application service with the core of Spring MVC [32]. Spring MVC has the responsibility of handling requests for recommendations. These requests are originated from an active researcher and are sent through RESTful services to Spring MVC. After that, Spring MVC starts to retrieve the required information by querying the PALM database based on the chosen recommendation method. The next step is sending a file that consists of the required information to the modules of the recommendation engine, namely Gephi Toolkit [33] and Apache Mahout [34]. The sent files have different contents based on the intended task. For the recommendation that applies user-based collaborative filtering, Mahout manages the whole recommendation procedure and sends the result back to Spring MVC. For SNA-based recommendations, Gephi computes the centrality measures and sends the result to the implemented services in Spring MVC for providing the final list of recommendations. These services are responsible for computing Jaccard similarity, add the result of SNA centrality measure to them, and offer a list of recommendation. Next, the outcome of recommendations is converted to JSON format by Spring MVC and is sent to the recommendation interface. The provided interface, as the fourth component, handles the task of visualizing recommendation data to the active researcher.

C. Recommendation Generation

In this study, we implemented four different CF recommendation algorithms: User-based CF, Trust-based CF and 2 different ways of SNA-based CF, as listed in Table I. In the following sections, we discuss the implementation of the proposed algorithms in some detail.

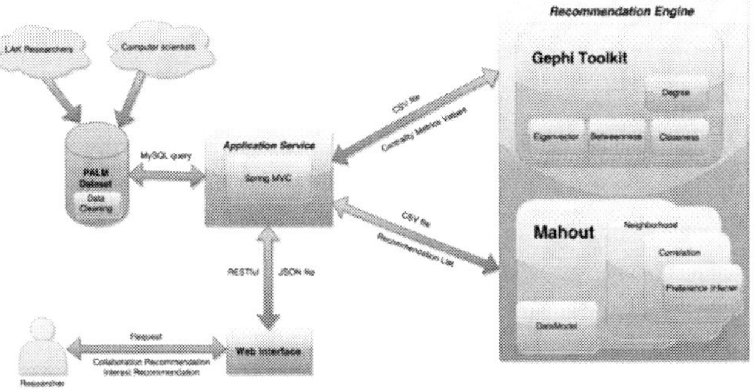

Figure 1. PALM Recommender System Architecture

TABLE I. IMPLEMENTED ALGORITHMS FOR COLLABORATION RECOMMENDATION

Rec. No	Rec. Method
1	User-based CF
2	Trust-based CF
3	SNA-based RS on Co-authorship Network
4	SNA-based RS on Interest Network

1) User-based CF: This algorithm uses the entire user-item matrix of the PALM dataset to find similar users. To do recommendation, first a file that represents information about users and their associated preferences for items is created. In this file, each line has the format of "userID, itemID, value" that is assigned to a particular researcher. UserID means the ID of a researcher, itemID shows the interest ID that is saved in the PALM database and value means the score assigned the researcher's interest. A service in Spring MVC is responsible for creating this file by a query to the MySQL database. To apply user-based CF for a researcher, the created file is used by Mahout to find 10 researchers who have similar interests with the active researcher. The recommended researchers are not from the list that the active researcher published a paper with them before.

2) Trust-based CF: In this algorithm, the trust information of co-authorship networks is used to implement trust-based CF recommendation. Here, researchers are clustered based on information of indirect co-authors in 2-depth co-authorship networks to identify the trust network of an active researcher. For a particular researcher, the first depth of the co-authorship network contains his direct co-authors and the second depth contains his indirect co-authors; i.e. the co-authors of his co-authors. To provide a recommendation based on this category, a file that represents information about indirect nodes in 2-depth co-authorship network of a particular researcher is created by a service in Spring MVC. This file represents information about researchers and their associated preferences for items in the same format "userID, itemID, value" as above. As compared to the user-based CF, only researchers from the trust network are listed in the file. This file builds the input for collaboration recommendation computation, which is done by Mahout. The recommendation of potential collaborators for an active researcher is then collected from the list of researchers who are in the second depth of the co-authorship network.

3) SNA-based RS on Co-authorship Network: The primary component of this algorithm is again the 2-depth co-authorship network of the active researcher. Two elements affect the result of this recommendation method. One is the degree network centrality measure and the other one is Jaccard similarity. We combine these elements to recommend potential collaborators, as defined in the formula below. $P(u, v)$ means the prediction value for recommending user v to the user u.

$$P(u, v) = C(v)_{degree} + Sim(u, v)_{Jaccard} \quad (1)$$

The procedure of recommendation for this algorithm starts by creating a file. This file includes the information of the 2-depth co-authorship network of the active researcher. This file is saved in a CSV format, and each line of this file contains two elements that are separated by a comma: the researcher ID and ID pairs showing the co-authorship relation between two researchers. This file build the input for the SNA tool Gephi. By default, graphs that are imported to Gephi from a CSV file are directed graphs but the co-authorship networks are logically undirected networks as if two researchers published a paper with each other, both of them has a connection to each other. Therefore, before computing centrality measures based on the imported graph by Gephi, the undirected graph option is selected.

The second step in this algorithm is to compute centrality metrics using Gephi toolkit. The implemented centrality metrics algorithm in Gephi finds the result of degree centrality measure for each node in the graph. After that, the result is normalized and is saved for further computation. The normalization for the degree is computed as the degree value divided by the number of all nodes in the network minus one.

The third step is to compute Jaccard similarity between the interests of the active researcher and those of the other researchers in the graph. Cold start researchers have the Jaccard similarity of zero or very low with all the other researchers in the network. At the end, the result of Jaccard similarity is normalized and is saved for further computation.

The computed degree centrality and Jaccard values are computed for each node in the graph. The fourth step is to add these two elements together and compute an individual value for each node in the graph. The result is then sorted from highest to lowest value.

At the end, top ten researchers in this graph are listed for collaboration recommendation. This list should be new for the active researcher. Therefore, the recommended list should be checked with the list of direct co-authors before recommending. If someone from the co-author list exists, then this item is replaced with the next top rated researcher.

4) SNA-based RS on Interest Network: The primary component of this algorithm is the interest network. This network is created based on two aspects, co-authorship relationships and correlation between interests. To create an interest network, first, the 3-depth co-authorship network of the active researcher is built and all nodes in this graph are detected. After that, the five top interests of each node are picked. The interests that occur together for a researcher are then connected to each other to form the final interest graph. An example of such graph can be seen in Figure 2. The first step for recommendations in this algorithm is to create a file that contains information about relations between interests in the created interest network. Each line of this file has the structure of "interestID,interestID" reflecting two interests that occur together. The interest network is logically an undirected graph. Therefore, Gephi is set to realize two-way connections between nodes in this graph. In this algorithm, first, a list of interests based on degree centrality in interest network is computed. The first ten interests that have the highest degree values in the graph and that do belong to the actual interests of the active researcher are selcted as potential interest list. The collaboration recommendation list is then selected from the indirect co-authors in the 3-depth co-authorship network of the active researcher based on the potential interest list. For each interest in the potential interest list, the indirect co-author who has the top score for this interest is recommended.

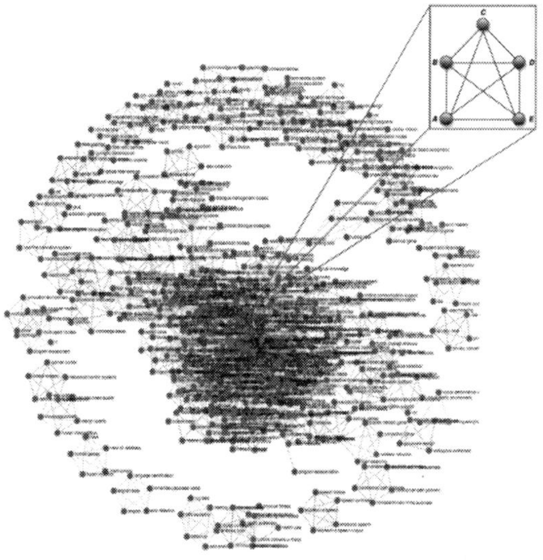

Figure 2. Example of Interest Network

IV. Evaluation Results

We conducted a user evaluation on the four recommendation methods, discussed in the previous sections. Eight users participated in this evaluation and all have a profile on PALM. The particpants in this study are Ph.D. students, professors and researchers at RWTH Aachen University. All of them have published at least one research and thus have a co-authorship network.

A. Evaluation Methodology

A questionnaire is prepared to do user evaluation based on the ResQue (Recommender systems quality of user experience) framework for user-centric evaluation of recommender systems [35]. A wide variety of questionnaire statements are provided in the ResQue framework. Eight sample questions from the suggested questionnaire statements are selected. Researchers are asked to assign their answer based on 1-5 Likert scale while answering questions. In this Scale, "Strong disagree" means number 1 and "Strong agree" means number 5. The category of questions can be seen in the following list.

1) Ability to recommend: The system can provide a recommendation for me (Coverage). (Y/N)
2) Accuracy: In my opinion, the system can recommend to me 1-3 / 4-6 / 7-10 relevant Collaborators.

3) Relative accuracy: The recommendation I received better fits me than what I may receive from a colleague
4) Novelty: The collaborators recommended to me are novel and interesting
5) Diversity: The collaborators recommended to me are diverse
6) Context Compatibility: The collaborators recommended to me considered my personal interests.
7) Perceived usefulness: I feel supporting to find proper new collaborators with the help of recommender.
8) Attitudes: Overall, I am satisfied with the recommender.

B. Discussion of The Results

A summary of the average scores per question and per algorithm are given in Figure 3. The first question investigates the sparsity and cold start problems by measuring coverage. The result of coverage performance checks the possibility of providing a recommendation list, not the quality of recommended items.

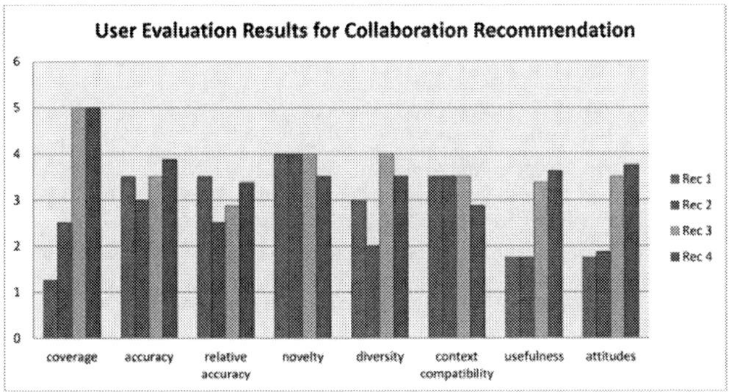

Figure 3. User evaluation average results for collaboration recommendation

The ranking of the examined algorithms based on coverage performance are presented in Figure 4. As it can be seen, SNA-based RS on co-authorship network and SNA-based RS on interest network have the highest coverage value and they could provide recommendations for most of the participants. These results show that the SNA-based RS methods can indeed provide a solution to the sparsity and cold start problems in CF RS.

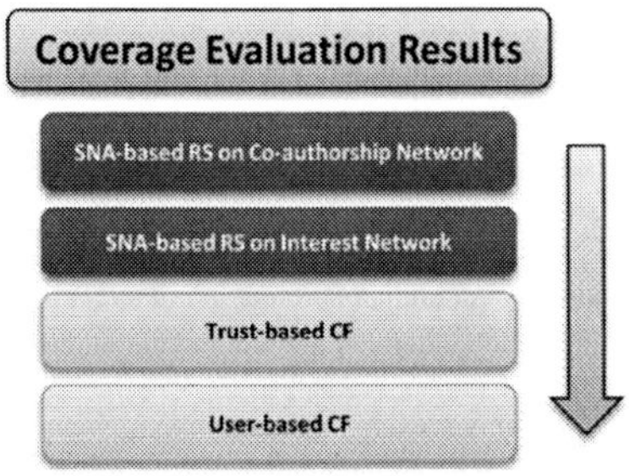

Figure 4. Ranking of Recommendation Algorithms based on Coverage

The evaluation results of accuracy, relative accuracy, diversity, and usefulness show that the SNA-based RS algorithms perform better than the trust-based CF while, in novelty and context compatibility, they performed with almost the same results. Moreover, the results of this evaluation show that not all SNA-based RS algorithms perform better than user-based CF algorithm. They performed equally or worse in accuracy, relative accuracy, novelty and context compatibility. The user-based CF algorithm performed equally or better than trust-based CF algorithm in all aspects except coverage and attitude.

In the attitude factor, the users were asked to evaluate their level of satisfaction based on previously asked factors (see Figure 5). The result shows that in general the evaluators were satisfied with the algorithm SNA-based RS on interest network, more than the other algorithms. SNA-based RS on 2-depth co-authorship network was evaluated far better than CF and trust-based CF and a little lower than SNA-based RS on interest network. Moreover, it can be seen that the level of satisfaction provided with the Trust-based CF algorithm achieved a slightly better result than the CF algorithm.

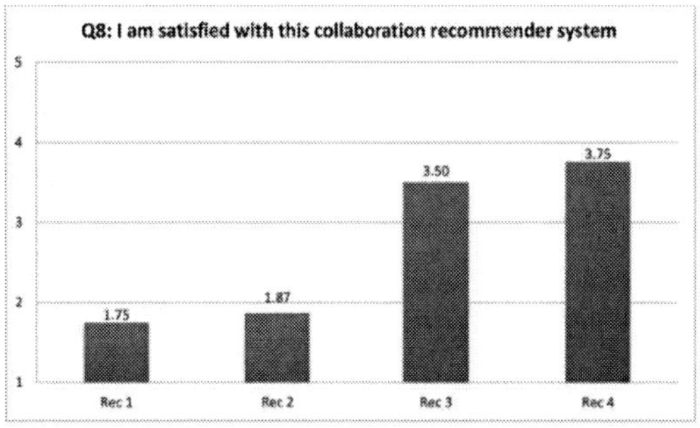

Figure 5. Results of Q8 - Satisfaction with the Recommender System

V. CONCLUSION AND FUTURE WORK

In this paper, we addressed recommendation in professional learning settings. We incorprated the interest and network informations and leveraged social network analysis (SNA) methods to deal with the sparsity and cold start problems in traditional collaborative filtering (CF) recommeder systems. We conducted a study to investigate SNA-based recommendation methods and compare their performance with both user-based CF and Trust-based CF. The user evaluation results based on the ResQue framework confirmed that SNA-based CF recommendation outperform traditional CF methods in terms of coverage and thus can provide an effective solution to the sparsity and cold start problems. The evaluation further proved that using SNA metrics in recommender system could improve the performance better than using social networks as the source of trust information for CF.

While our early results are encouraging for generating effective recommendations in professional learning environments based on interest and network information, there are still a number of areas we would like to improve. This work focused on collaboration recommendation while other types of recommendation like interest recommendation can be explored as well. Moreover, an offline evaluation based on precision, recall and f-measure can be done and compared with the results of user evaluation. Additionally, in addition to degree centrality, we can inverstigate other types of network centrality metrics such as closeness, betweenness and eigenvector.

Furthermore, other types of networks, such as 3-depth co-authorship networks can be added as a source of information for trust-based and SNA-based CF recommendation.

ACKNOWLEDGEMENTS

The authors acknowledge the support of the German Federal Ministry of Education and Research through the PRiME Project (https://prime.rwth-aachen.de/).

REFERENCES

[1] M. A. Chatti, H. Thüs, C. Greven, and U. Schroeder, "Layered knowledge networking in professional learning environments," in Proceedings of the 7th International Conference on Computer Supported Education (CSEDU 2015), vol. 2, 2015, pp. 363–371.

[2] M. A. Chatti, U. Schroeder, and M. Jarke, "Laan: convergence of knowledge management and technology-enhanced learning," IEEE Transactions on Learning Technologies, vol. 5, no. 2, 2012, pp. 177–189.

[3] M. A. Chatti, S. Dakova, H. Thüs, and U. Schroeder, "Tag-based collaborative filtering recommendation in personal learning environments," IEEE Transactions on Learning Technologies, vol. 6, no. 4, 2013, pp. 337–349.

[4] K. Verbert et al., "Dataset-driven research for improving recommender systems for learning," in Proceedings of the 1st International Conference on Learning Analytics and Knowledge, LAK 2011, 2011, pp. 44–53.

[5] N. Manouselis, H. Drachsler, R. Vuorikari, H. Hummel, and R. Koper, "Recommender systems in technology enhanced learning," in Recommender Systems Handbook, L. R. P. B. Kantor, F. Ricci and B. Shapira, Eds. Springer, 2011, pp. 387–415.

[6] F. Ricci, L. Rokach, and B. Shapira, Introduction to recommender systems handbook. Springer, 2011.

[7] G. Adomavicius and A. Tuzhilin, "Toward the next generation of recommender systems: A survey of the state-of-the-art and possible extensions," Knowledge and Data Engineering, IEEE Transactions on, vol. 17, no. 6, 2005, pp. 734–749.

[8] G. Linden, B. Smith, and J. York, "Amazon. com recommendations: Item-to-item collaborative filtering," Internet Computing, IEEE, vol. 7, no. 1, 2003, pp. 76–80.

[9] J. L. Herlocker, J. A. Konstan, A. Borchers, and J. Riedl, "An algorithmic framework for performing collaborative filtering," in Proceedings of the 22nd annual international ACM SIGIR conference on Research and development in information retrieval. ACM, 1999, pp. 230–237.

[10] B. Sarwar, G. Karypis, J. Konstan, and J. Riedl, "Item-based collaborative filtering recommendation algorithms," in Proceedings of the 10th international conference on World Wide Web. ACM, 2001, pp. 285–295.

[11] P. Massa and P. Avesani, "Trust-aware recommender systems," in Proceedings of the 2007 ACM conference on Recommender systems. ACM, 2007, pp. 17–24.

[12] M. Jamali and M. Ester, "Trustwalker: a random walk model for combining trust-based and item-based recommendation," in Proceedings of the 15th ACM SIGKDD international conference on Knowledge discovery and data mining. ACM, 2009, pp. 397–406.

[13] H. Ma, I. King, and M. R. Lyu, "Learning to recommend with social trust ensemble," in Proceedings of the 32nd international ACM SIGIR conference on Research and development in information retrieval. ACM, 2009, pp. 203–210.

[14] H. Ma, H. Yang, M. R. Lyu, and I. King, "Sorec: social recommendation using probabilistic matrix factorization," in Proceedings of the 17th ACM conference on Information and knowledge management. ACM, 2008, pp. 931–940.

[15] K. Kwon, J. Cho, and Y. Park, "Multidimensional credibility model for neighbor selection in collaborative recommendation," Expert Systems with Applications, vol. 36, no. 3, 2009, pp. 7114–7122.

[16] M. C. Pham, Y. Cao, R. Klamma, and M. Jarke, "A clustering approach for collaborative filtering recommendation using social network analysis." J. UCS, vol. 17, no. 4, 2011, pp. 583–604.

[17] M. Jamali and M. Ester, "Mining social networks for recommendation," Tutorial of ICDM, vol. 11, 2011.

[18] S. Wasserman and K. Faust, Social network analysis: Methods and applications. Cambridge university press, 1994.

[19] C. Lam, "Snack: incorporating social network information in automated collaborative filtering," in Proceedings of the 5th ACM conference on Electronic commerce. ACM, 2004, pp. 254–255.

[20] J. Li, F. Xia, W. Wang, Z. Chen, N. Y. Asabere, and H. Jiang, "Acrec: a co-authorship based random walk model for academic collaboration recommendation," in Proceedings of the companion publication of the 23rd international conference on World wide web companion. International World Wide Web Conferences Steering Committee, 2014, pp. 1209–1214.

[21] H.-H. Chen, L. Gou, X. Zhang, and C. L. Giles, "Collabseer: a search engine for collaboration discovery," in Proceedings of the 11th annual international ACM/IEEE joint conference on Digital libraries. ACM, 2011, pp. 231–240.

[22] T. Huynh et al., "Scientific publication recommendations based on collaborative citation networks," in Collaboration Technologies and Systems (CTS), 2012 International Conference on. IEEE, 2012, pp. 316–321.

[23] E. Spertus, M. Sahami, and O. Buyukkokten, "Evaluating similarity measures: a large-scale study in the orkut social network," in Proceedings of the eleventh ACM SIGKDD international conference on Knowledge discovery in data mining. ACM, 2005, pp. 678–684.

[24] G. R. Lopes, M. M. Moro, L. K. Wives, and J. P. M. De Oliveira, "Collaboration recommendation on academic social networks," in Advances in Conceptual Modeling–Applications and Challenges. Springer, 2010, pp. 190–199.

[25] J. Palau, M. Montaner, B. López, and J. L. De La Rosa, "Collaboration analysis in recommender systems using social networks," in Cooperative Information Agents VIII. Springer, 2004, pp. 137–151.

[26] E. Davoodi, M. Afsharchi, and K. Kianmehr, "A social network-based approach to expert recommendation system," in Hybrid Artificial Intelligent Systems. Springer, 2012, pp. 91–102.

[27] E. Castillejo, A. Almeida, and D. López-de Ipiña, "Social network analysis applied to recommendation systems: Alleviating the cold-user problem." in UCAmI. Springer, 2012, pp. 306–313.

[28] B. Fan, L. Liu, M. Li, and Y. Wu, "Knowledge recommendation based on social network theory," in Advanced Management of Information for Globalized Enterprises, 2008. AMIGE 2008. IEEE Symposium on. IEEE, 2008, pp. 1–3.

[29] B.-R. Dai, C.-Y. Lee, and C.-H. Chung, "A framework of recommendation system based on both network structure and messages," in Advances in Social Networks Analysis and Mining (ASONAM), 2011 International Conference on. IEEE, 2011, pp. 709–714.

[30] C. Yang, J. Sun, and Z. Zhao, "Personalized recommendation based on collaborative filtering in social network," in Progress in Informatics and Computing (PIC), 2010 IEEE International Conference on, vol. 1, Dec 2010, pp. 670–673.

[31] M. A. Chatti, D. Dugošija, H. Thüs, and U. Schroeder, "Learner modeling in academic networks," in Proceedings of The 14th IEEE International Conference on Advanced Learning Technologies (ICALT 2014), 2014, pp. 117–121.

[32] Spring framework. Last accessed March 14, 2016. [Online]. Available: http://spring.io/

[33] Gephi. Last accessed March 14, 2016. [Online]. Available: http://gephi.github.io/toolkit/

[34] Mahout. Last accessed March 14, 2016. [Online]. Available: http://mahout.apache.org/

[35] P. Pu, L. Chen, and R. Hu, "A user-centric evaluation framework for recommender systems," in Proceedings of the fifth ACM conference on Recommender systems. ACM, 2011, pp. 157–164.

Setting the Climate: The Impact of Multimedia on Online Learning

Hwangji S. Lu
Department of Business Administration
Colorado Technical University
Aurora, CO, USA
E-mail: Hlu@faculty.ctuonline.edu

Abstract—**The innovation of information technology has transformed the education world. Multimedia has been integrated into online classrooms in various ways. The use of multimedia could result in a positive impact on student's learning experience. A master's course offered exclusively online is redesigned to incorporate multimedia into course content, courses delivery, and assessments. The aim of this case study is to investigate the relationship between student's satisfaction, as well as student's learning outcomes, and the effectiveness of the multimedia-enhanced course. Student's performance, student's engagement, and student's stratification show improvement in the redesigned course. The implications, limitations and further research are also discussed in this paper.**

Keywords-multimedia; online learning; learner-centered teaching; student engagement; student satisafction.

I. INTRODUCTION

With the advance of the Internet, distance learning in the higher education has developed its popularity in the world [1]. The Internet has shortened the distances among people, while distance learning transforms the way education has been delivered and defined; this new way of interactive teaching uses the latest technologies to deliver the instructional materials to learners [2]. Thus, the geographical boundaries and scheduling conflicts are no longer the obstacles to learning. The paradigm has shifted to a learning environment that promotes learning through the interactivity feature of the technology [2][3][4].

The research described in this paper investigates the effectiveness of a multimedia-enhanced online course. A literature review on the impact of multimedia and learner-centered teaching will be presented. The research methodology, results, and discussion will be reviewed. Finally, implication, limitation, and further research will be examined.

II. THEORETICAL FRAMEWORK

A. Multimedia

Multimedia refers to the combinations of different types of media that appeal to more than one perceptual sense to convey information; the examples of media include sound, text, animation, audio, video, image, and mixes of all these objectives [1]. With the rapid development of telecommunication technology, multimedia has been increasingly used in education, especially in the online environment, as it provides the learners with an alternative means to acquire new knowledge. Four main benefits of multimedia have been attributed to better learning outcomes.

- Multimedia can help students with various learning styles learn better because multimedia instructional materials are more dynamic than text-oriented online classrooms [3][5].
- Multimedia can engage the learners to keep learning [3]. As an effective instructional tool, multimedia is playing an active role in education because the content delivery of multimedia is more vibrant and can draw the learners' attentions better.
- The use of multimedia fosters deeper learning [3]. Multimedia instructional materials, indeed, help learners better comprehend key course ideas by stimulating learning at both cognitive and emotional levels—reaching a deeper learning.
- The multimedia tools help transform the traditional instructor-centered teaching toward learner-centered teaching [2][3].

B. Learner-Centered Teaching

In the learner-centered environment, students play an active role in the learning process. They are actively engaged in constructing new meaning within the context of their current knowledge and experience. When learners construct their acquired knowledge successfully, they tend to work in collaboration with others [6]. Learners share their commitments to learning and see collective learning as an imperative part of their educational experience. Learner-centered instructors also promote the development of a learning community to engage learners and provoke the learners' critical thinking and problem-solving skills [3][6]. However, this approach can work well only for the mature and self-efficient learners [7].

III. CASE STUDY

An U. S. university offers the master's program of healthcare administration exclusively online. The original courses relied solely on text, requiring a large amount of reading and writing. Such a course design may have a negative impact on students' learning and satisfaction. In 2014, the author redesigned a healthcare administration course in the master's program. The redesigned course has incorporated multimedia into course content, course delivery, assignments, and e-textbook. Assessing the effectiveness of the redesigned course and student's learning outcomes is needed to reflect the depth and breadth in instructional design principles. Thus, two research questions are raised: (1) How do multimedia instructional materials enhance student's learning? (2) What are the relationships between multimedia instructional materials and student's satisfaction? The purpose of this study is to examine the association between the effectiveness of this redesigned course and student's satisfaction, as well as student's learning outcome.

A. Research Methodology

The data were analyzed with a comparison between FY13-14 and FY14-15 courses. Simple comparative tests including analysis of variance (ANOVA) were performed using Statistical Package for the Social Sciences (SPSS) software. Student achievement was evaluated by a 10 to15-page final research paper. Student engagement was measured by the number of posts and time spent per discussion board in the five selected discussion boards. Students' satisfaction was investigated using the University's standardized end-of-course evaluation survey.

B. Results and Discussions

1) Student Achievement: As shown in Figure 1, the mean score of the final research paper from the FY14-15 courses (n = 621) was 23.1, which is statistically higher ($p < 0.001$) than 22.3 of the FY13-14 courses (n = 695).

2) Student Engagement: Figure 2 exhibits a signficant lower ($p < 0.05$) number of postings, 3.27, per discussion board in FY14-15 comparing to 3.39 in FY13-14. This might result from the impact of a new university policy. Two months after this revised course was implemented, the univiersity changed its discussion board expectation for the instructors by reducing the requrired postings. Research studies have shown that instructor's intervention affects the quantity of students' posts in the discussion boards [8][9]. The result from this research study is in accordance with other research findings. Even though students in the FY14-15 courses posted fewer responses, they indeed spent signficantly longer time reading their peers' postings. Students in FY14-15 courses spent 158.2 mintues per discussion board in the five selected discussion boards comparing to 106.06 mintues in FY 13-14 courses ($p < 0.001$) displayed in Figure 3.

3) Student Satisfaction: Figure 4 shows students' perception and feedback on the course in the 16-item end-of-course survey. The overall satisfaction score, 3.46, in the FY14-15 courses (n = 156) is higher than 3.38 in the FY13-14 courses (n = 134) ($p < 0.05$).

C. Conclusions and Implications

Despite the fact that students' learning styles influence the outcomes of the collaborative learning [7], the findings from this study show positively on students' performance, engagement, and satisfaction. The findings suggest that with the exponential development of multimedia technology, educators might integrate it into the course content and course delivery to engage learners in a deeper learning, as well as raise learners' interest and satisfaction in the online environment. Educators might also take advantage of a wide variety of multimedia learning tools to improve the quality of online experience, foster a sense of community, and prepare learners to be lifelong learners with critical thinking and problem-solving skills.

D. Limitations

Several multimedia creations are used to enhance the course, and there is no way of knowing exactly which multimedia is responsible for the improvement. Additionally, there are potential confounding factors, such as student's job status, student's family issue, instructor's profile, and instructor's teaching style, all of which may interfere with students' learning and objective evaluation on the course.

E. Future Reseach

The examination of the correlation between students' attitudes about multimedia learning materials and their actual academic achievement is demanded. There is a need to investigate the relationship between the instructor's teaching style and students' achievement, students' engagement, as well as students' satisfaction. There is also a need to explore the association between the instructor's profile, such as age, gender, race or ethnicity, and students' achievement, students' engagement and students' satisfaction.

REFERENCES

[1] Y. W. Li, X. Wang, and M. Yu, "A research on cultivating method of college students' online learning ability," International Journal of e-Education, e-Management and e-Learning, vol. 1, no. 1, April 2011, pp. 69-74.

[2] F. Leow and M. Neo, "Interactive multimedia learning: Innovating classroom education in a Malaysian University," The Turkish Online Journal of Educational Technology, vol. 13, no. 2, April 2014, pp. 99-110.

[3] Y. W. Li, "Transforming conventional teaching classroom to learner-centred teaching classroom using multimedia-mediated learning module," International Journal of Information and Education Technology, vol. 8, no. 2, 2016, pp. 105-111. doi:10.7763/IJIET.2006.V6.667

[4] M. Neo, K. T. Neo, and H. Y. Tan, "Applying authentic learning strategies in a multimedia and web learning environment (MWLE): Malaysian students' perspective," The Turkish Online Journal of Educational Technology, vol. 11, no. 3, July 2012, pp. 50-60.

[5] M. V. Miller. (2011, June). "A system for integrating online multimedia into college curriculum" Journal of Online Learning and Teaching, vol. 7, no. 2, June 2011, pp. 294-296.

[6] M. Weimer, Learner-centered Teaching: Five Key Changes to Practice (2nd ed.). San Francisco, CA: Jossey-Bass, 2012.

[7] P. Serdyukov, "Does online education need a special pedagogy?," Journal of Computing and Information Technology, no. 1, 2015, pp.61-74. doi:10.2498/cit.1002511

[8] A. Picciano, "Beyond student perceptions: issues of interaction, presence, and performance in an online course," Journal of Asynchronous Learning Networks, vol. 6, no. 1, 2002, pp. 21-40.

[9] T. Russo and S. Benson, "Learning with invisible others: Perceptions of online presence and their relationship to cognitive and affective learning," Educational Technology & Society, vol. 8, no. 1, 2005, pp. 54-62.

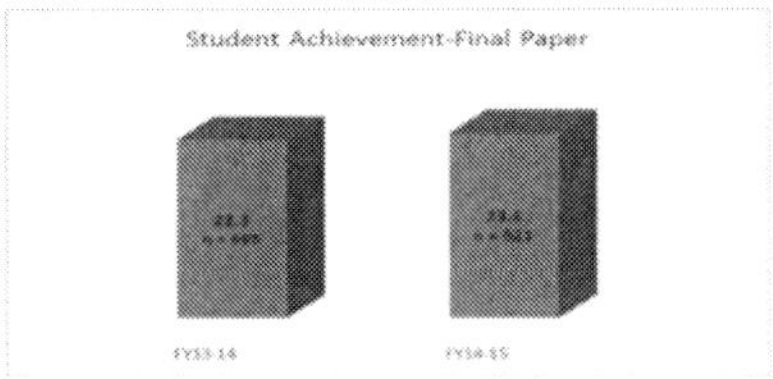

Figure 1. Mean scores of final reach papers from FY13-14 and FY14-15 ($p<0.0001$).

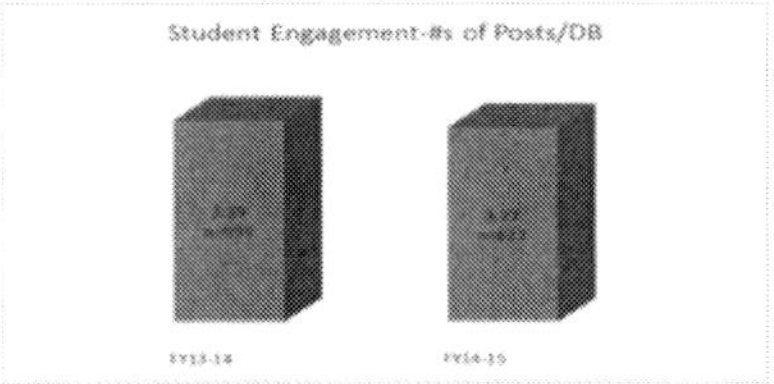

Figure 2. Average numbers of posts per discussion board from FY13-14 and FY14-15 ($p<0.05$).

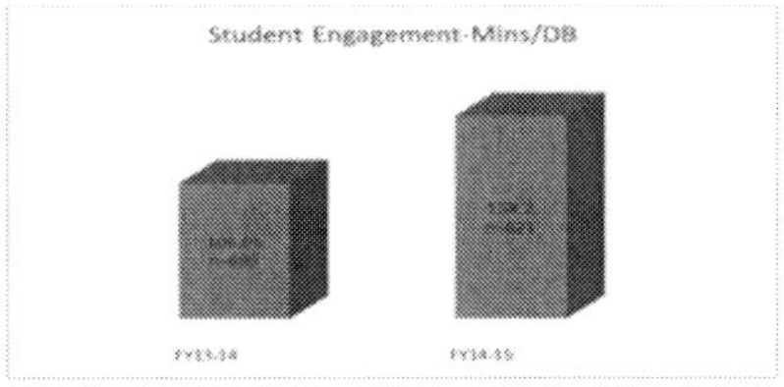

Figure 3. Average time spent per discussion board from FY13-14 and FY14-15 ($p<0.0001$).

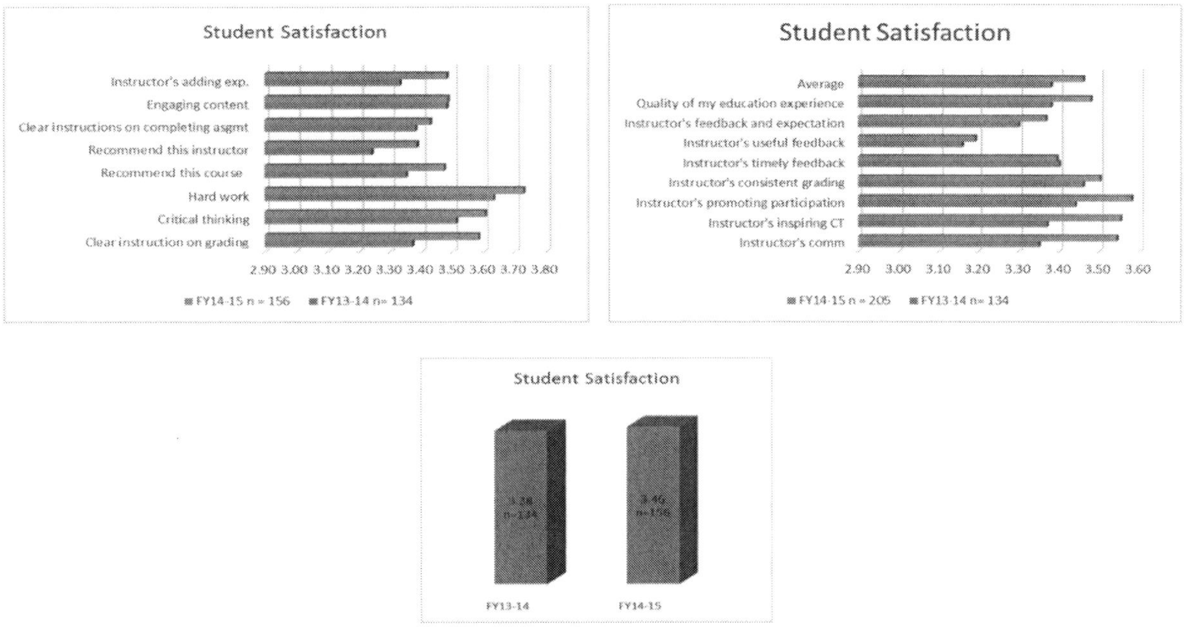

Figure 4. Student satisfaction scores from FY13-14 and FY14-15.

Situated Learning: A Theoretical Base for Online Learning

Wikipedia Translation into Oshikwanyama at a Namibian school

Aletta Mweneni Hautemo
Faculty of Education
University of Namibia
Windhoek, Namibia
email: alettanghelo@gmail.com

Prof Lorenzo Dalvit
Education Department
Rhodes University
Grahamstown, South Africa
email: l.dalvit@ru.ac.za

***Abstract*—This paper provides an in-depth literature review on situated learning and its conceptual model of cognitive apprenticeship and their influence on learning in an Information and Communication Technology (ICT) domain. These are used as epistemological basis to reflect on an intervention involving the translation of Wikipedia content into Oshikwanyama, an indigenous Namibian language in a high school context. This intervention follows a series of research works on ways to engage and integrate ICTs in African indigenous language classrooms. Cognitive apprenticeship principles provide participatory units of analysis which help to explicate the socially mediated learning process, in which all the elements co-contribute to learning in a community of practice using interactive multimedia such as the Internet. The paper argues that situated learning provides a useful theoretical and analytical lens through which a set of authentic activities – reflecting on the way knowledge is constructed and used in real life – can be explored in the classroom. Its key advantages seem to be access to expert performances, modeling of the processes, providing learners with multiple roles and perspectives, supporting collaborative construction of knowledge through coaching and scaffolding.**

Keywords-Information and Communication Technology; Situated Learning; Cognitive Apprenticeship; Wikipedia; Online learning; Translation.

I. INTRODUCTION

Learning environments are loaded with powerful digital devices connected to the Internet, which have revolutionized the way people interact, exchange messages, teach and learn. The web increasingly features "millions of web pages, site-archives, portals, databases and much more for ascertaining a kind of harvested-knowledge where learners can learn by themselves to construct knowledge" [1]. E-learning requires new skills, competencies and attitudes amongst teachers who are the designers and developers of classroom materials. This paper looks at the pertinence of situated learning theory [2], and its model of cognitive apprenticeship and its contribution to and implications for ICT use in the language classroom.

This theoretical background follows a qualitative case study aiming to investigate the use of Wikipedia translation as an additional teaching and learning tool. The intention of this study is to represent the complexity of Wikipedia translation in an Oshikwanyama first language classroom, by providing an in-depth representation of online translation as a real-time activity and engaging learners in interactive and collaborative learning mediated by ICT. We concentrate on the impact that ICT tools have on learning, and the motivation Wikipedia translation has on learners to learn Oshikwanyama. The study involved 32 high school learners who were involved in a survey on the accessibility to and use of ICT devices in Oshikwanyama First Language (elml, 2012), a basic computer training for learner participants and finally the Online Wikipedia translation project.

Therefore, the main aim in exploring this theoretical framework is to try to situate eLearning in the Oshikwanyama classroom as ICT integration across the curriculum is stipulated in the Namibian ICT policy for education [3] which maintains that teachers must try and find contexts in which to integrate ICT and ensure that it makes sense to learners so that they appreciate a new mode of learning. This paper is divided into five sections. Section two reviews literature covering the ontological and epistemological frameworks of situated learning and the model of cognitive apprenticeship. Section three discusses the methodology of the study, and section four presents a critical discussion of the findings. The final section concludes the study.

II. LITERATURE REVIEW

This literature review discusses situated learning framework based on its ontological perspectives and its model of cognitive apprenticeship and its influences on ICT integration in the classroom with respect to the use of Wikipedia translation.

i. Ontological and epistemological underpinnings

Situated learning stems from Vygotsky's social development theory [4], [5], in which learning (including language learning) is viewed as "the appropriation of socially-derived forms of knowledge; which are constructed through the exchange between persons and social and cultural circumstances" [6]. "Situation" encompasses aspects of the physical, social and cultural environment, including communication with peers during the learning process [7]. In situated learning, knowledge and skills are created in contexts that reflect how knowledge is obtained and applied in everyday situations [3].

Situated learning maintains that "knowledge is not a static symbolic representation, 'stored' in the brain of an individual, it is situated, being a product of the activity, context, and culture in which it is developed and used" [8]. Individuals, culture and languages are considered as a whole, co-existing as joint members of the knowledge construction community. ICT integration requires knowledge to be constructed through the interactions of the students within their corresponding socio-cultural environment. ICT tools that include the use of computers have the potential to alter and replace traditional forms of teaching and learning and serve as a vehicle for situated learning [9].

Lave [2], asserts that in situated learning, "knowledge is conceived as a set of tools stored in memory, carried around by individuals who take the tools and use them ... after which they are stored away again without change at any time during the process". This relates well with the use of ICT tools in the language classroom. ICT may be used as an effective and attractive means of presentation, and more importantly, as a way to facilitate peer interaction in and out of the classroom. From the situated learning perspective, "integration of technology into instruction does not just mean to teach students how to use a piece of technological equipment or to teach students by drill and testing" [10]. It is rather a plan to use technological resources to assist students to construct meaningful knowledge by creating social, collaborative, inquiry-based activities and engage learners in critical and higher order thinking.

The computer plays a mediating role, providing a medium for linguistic and notational expression, especially in the language classroom [11]. ICT plays a significant role in enhancing social interactivity among learners and presenting information/ideas effectively for easy processing. This further means that ICT not only enables the transmission of the teacher's understanding to the students, but it is a medium through which teachers and students' understanding can be enhanced through social learning activities.

In proposing their model, Brown, Collins and Duguid [12] argue that meaningful learning will only take place if it is embedded in the social and physical context within which it is used. The core idea in situated learning is that learning is inherently social in nature [13]. This means that in situated learning, learning is shaped by the nature of the interactions among learners, the tools they use within these interactions, the activity itself, and the social context in which the activity takes place. These core ideas of situated learning are relevant for ICT use in the language classroom.

ii. Cognitive apprenticeship as a model for situated learning

Cognitive apprenticeship [14], [2], [3], is a model of learning based on the situated learning theory. This model is designed to "acculturate students into authentic practices by practitioners in their everyday work" [14]. In cognitive apprenticeship, learners collaborate with one another and their teacher to reach shared understandings. According to Lave [2], "Apprentices learn to think, argue, act and interact in increasingly knowledgeable ways with people who do something well, by doing it with them as legitimate, peripheral participants". Apprenticeship is not just a process of internalizing knowledge and skills, it is the process of becoming a member in a community of practice [15].

In cognitive apprenticeship, (i) learning occurs naturally through activities, contexts and cultures, (ii) concepts taken from the natural contexts and applications are taught, and (iii) more "apprentice-like' examples are presented [3]. This means that learning is seen as the notion of the apprentice observing the 'community of practice'. A community of practice helps learners to participate in a legitimately peripheral way, which allows them to have a broad access to arenas of mature practice. As learning happens the involvement in the culture increases, the learners participate in what is called, a 'legitimate peripheral anticipation' [2], [3] which enables them to progressively gather the culture of the group and get the meaning of what it takes to be a member.

Lave and Wenger [3], adopted Vygotsky's Zone of Proximal Development (ZPD) [5] in developing this model. According to Vygotsky the ZPD refers to "the distance between the actual developmental level as determined by independent problem solving and the level of potential development as determined through problem solving under adult guidance or in collaboration with more capable peers". Cognitive apprenticeship requires that a more experienced member of the community of practice is involved to plan and manage the learning situation [13]. This provides an opportunity for guided activities, which are offered in collaborative learning environments. A more knowledgeable other (the teacher or an experienced peer) and cultural artefacts (ICT tools and language) are regarded as important social components for communication.

The concept of cognitive apprenticeship can only promote understanding of the theories of teaching with ICT but it has little influence on the actual practice of using them in daily classroom teaching. Li and Ngan [16], claim that "teachers will never be competent in using ICT in teaching and learning if they are not given the opportunities to observe other more experienced teachers using ICT in teaching". In an intervention conducted at a Namibian school, to use English Wikipedia translation in the Oshikwanyama first language classroom the teacher needs to be knowledgeable in carrying out online lessons, time managements and more especially if they want to complete the lesson objectives, and be aware of cultural artifacts such as the use of language and the Wikipedia translation toolkit.

Stages of cognitive apprenticeship

Five extended stages of cognitive apprenticeship are proposed by Brandt, Falmer and Buckmaster (1993) as cited in [13]. These are analyzed in sequential phases, in the figure below:

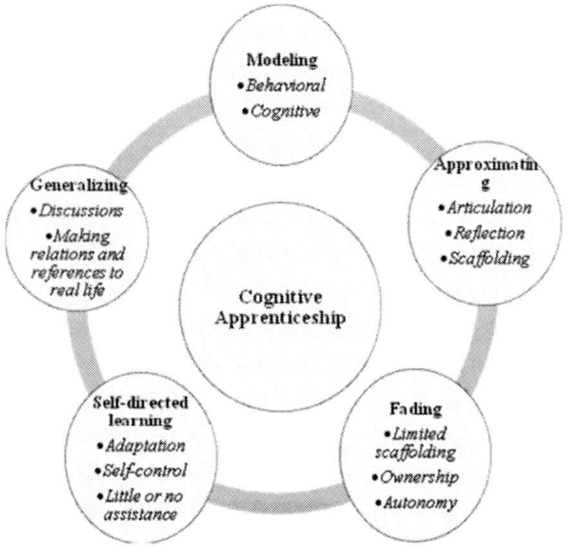

Figure 1. Cognitive Apprenticeship as a model for situated learning

Modelling is one of the strong attributes of situated learning [1], [7]. Modelling assists learners in observing the activity performed by an experienced member of the community and cognitively to allow the experienced member to share knowledge with the inexperienced members [9].

Thus, in cognitive apprenticeship, a teacher models the expert strategies needed to execute the function effectively e.g. the teacher demonstrates how to use certain ICT tools such as the Internet to translate English Wikipedia content and how to use different strategies in translating from the source language to the target language and scaffolds learners throughout the activity. Scaffolding in cognitive apprenticeship, requires a modification of the learning context to suit the individual learner or situation [13]. Scaffolding is collaborative in nature, it requires the task to be located within the learner's ZPD and gradual support of the learners' competence is essential.

Development of eLearning classroom environment for Situated Learning

Situated learning emphasizes the idea that "much of what is learned is specific to the situation in which it is learned" [3]. In cognitive apprenticeship, learning occurs while learners are working on tasks that are slightly more difficult than those they can manage independently, requiring the aid of their peers and instructors to succeed, [17], [18]. Therefore, situated learning can be considered experimental learning since learners learn by doing.

Integrating ICT in the first language classroom can be a daunting task for teachers. Teachers may struggle to decide on appropriate learning contexts, learning content and learning strategies to carry out online activities successfully. Situated learning may offer some of the most helpful strategies to deal with the effective development of learning situations.

Wikipedia translation is an activity grounded in everyday situations such as traditional translation with pen and paper in the language classroom, and the professional translation or localisation of the Internet content by professional translators. Thus, it is learning that could be transferred to other situations such as the Oshikwanyama language classroom using the English Wikipedia content. In this way, knowledge is transferred to similar situations, and learning becomes a result of a social process which is not separated from the world of action but exists in robust, complex, social environments made up of actors, actions and situations. Situated learning happens in a community of practice [3]. Thus, the situated cognitive use of technology could work best in complex situations that require transferring lower level skills to higher order thinking skills as there are many players (teachers and learners) that could contribute to the body of knowledge.

III. METHODOLOGY

This case study was conducted in a northern Namibian school located in the Oshana region. The group that was involved in this research study comprised 32 learners (21 girls and 11 boys) who are, (1) Grade 12 Oshikwanyama First language learners, (2) doing both English Second Language and Oshikwanyama First Language on the Higher Level. The group was chosen because of their language proficiency, which was necessary to carry out the translation from English to Oshikwanyama. Although not all the participants speak Oshikwanyama as their mother tongue at home, they were all taught Oshikwanyama throughout their schooling (from grade 1 to grade 12). In addition, two language teachers at the school participated as co-observers and reviewers of the translated Wikipedia texts/pages on different occasions.

This Wikipedia translation project was conducted in a large, well-ventilated computer laboratory, which consisted of 32 computers and a printer. The data was created through the translation of Wikipedia pages. The respondents had an opportunity to translate Wikipedia content into Oshikwanyama First Language in groups of 3-4 members. This was also done in two stages. Firstly, the participants were given a two-day basic computer literacy course. Afterwards the Wikipedia translations were carried out on four consecutive days. The researcher as a participant observer facilitated the translation. Daily reflection questionnaires were given to the participants to reflect on daily translation activities and an in-depth focus group interviews were conducted at the end of the translation exercise for overall evaluation of the project.

IV. FINDING AND DISCUSSION

This section presents the findings which a discussed based on the characteristics or elements of situated learning environments in which they were analyzed [19][20].

a. *Authentic contexts*

Situated learning attempts to promote learning within the nexus of activity, tools and culture through collaboration and social interaction [12]. A physical and conceptual structure of the classroom, which comprises different ICT media was needed to facilitate the translation activity and was presented for learners to explore. A Wikipedia account was opened for their group, which gives the participants a range of activities to choose from and which could be edited at a time convenient to the learner outside the classroom.

Although learning should be organized in authentic settings for learners to apply "abstract concepts and self-contained examples" [14], the participants were optimistic about translating Wikipedia content, thus concerns were raised about the area of the learning context (i.e. online material) versus the number of learners with computer knowledge or background. Conversely, some respondents felt that learning on Wikipedia was interesting because they would gain knowledge about working with online activities and they believed this would improve their performance.

The participants also observed that although Wikipedia might be a good platform for learning languages and translation activities in the classroom there were risks attached. Some participants asserted that Wikipedia is a free encyclopedia, and thus its content is not reliable because it might be full of inaccuracies. It has transpired that during the translation activity, some learners were not truthful with their translation because they omitted and deleted relevant information. The participating teachers commented that this is risky in the classroom context, if the translation is to become a classroom activity, this would lead to learners failing. They pointed out that, when using activities like Wikipedia translation, learners must be given strict rules and a thorough explanation on assessment procedures. The activities must be treated in the same manner as any other classroom activity.

Time management was one of the contextual key issues which the participants highlighted as a critical factor in learning with authentic content in an authentic context. The participants observed that doing a Wikipedia activity was time-consuming.

b. *Authentic activities*

Cognitive apprenticeship methods try to acculturate students into authentic practices through activity and social interaction in a way similar to that evident – and evidently successful – in craft apprenticeship [12]. This means that in innovative teaching such as web-based teaching, the focus is placed on problem-solving, deliberate attempts are made to generate meaning and show understanding of the nature of the activity. Authentic Wikipedia activities, which are readily available on the Wikipedia portal, were introduced to the learners. Learners opened a Wikipedia account in their groups, which enabled them to access a wide range of online articles in English that they could edit and translate into Oshikwanyama. Learners were given the autonomy to select the articles that they wanted to translate, although they were asked to look at articles within their own context (Namibia, African people, countries or villages and articles within their social circles (the country's or continent's celebrities). Thus, the activity required cooperative engagement in the task and sustained thinking over the process and strategies of translation, using ICT.

Although learners were given the freedom to choose any article they wanted to translate, some of them pronounced their dissatisfaction with authentic articles. Learners came across some of the articles that were social but not educational and unnecessarily long. Some of the articles chosen were written in advanced, complex languages, which many failed to translate adequately, and which led to the meaning being mistranslated and message distorted. The findings indicate that learners were concerned about the value the article added to their education and knowledge. Articles that were not deemed educational were a demotivating factor, which they translated just for the sake of finishing.

c. *Expert performance*

Wikipedia translation is a new phenomenon in an African first language classroom. As such, it needs to be guided through expert thinking and modelling in order to move learners from being less knowledgeable to more knowledgeable. Learners need to have access to the observations of real-life, real-time translation episodes being performed by the teacher or an experienced online translator.

This Wikipedia translation project followed a spiral of activities designed to ensure that learners understood what was required of them. First, the two-day basic computer literacy training introduced learners to key areas of focus, with skills such as basic keyboard use, Internet searching or browsing, and the Wikipedia portal itself. Thus the participants had an opportunity to work on the project surrounded by experts in languages and in ICT, who guided and supported them and in some cases demonstrated learning and decontextualised instruction and strategies for them.

d. *Multiple roles and perspectives*

Situated learning provides the students with a chance to generate their own solution paths in which they take on roles as creative members of the community, who discuss, reflect upon, evaluate and validate learning procedures through collaboration [12]. In this project, multiple perspectives were provided in different ways. One way was that learners were assigned to work in collaborative groups in which each learner brought his/her perspective, experience and understanding of using ICT skills and language skills to the group. Another perspective concerned ICT skills versus the language skills and translation strategies among the participants and lastly, the participants' overall views on the Wikipedia translation process and the translation.

The whole design of the activity, the computers and Wikipedia itself brought in that natural curiosity of learners. Learners usually consult Wikipedia as a source of information on the Internet, or as an educational platform. This activity enabled them to search for and contribute to a wide range of knowledge collaboratively; in which the opportunity to share, debate, create or develop new knowledge was enhanced. Furthermore, learners got a chance to get different perspectives on ICT and languages from their peers. This enabled them to rely on the team's efforts because the successful completion of the task depended on group cooperation, time management and the translations strategies used.

e. Collaborative learning

Collaborative learning is the process of students working in teams to pursue knowledge and learning [7]. In collaborative learning, information, ideas, and problem solving are actively shared among the team members. In situated learning, learners participate and become intimately involved with a culture of learning, interacting with the community and learning to understand and participate in its history, assumptions, and cultural values and rules [3]. In translating Wikipedia pages, heterogeneous groups were organized with learners given the freedom to choose their partners. To many, group work was a serious arena for knowledge building and co-contribution to the translation activity. One advantage was that the learners learnt by articulation and negotiation of meaning, by which they were able to let other group members feed them with the knowledge and then they combined that knowledge to make decisions on how to translate. Although, most of the learners enjoyed working in groups, some were not satisfied with their group performance. Individual preferences in the group, time wasting were some of the disadvantages that the participants alluded to.

f. Reflective learning

A situated learning environment would require students to reflect upon a much broader base of knowledge to solve their problems, and this can be done when the student is able to predict, hypothesize, and experiment to produce a solution [17]. The translation was designed based on authentic context and authentic activities that required learners to reflect on their experience and beyond. Learners were given a daily reflection task to note their views, feelings and think about their strengths and weaknesses. In addition, the interview conducted with them served as a reflective tool that enabled learners to look back at the activity they had just finished, and reflect upon learning languages, using ICT and the motivation from engaging in the Wikipedia translation exercise. Some learners were excited about the whole experience and the outcome of the translation, and wished that their parents or grandparents could see and read their translation, because although it was not a perfect translation, they wrote it in a way that anyone could understand the meaning. This meant that even though this was intended to be a classroom activity, learners were optimistic about the diverse knowledge and understanding that it could carry out there for other people to get information in their own indigenous languages.

g. Articulation of learning skills

Articulation is needed in situated learning in order to enable tacit knowledge to be made explicit [19]. This articulation is procedural in the ICT context such as the Wikipedia translation where tools are used to produce knowledge, and where a learner as a novice becomes an apprentice to learning. In this translation activity, learners were not only given an opportunity to interact with computers, they were also given a chance to interact with each other, and interact with the Wikipedia content that they were translating. These learners had the opportunity to view the task from different aspects and use different strategies to translate the sentences. The activity was designed in such a way that allowed learners to learn in a social situation through group work, where they discussed the translation and strategies and tackled the whole process collaboratively. Many students were able to draw from their individual experience (tacit knowledge) and use it to provide effective strategies. They alluded to the way they tackled translations, mostly focusing on the area of failure experienced in the previous sessions.

h. Coaching and scaffolding

Scaffolding learning advocates that people learn in a community of practice, where learning requires development through ZPD [2]. This means that learners and novice members of the community need teachers to provide different forms of support for learning, through intrinsic scaffolding and coaching [19]. Learners were allowed to work in collaborative groups where more experienced others could assist in the learning process. The presence of a facilitator, an experienced teacher of English and Oshikwanyama who has advanced ICT skills helped learners to comfortably engage with the online activity. The presence of an additional teacher also contributed to the success of the translation. Learners were able to consult and ask the meaning of the words that they totally failed to translate. In some cases, learners asked for clarity when it came to the spelling of words or using the website.

i. Authentic assessment of learning within the task

Assessment involves the process in which learning outcomes are assessed and evaluated. In teaching through

ICT integration, authentic assessment requires "student time and effort in collaboration with others and, as with authentic activities, requires complex, well-structured challenges that involve judgment and a full array of tasks within the assessment seamlessly integrated in the activity" [20]. During the translation, learners were involved in the process of error analysis in which they were asked to identify different errors. This helped learners to correct those errors immediately and choose the most suitable/closest terms. After learners finished with the translation, they were involved in retrospective assessment in which they were asked to read the passage (several groups 3 out of 8 read aloud for the whole class) and then compared it with the source text. In this way the whole group was given the opportunity to judge their translation, check for accuracy and its effectiveness in case it was decided that the Wikipedia translation process become part of Oshikwanyama curriculum.

V. CONCLUSION

In this paper, we provided a qualitative analysis of literature based situated learning and the model of cognitive practices through the lenses of eLearning and Language learning. The use of English Wikipedia translation into Oshikwanyama was explored. The review indicates that, as an educational platform, Wikipedia presents a good chance of involving learners as apprentices into new and practical learning in an authentic context using authentic content, collaboratively. The adoption of situated learning ensures the enculturation of beliefs and improved self-esteem of learners. Furthermore, situated learning widens the zone of proximal development (ZPD), helping learners to carry out an activity and achieve learning in an ICT integrated environment.

REFERENCES

[1] G. M. Kundi, and A. Nawaz. From objectivism to social constructivism: The impacts of information and communication technologies (ICTs) on higher education. Journal of Science and Technology Education Research, vol. 2, no. 1, 2010, pp. 30-36.

[2] J. Lave. Cognition in practice: Mind, mathematics and culture in everyday life. New York: Cambridge University Press. 1988.

[3] J. Lave, and E. Wenger. Situated learning: legitimate peripheral participation. Cambridge: Cambridge University Press. 1991.

[4] L. S. Vygotsky. Thought and language. Cambridge, MA: MIT Press. 1962.

[5] L. S. Vygotsky. Mind in society: The development of higher psychological processes. Cambridge, MA: Harvard University Press. 1978.

[6] S. Billet. Situated learning: Bridging socio-cultural and cognitive theorizing. Learning and Instruction, vol. 6, no. 3, 1996, pp. 263-280.

[7] R. Cobcroft. Literature review into mobile learning in the university context. In Mobile learning literature review, Queensland University of Technology. 2006.

[8] A. Tretiakov. A. Kinshuk, and T. Tretiakov. Designing multimedia support for situated learning. In V. Devedzic, J. M. Spector, D. G. Sampson & Kinshuk A.(Eds.), The 3rd IEEE International Conference on Advanced Learning Technologies, conference proceedings (pp. 32-36), Los Alamitos, USA. 2003.

[9] C. Salomonidou. Constructivist design and evaluation of interactive educational software: A research-based approach and examples. The Journal for Open and Distance Education and Educational Technology, vol. 5, No. 1. 2009. pp. 6-24.

[10] M. Koc. Questioning technology use in educational reform: From ideological theoretical and practical perspective. Malaysian Online Journal of Instructional Technology. Vol. 2, no. 2. 2005. pp. 72-81.

[11] D. R. Garrison. Self-directed learning: Toward a comprehensive model. Adult Education Quarterly, vol. 24, no. 1, 1997. pp. 18-33.

[12] J. S. Brown, J. S., A. Collins, and P. Duguid. Situated cognition and the culture of learning. Educational Researcher, vol. 18 no. 1. 1989. pp. 32-42.

[13] D. C. Hung, K. Looi, and T. S. Koh. Situated cognition and communities of practice: First-person "lived experiences" vs. Third-person perspectives. Education Technology and Society, vol. 7 no. 4, 2004. pp. 193-200.

[14] L. Ilomäki, The effect s of ICT on school: Teachers' and students' perspectives. Unpublished PhD thesis, University of Turku. 2008. Retrieved on 20 November 2015 from https://www.doria.fi/bitstream/handle/10024/42311/B314.pdf ?sequence=3.

[15] M. Kageto, and S. Sato. Rethinking the university learning environment: How to enrich students' education through a constructivist learning environment. International Journal for Educational Media and Technology, vol. 4 no. 1, 2010, pp. 67-78.

[16] K. M. Li, and M. Y. Ngan. Learning to teach with information and communication: Technology in a teacher induction program. International Journal of Technology in Teaching and Learning. vol. 5, no. 1, 2009, pp. 49-61.

[17] C. A. Hansman. Context-based adult learning. In S. Merriam (Ed.), The new directions on adult learning theory: New directions for adult and continuing education. San Franscisco: Jossey-Bass. 2001.

[18] A. Collins, J. S. Brown, and S. E. Newman. Cognitive apprenticeship: Teaching the crafts of reading, writing, and mathematics. In L. B. Resnick (Ed.), Knowing, learning and instruction: Essays in honour of Robert Glaser (pp. 453-494). Hillsdale, NJ: Lawrence Erlbaum, 1990.

[19] J. Herrington, J. and R. Oliver. An instructional design framework for authentic learning environments. Educational Technology Research and Development, vol 48, no 3, 2000. pp. 22-48.

[20] J. Herrington, and R. Oliver. Critical characteristics of situated learning: Implication for the instruction design of multimedia. In J. Pearce & A. Ellis (Eds.). Learning with technology (pp. 253-263). Parkville. Vic: University of Melbourne, 1995.

A Systematic Analysis of Peer Assessment in the MOOC Era and Future Perspectives

Usman Wahid, Mohamed Amine Chatti, Ulrik Schroeder
Informatik 9 (Learning Technologies),
RWTH Aachen University, Germany
e-mail: {wahid; schroeder}@cil.rwth-aachen.de; chatti@informatik.rwth-aachen.de

Abstract— **Massive Online Open Courses (MOOCs) have become a cost and time effective choice for learners all across the globe. This has led to new challenges for teachers such as providing valuable and quality assessment and feedback on such a large scale. Recent studies have found peer assessment where learners assess the work of their peers to be a viable and cost effective alternative to teacher/staff evaluation. This study systematically analyzes the current research on peer assessment published in the context of MOOCs and the online tools that are being used in MOOCs for peer assessment. 48 peer reviewed papers and 17 peer assessment tools were selected for the comparison in this study and were assessed on three main dimensions, namely, system design, efficiency and effectiveness. In the light of the comparison and discussion of current research in terms of these categories, we present future visions and research dimensions to improve the peer assessment process in MOOCs.**

Keywords-Open Assessment; Peer Assessment; MOOC; Blended Learning; Peer Reviews, Online Assessment.

I. INTRODUCTION

The advent of Massive Online Open Courses (MOOCs) has revolutionized the field of technology-enhanced learning (TEL). MOOCs enable a massive number of learners from all over the world to attend online courses irrespective of their social and academic backgrounds. MOOCs have been classified in different forms by researchers, including cMOOCs, xMOOCs [1]. cMOOCs allow the learners to build their own learning networks by using blogs, wikis, Twitter, Facebook and other social networking tools outside the confines of the learning platform [2]. Whereas xMOOCs follow a more institutional model, having pre-defined learning objectives e.g., Coursera, edX and Udacity. Apart from these sMOOCs and bMOOCs have also been introduced as variations of the MOOC platform with sMOOCs catering to a relatively smaller number of participants and bMOOCs combining the in-class and online learning activities to form a hybrid learning environment [1].

Irrespective of the classification, MOOCs require their stakeholders to address a number of challenges including and not limited to the role of university/teacher, plagiarism, certification, completion rates, innovating the learning model beyond traditional approaches and last but not the least assessment [3]. Assessment and Feedback are an integral part of the learning process and MOOCs are no different in this regard. However, in the case of MOOCs assessment presents a bottleneck issue due to the massiveness of the course participants and requires increased resources on part of the teachers. This limitation causes many MOOCs to use automated assessments. Peer assessment offers a scalable and cost effective way of providing assessment and feedback to a massive amount of learners where learners can be actively involved in the assessment processes [4]. A significant amount of research is directed towards exploring peer assessment in MOOCs discussing many issues such as the effective integration of peer assessment in MOOC platforms and the improvement of the peer assessment process.

It is evident that peer assessment is a viable assessment method in MOOCs hence, the need for scouting available systems and studies becomes paramount in importance as it could be beneficial for future developments as well as provide a good comparison of available tools. In this study, we look at the state of art in peer assessment in the MOOC era, perceived benefits and challenges of peer assessment. We also look at different tools for peer assessment and the manner in which they try to address the different challenges and drawbacks. The remainder of this paper is structured as follows: Section II introduces peer assessment. Section III is a review of the related work. Section IV describes the research methodology and how we collected the research data. In Section V, we review and discuss the current research based on several dimensions. Section VI summarises the results of our findings. Section VII presents challenges and future perspectives in peer assessment. Finally, Section VIII gives a conclusion of the main findings of this paper.

II. PEER ASSESSMENT

In recent years, student assessments have shifted from the traditional testing of knowledge to a culture of learning assessments [5]. This culture of assessment encourages students to take an active part in the learning and assessment processes [5]. Peer assessment is the flag bearer in this new assessment culture. Peer assessment, is defined by Topping as "an arrangement in which individuals consider the amount, level, value, worth, quality or success of the products or outcomes of learning of peers of similar status" [6].

Peer assessment has been leveraged in a wide range of subject domains over the years [7]. According to Somervell [8], at one end of the spectrum peer assessment may involve feedback of a qualitative nature or, at the other, may involve students in the actual marking process. This exercise may or may not entail previous agreements over criterion. It may involve the use of rating instruments, which may have been designed by others before the exercise, or designed by the user group to meet its particular needs. The use of peer assessment not only reduces the teacher workload; it also brings many potential benefits to student learning. These benefits include a sense of ownership and autonomy, increased motivation, better learning and high level cognitive and discursive processing [7].

Despite these potential benefits, peer assessment still has not been able to have strong backing from either teachers or students. Both parties have pre-conceived notions of low reliability and validity on their minds when discussing peer assessment [9]. A number of possible factors have been identified for the lack of effectiveness of peer assessment in MOOCs including the scalability issue, diversity of reviewers, perceived lack of expertise, lack of transparency and fixed grading rubrics [10]. The aim of this paper is to examine the available literature and tools for peer assessment, provide a systematic analysis and provide a bigger picture of the research domain.

III. Related Work

Peer assessment in MOOCs is still an emerging field, hence we did not find any research directly related to our work. Luxton-Reily [11] made a systematic comparison of a number of online peer assessment tools in 2009, but the study was conducted with limited dimensions for comparing the tools. The study examined tools including legacy systems, and divided the tools in different categories; namely generic, domain specific and context specific. The study identifies the problem that majority of online tools have been used in computer science courses, and most of the tools could not be used outside the context in which they were developed. This context limitation prevents these tools from being widely adopted which gives rise to the need for more general-purpose tools. Luxton-Reily also stressed the need to investigate the quality of the feedback provided by students [11].

IV. Methodology

The research methodology used for this study is divided in two parts; namely, identification of eligible studies followed by a cognitive mapping approach to find criterion for categorizing and analyzing peer assessment tools.

A. *Identification of Eligible Studies*

We applied the significant research method of identifying papers from internet resources in our study [12]. This method was carried out in two rounds. Firstly, we conducted a search in 7 major refereed academic databases. These include Education Resources Information Center (ERIC), JSTOR, ALT Open Access Repository, Google Scholar, PsychInfo, ACM publication, IEEEXplorer, and Wiley Online Library. We used the keywords (and their plurals) "Peer Assessment", "Peer Review", "Assessment in MOOC", and "Peer Assessment in MOOC". As a result, 87 peer-reviewed papers were found. In the second round, we identified a set of selection criteria as follows:

1- Studies must focus on using peer assessment preferably in a MOOC setting.

2- Studies that focus on design of peer assessment systems or that detail the setting in which peer assessment should be carried out were included.

3- Studies focusing on peer assessment in a manual setting were excluded.

4- Tools older than 10 years have not been included in the study, however, tools having current support are included.

This resulted in a set of 48 research papers/studies on peer assessment in MOOCs and a list of 17 peer assessment tools. These tools include Peer Studio [13], Cloud Teaching Assistant System (CTAS) [14], IT Based Peer Assessment (ITPA) [15], Organic Peer Assessment [16], EduPCR4 [17], GRAASP Extension [18], Web-PA [19], SWoRD (Peerceptiv now) [20], Calibrated Peer Reviews (CPR) [21], Aropä [22], Web-SPA [23], Peer Scholar [24], Study Sync [25], Peer Grader [26] and L²P (Lehr und Lern Portal, RWTH Aachen) Peer Reviews [10]. We also took a look into some open systems that could be used in MOOCs as well, namely: TeamMates [27] and TurnItIn [28].

B. *Cognitive Mapping Approach*

Cognitive mapping is a method that enables researchers to classify and categorize things into several dimensions based on the research questions [29]. For the sake of our study, we scouted the literature to form a directed cognitive map for each study identifying main ideas that talked about peer assessment. These maps were later analyzed for distinct cluster of concepts, grouping similar terms and ideas. After analyzing the clusters, we were able to identify certain dimensions namely system design, efficiency and effectiveness (see figure 1) which were all part of the discussed peer assessment systems. These dimensions provide an easy and efficient way to assess different peer assessment tools/studies.

FIGURE 1. PEER ASSESSMENT CLASSIFICATION MAP

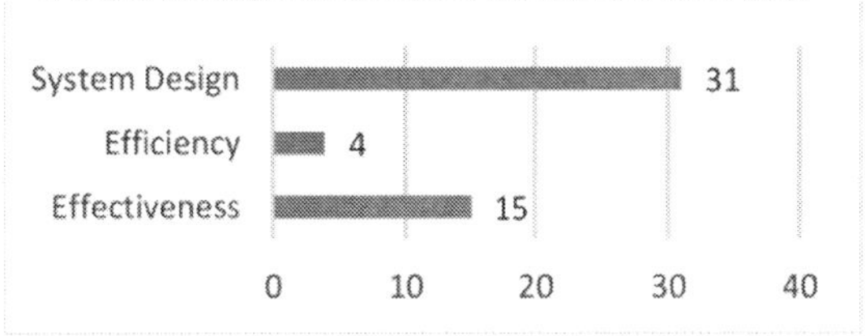

V. Discussion

This section deals with the critical analysis of the peer assessment literature based on the cognitive mapping dimensions derived in the previous section. In order to capture the information gained from the literature analysis, we partitioned these three categories into ten sub-categories. For the critical discussion part, we discuss the way in which certain tools cater to different dimensions (if at all).

A. *System Design*

A lot of effort has been put into the design of peer assessment systems, design of certain features provided by the system and the manner in which they are implemented. Nearly 70% of the studies deal in one way or the other with system or a feature design in peer assessment. In the following sections, we discuss some key features of peer assessment systems and the way; different tools realize them.

1) Anonymity: Anonymity is a key feature that is to be kept in mind while designing any peer assessment system, as it safeguards the system against any type of bias (gender, nationlity, friendship etc.) to play a factor in the assessment from peers. There are three levels of anonymity namely, single blind: assessor knows the assessee but the assessee has no idea of the assessor, double blind: both assessor and assessee are unaware of each other and finally no anonymity in which the identity of both the assessor and assessee are known to each other. Most of the systems reviewed in this study follow the principle of double blind reviews to remove bias, however TurnItIn [28] and Study Sync [25] only implement the single blind reviews.Whereas, organic peer assessment [16] has no mention of the feature at all.

2) Delivery: This feature entails the delivery mode of the review, whether it is delivered indirectly (as is the case in most of the MOOC courses), or directly face to face (could be a situation in a bMOOC). All the reviewed systems only support indirect feedback at the moment.

3) Grading Weightage: Almost two third of the reviewed systems assign a pre-defined weightage to the review from the peers in the overall grade. This means that the final grade is calculated by combining the grade from the peers and the instructor and assigning certain weightages to each of them.

Channel: Researchers believe that more reviews help the assessee to have multiple inisghts about their work and learn from them instead of a single point of view being forced upon them. All the reviewed systems provide multi-channel feedback support for the reviews. A study conducted at Stanford and University of California proposed a process of selecting an appropriate number of reviewers needed for each submission by making use of an automated system. Initially, the student grade is predicted by a machine learning algorithm which then estimates the confidence value. This value is used to determine the required number of peer graders [30]. This automated process aims at putting manageable load on peers by trying to reduce the number of peers required for each submission.

Review Loop: The purpose of this feature is to allow the students to work on their assignments in multiple iterations in order to improve the final product and have a better learning outcome. Although, researchers claim it to be a very important feature for any peer assessment tool, only a handful of the reviewed tools actually implement more than one review loops. These systems include PeerStudio [13], EduPCR4 [17], Peerceptiv [20], Aropä [22], Web-SPA [23] and Peer Grader [26]. Peer grader is unique in this respect as it allows for a communication channel between the author and the reviewer to help the authors improve their submissions [26].

4) Collaboration: Collaboration means the ability of the tool to allow students to form and work in small groups. Although many MOOC platforms make use of discussion forums and wikis to enable collaboration and idea sharing between the students, but we found that only three systems actually allow the students to form groups and submit their work in groups. Team mates [27] is an open source tool that allows the students to form smaller groups and submit their work. Also L^2P Peer reviews [10], makes use of a separate module Group Workspace in their learning management system to manage student groups.

B. Efficiency

In this section, we list the features that contribute to the overall efficiency of the system. These features allow the system to be more efficient for its users and help them get the most value out of the system.

1) Feedback Timing: Research has shown that the optimal timing of a feedback is early in the assessment process, as it gives the learners more time to react and improve. Peer Studio, proposes an effective way to reduce the review response time. The learners can submit their work any number of times for a peer review and get the review by reviewing the work of others. A study conducted on the usefulnes of the system concludes that the students in the Fast Feedback condition did better than the No Early Feedback condition group. It also states that on average students scored higher by 4.4% of the assignment's total grade, hence proving the usefulnes of early feedback [13].

C. Effectiveness

Several researchers in TEL have explored how to design effective peer assessment modules with a higher level of user satisfaction. We identified certain features that contribute to the effectiveness of the reviews provided by the peers, which are discussed in the following sections.

1) Rubrics: Rubrics provide a way to define flexible task specific questions that could include descriptions of each assessment item to achieve fair and consistent feedback for all course participants. Studies suggest that asking direct questions for the peers to answer, in order to assess the quality of someone's work enables the reviewer to easily reflect on the quality of submitted work in a goal oriented manner [10]. Hence, a flexible rubric system becomes a must have feature for any good peer assessment system. In our study, we found that majority of the reviewed systems offer this feature in one way or the other with a notable exception of Peer Grader.

A variation of the use of rubrics is the way peer studio tool handles them. The tool allows the teachers to define rubrics and then enforces the students to answer these questions in a better way by using a technique they call scaffolding comments [13]. The system does this scaffolding by making use of short tips for writing comment below the comments box.

2) Validation: A number of studies have been carried out on the validation aspect of the reviews provided by peers, i.e., on methods to make sure that the feedback provided by the peers is valid and of a certain value. Luo et al. [7] conducted a study specifically on Coursera platform to evaluate the validity of the reviews from peers. In their study they propose that increasing the number of reviewers and giving prior training to the reviewers are some techniques that could be used to bolster the validity of the reviews. Peerceptiv measures the validation of reviews to a submission by simply calculating the agreement rate between different reviewers. It takes score difference, consitency and the spread of scores into consideration for evaluating the validity of reviews [20].

3) Reviewer Calibration: Calibrated peer reviews (CPR) [21] along with some other studies carried out in MOOCs [31] propose a different method to achieve system effectivness, namely, reviewer calibration. In this method, the reviewers are required to grade some sample solutions which have been pre-graded by the instructor to train them in the process of providing reviews.

4) Reverse Reviews: Another interesting method to verify the effectiveness of the reviews is to use the reverse review method. Peer Grader [26] and EduPCR4 [17] tools make use of this method to allow the original authors of the reviewed submissions to rate the reviews they reeived from their peers. The students can specify whether the review helped them in improving their submission, or was of a certain quality, or helped them understand the topic clearly. This review is then taken into consideration at the time of calculation of the final grade, so the peers who provided better reviews have a chance to better their assignment score.

VI. SUMMARY

Table I shows a summary of evaluation of different tools against the dimensions identified in Section IV. The table shows that nearly all the tools reviewed in our study follow a similar system design varying slightly based on the context in which they are used. The only major discrepancy in most tools is their inability to allow students to work in groups (for assignment submission and reviews). Another pattern emerging from studying the table is that more and more tools are giving weightage to the student reviews in the overall grade of the students. This means that the teachers have to be sure about the validity and quality of the student reviews, and the system has to provide features for its insurance. Another useful observation is the usage of assessment rubrics by the tools to help students in the review process. As identified by Yousef et al. [10] rubrics are an easy way to provide learners with task specific questions, allowing achievement of fair and consistent feedback for all course participants.

In the comparison for the validation, we mention all the tools for which a study has been conducted for the validation of peer reviews. It does not specify that the tool have some in-built validation mechanism for the reviews provided by peers. Table I also highlights an important trend in the field of peer assessment for MOOCs. It shows that most systems are moving on from the basic system design and looking for ways to improve the efficiency and effectiveness of the system. This leads to the use of innovative ways to ensure the quality of reviews, and a focus to find ways on improving the overall user experience and learning.

VII. CHALLENGES AND FUTURE VISION

MOOCs with their large number of participants pose a challenge when it comes to assessment and feedback, and peer assessment offers a viable solution to the problem. However, peer assessment itself faces a number of challenges including scalability, reliability, quality and validation. A number of studies have focused on overcoming these limitations, as outlined in the previous section but there is still a lot of room for improvement.

The challenges faced by peer assessment are inherent from the challenges of open assessment in general, and the field of learning analytics offers a number of techniques to overcome these challenges. In this section, we try to offer some solutions from the field of learning analytics, which could be used to overcome some peer assessment challenges.

1) Scalability: The massive number of participants in the MOOC courses requires the feedback provided to students to be scalable as well. This requires the use of certain measures to decrease the time required by the teacher to provide useful feedback to the student submissions. Although peer assessment tries to lessen the teacher's burden but still the teacher has to be in the loop to ensure quality feedback. To overcome this issue of scalability, we could make use of clustering techniques. We could cluster similar submissions

TABLE I. A SYSTEMATIC COMPARISON OF PEER ASSESSMENT TOOLS

	System Design						Efficiency	Effectiveness			
Tools	**Anonymity**	**Delivery**	**Grading Weightage**	**Channel**	**Review Loop**	**Collaboration**	**Time/Rapid Feedback**	**Rubrics**	**Validation**	**Reviewer Calibration**	**Reverse Reviews**
Peer Studio [13]	Double	InDirect	Yes	Multiple	Multiple	No	Yes	Yes	Yes	No	No
CTAS [14]	Double	InDirect	Yes	Multiple	Single	-	No	Yes	Yes	No	No
ITPA [15]	Yes	InDirect	No	Multiple	Single	-	No	Yes	Not measured	No	No
Organic PA [16]	No	InDirect	No	Multiple	Single	-	No	No	Yes	No	No
EduPCR4 [17]	Double	InDirect	Yes	Multiple	Double	-	No	Yes	Not measured	No	Yes
GRAASP extension [18]	No	InDirect	Yes	Multiple	Single	-	No	Yes	Yes	No	No
Web-PA [19]	Yes	InDirect	Yes	Multiple	Single	Yes	No	Yes	Not measured	No	No
SWoRD/Peerceptiv [20]	Double	InDirect	Yes	Multiple	Double	Yes	No	Yes	Yes	No	No
CPR [21]	Double	InDirect	Yes	Multiple	Single	No	No	Yes	Yes	Yes	No
Aropä [22]	Yes	InDirect	Yes	Multiple	Double	-	No	Yes	Yes	No	Yes
Web-SPA [23]	Yes	InDirect	No	Multiple	Double	Yes	No	Yes	Yes	No	No
Peer Scholar [24]	Double	InDirect	Yes	Multiple	Single	No	No	Yes	Yes	No	No
Study Sync [25]	Single	InDirect	No	Multiple	Single	No	No	Yes	Yes	No	No
Peer Grader [26]	Double	InDirect	Yes	Multiple	Double	No	No	No	Yes	No	Yes
L²P Peer Reviews [10]	Double	InDirect	Yes	Multiple	Single	Yes	No	Yes	Yes	No	No
Team Mates [27]	Double	InDirect	No	Multiple	Single	Yes	No	Yes	Not measured	No	No
TurnItIn [28]	Single	InDirect	No	Multiple	Single	No	No	Yes	Yes	No	No

together and in case of peer assessment, the similar reviews (including rubric answers) could be clustered together to form a single unit. The teacher could easily grade the clusters, in turn saving valuable time.

Another solution to the problem of scalability could be the use of word clouds by extracting important parameters from the submitted work of students. This could help the teacher by providing an overview of the submission and giving a fair idea about the contents. Hence, a teacher could decide if the submission requires in depth review or they could grade based on the provided information.

2) Reviewer Credibility/Reliability: There have been cases identified in peer assessment studies, where students don't take the process of reviewing others work seriously. This leads to invalid reviews and casts a doubt over the credibility of the reviews being provided to students. In this scenario, the teacher must be in the loop to ensure valid reviews. One solution to this could be to rate the reviewers using the reverse review method. This way we could identify possible bad reviewers and screen them out for further reviews or they could be urged to provide better reviews.

3) Validity: We have already seen the usage of calibration to improve the validity of the reviews. Raman and Joachims make use of a statistical method in their study to ensure the validity of the reviews. They use Bayesian ordinal peer grading to form an aggregated ordering for all the submissions in a course room. The difference in ranking from different peers is also taken into account to ensure the effectiveness and validity of reviews [32]. Another approach could be the use of automated assessment, as is the case in automatic essay grading systems. The system takes into account the grade from one human reviewer and the automated assessment grade. If the difference in grades from both sources is greater than a certain threshold, then the system asks for an additional review from a human grader [33]. This technique could be applied to the peer reviews, and if the disagreement between the review from peer and the automated assessment is significant, the system could mark the submission for grading by the teacher or ask for a review from some other peer as well.

4) Quality: Rubrics provide an easy way of improving the quality of the reviews [10]. The peer assessment system could enhance this by providing a way for the teacher to specify common mistakes that students make, so that the reviewer could look for these and in turn improve review quality.

5) System Configuration: Another improvement to the peer assessment tools could be to allow the user to configure different settings from a central location rather than making it a part of system design. Majority of peer assessment systems in use today have pre-defined configuration in features like anonymity, review loops, grading weightage etc. These pre-configured settings make it difficult for the tool to be used in a more generic way and in different contexts. Hence, a tool that allows its users to configure all these settings could be a lot more useful across different domains and have a higher acceptance rate from users across the glo.

VIII. CONCLUSION

Peer assessment is a rich and powerful assessment method used in technology-enhanced learning (TEL) to improve learning outcomes as well as learner satisfaction. In this paper, we analysed the research on peer assessment published in the MOOC era, and the tools that could be used to provide peer assessment capabilities in a MOOC. A cognitive mapping approach was used to map the selected studies on peer assessment into three main dimensions namely, system design, efficiency and effectiveness. The following is a summary of the main findings in our study as well as aspects of peer assessment that need further research, according to each dimension.

A. System Design

The analysis of the peer assessment research showed that majority of the systems are designed on similar lines to each other, differing in only a small number of features or the way these features are implemented. Despite these possible differences in implementation, the general idea for different system features remains the same across different tools. However, several features concerning system design need a better acceptance across these tools: (1) Collaboration: The tools should allow the students to work in a collaborative environment and submit their assignments and even review in groups. (2) Review Loops: In our opinion, all peer assessment tools should provide at least double review loops to give students more chances of improvement and in doing so we leverage the peer assessment model in a better way to achieve positive results.

B. Efficiency

Studies have established the positive effect of timely feedback on student performance but the assessment tools are lagging far behind in this regard. In our opinion, tools should focus on efficient ways to decrease feedback time, and focus on more innovations to make the process more efficient.

C. Effectiveness

Several methods are being used in peer assessment to increase effectiveness of the reviews and in turn the learners' satisfaction with peer assessment. Although, rubrics, reviewer calibration and reverse reviews are good ideas to improve the effectiveness of the reviews; more research has to be put into measuring the validity of the reviews provided by peers. Future research needs to find new ways to record validity of reviews and improvements to this validity. The systematic comparison also reveals certain patterns and trends across the analysed tools. It points out the fact that most tools are quite similar in system design, and the way they carry out the peer assessment process. The difference arises in the way the apply validation and effectiveness techniques to the peer reviews. The study also highlights the shift in focus from basic system design to innovative ways of improving the quality and effectiveness of the reviews provided by peers.

The study concludes with providing a list of open challenges in the peer assessment process/systems and proposes certain techniques that could be applied to address these challenges. The proposed solutions include a number of techniques from the field of learning analytics including statistics, visualizations, and data mining techniques that could prove useful in improving the peer assessment process/tools.

REFERENCES

[1] G. Siemens, "MOOCs are really a Platform. Elearnspace (2012)." 2011.

[2] G. Siemens, "Connectivism: A learning theory for the digital age," 2014.

[3] A. M. F. Yousef, M. A. Chatti, U. Schroeder, M. Wosnitza, and H. Jakobs, "MOOCs-A Review of the State-of-the-Art," in *Proc. CSEDU 2014 conference*, 2014, vol. 3, pp. 9–20.

[4] R. O'Toole, "Pedagogical strategies and technologies for peer assessment in Massively Open Online Courses (MOOCs)," 2013.

[5] A. Planas Lladó, L. F. Soley, R. M. Fraguell Sansbelló, G. A. Pujolras, J. P. Planella, N. Roura-Pascual, J. J. Suñol Martínez, and L. M. Moreno, "Student perceptions of peer assessment: an interdisciplinary study," *Assess. Eval. High. Educ.*, vol. 39, no. 5. 2014, pp. 592–610.

[6] K. Topping, "Peer assessment between students in colleges and universities," *Rev. Educ. Res.*, vol. 68, no. 3, 1998, pp. 249–276.

[7] H. Luo, A. C. Robinson, and J.-Y. Park, "Peer grading in a mooc: Reliability, validity, and perceived effects," *Online Learn. Off. J. Online Learn. Consort.*, vol. 18, no. 2, 2014.

[8] H. Somervell, "Issues in assessment, enterprise and higher education: The case for self-peer and collaborative assessment," *Assess. Eval. High. Educ.*, vol. 18, no. 3, 1993, pp. 221–233.

[9] O. McGarr and A. M. Clifford, "'Just enough to make you take it seriously': exploring students' attitudes towards peer assessment," *High. Educ.*, vol. 65, no. 6, 2013, pp. 677–693.

[10] A. M. F. Yousef, U. Wahid, M. A. Chatti, U. Schroeder, and M. Wosnitza, "The Effect of Peer Assessment Rubrics on Learners' Satisfaction and Performance within a Blended MOOC Environment," in *Proc. CSEDU 2015 conference*, 2015, vol. 2, pp. 148–159.

[11] A. Luxton-Reilly, "A systematic review of tools that support peer assessment," *Comput. Sci. Educ.*, vol. 19, no. 4, 2009, pp. 209–232.

[12] A. Fink, *Conducting research literature reviews: from the Internet to paper*. Sage Publications, 2013.

[13] C. Kulkarni, M. S. Bernstein, and S. Klemmer, "PeerStudio: Rapid Peer Feedback Emphasizes Revision and Improves Performance," in *Proceedings from The Second (2015) ACM Conference on Learning@ Scale*, 2015, pp. 75–84.

[14] T. Vogelsang and L. Ruppertz, "On the validity of peer grading and a cloud teaching assistant system," in *Proceedings of the Fifth International Conference on Learning Analytics And Knowledge*, 2015, pp. 41–50.

[15] K. Lehmann and J.-M. Leimeister, "Assessment to Assess High Cognitive Levels of Educational Objectives in Large-scale Learning Services," 2015.

[16] S. Komarov and K. Z. Gajos, "Organic Peer Assessment," in *Proceedings of the CHI 2014 Learning Innovation at Scale workshop*, 2014.

[17] Y. Wang, Y. Liang, L. Liu, and Y. Liu, "A Motivation Model of Peer Assessment in Programming Language Learning," *arXiv Prepr. arXiv1401.6113*, 2014.

[18] A. Vozniuk, A. Holzer, and D. Gillet, "Peer assessment based on ratings in a social media course," in *Proceedings of the Fourth International Conference on Learning Analytics And Knowledge*, 2014, pp. 133–137.

[19] P. Willmot and K. Pond, "Multi-disciplinary Peer-mark Moderation of Group Work," *Int. J. High. Educ.*, vol. 1, no. 1, 2012, p. p2.

[20] J. H. Kaufman and C. D. Schunn, "Students' perceptions about peer assessment for writing: their origin and impact on revision work," *Instr. Sci.*, vol. 39, no. 3, 2011, pp. 387–406.

[21] P. A. Carlson and F. C. Berry, "Calibrated peer review/sup TM/and assessing learning outcomes," in *fie*, 2003, pp. F3E1–6.

[22] J. Hamer, C. Kell, and F. Spence, "Peer assessment using arop{ä}," in *Proceedings of the ninth Australasian conference on Computing education-Volume 66*, 2007, pp. 43–54.

[23] Y.-T. Sung, K.-E. Chang, S.-K. Chiou, and H.-T. Hou, "The design and application of a web-based self-and peer-assessment system," *Comput. Educ.*, vol. 45, no. 2, 2005, pp. 187–202.

[24] S. Joordens, S. Desa, and D. Paré, "The pedagogical anatomy of peer-assessment: Dissecting a peerScholar assignment," *J. Syst. Cybern. Informatics*, vol. 7, no. 5, 2009.

[25] D. L. White, "Gatekeepers to Millennial Careers: Adoption of Technology in Education by Teachers," *Handb. Mob. Teach. Learn.*, p. 351, 2015.

[26] E. F. Gehringer, "Electronic peer review and peer grading in computer-science courses," *ACM SIGCSE Bull.*, vol. 33, no. 1, 2001, pp. 139–143.

[27] G. Goh, X. Lai, and D. C. Rajapakse, "Teammates: A cloud-based peer evaluation tool for student team projects," 2011.

[28] S. Draaijer and P. van Boxel, "Summative peer assessment using 'Turnitin' and a large cohort of students: A case study," 2006.

[29] S. McDonald, K. Daniels, and C. Harris, "Cognitive mapping in organizational research In C. Casssell & G. Symon (Eds.), Essential guide to qualitative methods in organizational research" London: Sage, 2004, pp. 73-85.

[30] C. E. Kulkarni, R. Socher, M. S. Bernstein, and S. R. Klemmer, "Scaling short-answer grading by combining peer assessment with algorithmic scoring," in *Proceedings of the first ACM conference on Learning@ scale conference*, 2014, pp. 99–108.

[31] J. Wilkowski, D. M. Russell, and A. Deutsch, "Self-evaluation in advanced power searching and mapping with google moocs," in *Proceedings of the first ACM conference on Learning@ scale conference*, 2014, pp. 109–116.

[32] K. Raman and T. Joachims, "Bayesian Ordinal Peer Grading," in *Proceedings of the Second (2015) ACM Conference on Learning @ Scale*, 2015, pp. 149–156.

[33] H. Chen and B. He, "Automated Essay Scoring by Maximizing Human-Machine Agreement.," in *EMNLP*, 2013, pp. 1741–1752.

Persuasive Technologies for Efficient Adaptable Self-Education

Kids Smart Mobile School Project

Saad Abdessettar
École de Technologie Supérieure (ÉTS)
Montreal, Canada
e-mail: saad.abdessettar.1@etsmtl.ca

Mickaël Gardoni
École de Technologie Supérieure (ÉTS) / INSA
Montreal, Canada / Strasbourg, France
e-mail: mickael.gardoni@etsmtl.ca

Richard Hotte
Dept.: LICEF research center at Téluq University
Montreal, Canada
e-mail: richard.hotte@teluq.ca

Bessam Abdulrazak,
University of Sherbrooke
Sherbrooke, Canada
e-mail: bessam.abdulrazak@usherbrooke.ca

Abstract—**Persuasive Technologies could revolutionize the way education is delivered. It could enable serving kids who would probably never have the chance to even see a school. Millions of children still do not have access to school or teachers, especially in poor and developing countries. Thus, our research project aims at offering a persuasive mobile self-learning system that can be an alternative to standard school. We present in this paper the (KSMS) project. We focus on our vision of embedding persuasive technologies to enhance kids' education quality and efficiency, in a self-learning context.**

Keywords-Persuasive technology, Persuasive learning, Mobile learning, Pupil Perseverance, Pupil Motivation, Pupil Engagement

I. Introduction

Information and Communication Technologies (ICT) have changed our way of performing tasks in diverse domains such as economy, health, and higher education. This change affects even the way we live [1]. Still, the effectiveness of the ICT is not maximal due to the lack of efficient Human Machine Interaction (HMI) design. Several studies have emerged in the persuasive technologies science to address limitations of the HMI design. These studies resulted in numerous findings, constructs, methods and models, addressing problems related to persuasion and behavior or attitude changes. Persuasive technologies have a potential to revolutionize the Education [2-6]. Thus, we target in our *Kids Smart Mobile School* (KSMS) project, in collaboration with our industrial partner DATAWIND Inc. [36], to propose a low-cost solution for school access problems using mobile and persuasive technologies. The first target population of KSMS is the rural area in India.

In the rest of the paper is structured as follows. In Section II, we discuss the background of our research and our research project context. In Section III, we define our research question and originality. Section IV presents a summarized review of research studies and findings addressing the two main issues related to education (i.e., motivation and engagement) in primary and secondary school. Next, I Section V, we present an overview of relevant works in persuasive technologies for education, and then conclude the paper with a summarizing synthesis and a discussion of future perspectives.

II. Background

Adapting and using ICT for education is a current problem, particularly in developing countries. In Africa, for example, there have been numerous initiatives that target ICT for education. The list includes: use of tablets in colleges in Niger as a tool/medium for education, use of mobile phones in continuing training of primary teachers in Madagascar, etc. Unfortunately, there are still children in the world without access to school (primary and secondary). This situation is due to various reasons such as economy, social behavior, family structure, geographic condition, racial discrimination, and gender disparity [7]. Ardt et al. [7] highlight that gender disparities are critical in Bangladesh. They discussed that three million children between six and ten years (5% of children age of primary school) have never attended school. Ardt et al. [7] conclude that this situation is because those children are poor, from remote rural areas, without homes or, even from minority tribes. Kim et al. and Kim, P.H. [8, 9] discussed similar situations among indigenous of South America, seasonal or itinerant workers. They indicate that, among the underserved population in Latin America, a large number of the indigenous children are the poorest ones who hardly have access to formal school. Similarly, Achoka et al.[10] conclude that the failure in the access of young Kenyan children to primary education is due to poverty, inequality in gender and regional disparities.

Nowadays, around 124 million children and teenagers, between the ages of 6 and 15 years, have either never started school or have dropped out, according to UNESCO Institute of Statistics (UIS) [11]. The UIS discusses in a recent report that the main problem is (directly or indirectly) the lack of school access in rural and/or urban regions [11]. The UIS report also concludes that we can no longer rely only on 'usual' strategies based on more teachers, classrooms and textbooks. Thus, our KSMS project is an attempt to provide innovative education approaches. KSMS was defined in partnership between LICEF research center and his industrial partner DATAWIND. In the next section, we present a relevant state of the art of research studies related to the KSMS project.

III. Relevant Works

There exist a number of relevant research studies that focus on technological learning system to compensate the absence of school or teacher. Kam et al. [12] studied designing E-Learning Games for Rural Children in India. Kam et al. project's challenge was to design e-learning games that are both educational and pleasurable for their target learners. These children have limited familiarity with technology. Kam et al. [12] proposed the "receptive-practice-activation cycle" to be used as the conceptual model for designs. Another challenge was to design a balanced solution between fun and self-learning for rural children. Thus, those challenges gave high consideration to local environment and contextual information of the target learners.

EuroPLOT is another relevant project to compensate for the absence of school or teacher [13]. The project's team has developed Persuasive Learning and Technologies (PLOTs) and has evaluated them in four real-world case studies. The project covers different teaching scenarios of university education, adult learning in industry, informal learning at a museum, literature studies, and language learning. EuroPLOT explores to what extent persuasive learning objects and technologies could militate (simulate and alleviate) the functions of a persuasive teacher. The framework was designed based on Fogg's definition of CAPTOLOGY [14], and integrated the RAMP model (Relatedness, Autonomy, Mastery and Purpose) proposed by Marczewski [15] to enable engagement in the learning process. The learning diffusion strategies adopted in the EUROPLOT had diverse challenges. Indeed, the researchers and designers involved in the project had the challenge to deliver the teacher with the text, but at the same time to invest this teacher presence in the text with stronger persuasive power for learning.

Similar projects aiming at diffusing learning throughout technology and gaming environment have been undertaken. Plass et al. [16] present a research study that aims at designing a game (i.e., FactorReactor) to help practicing and automating arithmetic skills. The goal is to increase arithmetic fluency in middle-school-age students. Plass et al. argue that competitiveness increases in-game learning, whereas collaboration decreases performance during the experimental play session. They discuss that competition and collaboration elicit greater situational interest and enjoyment, and invoke a stronger mastery goal orientation. They conclude that, collaboration results in stronger intention and motivation to play the game again and to recommend it to others.

Similarly, Lerkkanen et al. [17] examined the extent to which teaching practices observed in kindergarten classrooms predict children's interest in reading and mathematics. They conclude that girls are more motivated than boys in reading. On the other hand, boys perform better than girls in tasks involving number sequences. Lerkkanen et al. [17] argue that for the observed teaching practices, the more child-centered and the less teacher-directed they are, the higher reading motivation is among children. Similarly, Hirvonen et al. [18] examined the developmental dynamics of task-avoidant behavior and math performance from kindergarten to Grade 4. They studied math performance and task-avoidant behavior development in tandem. Hirvonen et al. [18] argue that an increase in task-avoidant behavior is related to less improvement in math performance, and high initial level of task-avoidant behavior predicted less improvement and slower improvement in math later on.

To conclude, there is yet no research study that focuses on a technological learning system to compensate for the absence of school or teacher. Few existing studies focus on either complementing existing learning provided by standard schools, or on bringing new alternative learning (distant or hybrid) that always include teacher or tutor interaction with final learners. In the next section, we present our research project and research question, and then discuss our vision of persuasive technologies in KSMS.

IV. KSMS Project

KSMS's main goal is to create a learning system on mobile devices that will be adapted for individual self-learning. KSMS project targets particularly children in developing countries without access to teachers or school. Three main objectives are defined for KSMS project:

I. To provide autonomous learning for part of the elementary and/or secondary curriculum, with content definition and learning strategies adapted to a mobile device apps environment.

II. To design an educational game application based on serious game architecture to support learning contents.

III. To integrate persuasive design and HCI multimodal interaction design in the learning process. The main goal is to make the system more adaptive and more context-aware. This will allow guiding and impacting the learner's behavior, by helping him/her to control his/her own learning and to be continuously motivated to learn.

In this paper, we mainly focus on the third objective. More precisely, we intend to answer the following research questions: (i) How persuasive technologies can help stimulate pupil motivation and perseverance? (ii) At what extent should the targeted system consider contextual persuasion in order to ensure a learner centered strategy and an efficient self-determined education?

The KSMS project originality comes from the fact that the system is fully automated and will represent a unique source of learning for the target population. In other words, the final system will not be a complement to an existing learning system, such as school, classroom, learning resource or teacher. Instead, KSMS aims at providing all those components in an integrated architecture that can ensure the efficiency and the effectiveness of learning for the target population that is supposed to have limited or no access to teacher or school.

The third objective of KSMS project, which is the focus of this paper, is expected to compensate the absence of the school and the teacher. By persuasive learning, we refer to learning that is designed using persuasive technologies to impact the learner's engagement and ability to control his own learning. KSMS project is designed to integrate persuasive system design models and methods with the latest findings in education science field related to engagement and perseverance. Thus, the target solution is designed considering the autonomous fact of the learning provided, and also the challenge to ensure an equivalent quality of learning to Indian government standard as defined by the Central Board of Secondary Education in its international version.

We discuss next some definitions of motivation, its classes, and what factors can help to monitor and manage motivation and engagement in learning.

V. LEARNING MOTIVATION

Motivation refers to "the choices people make as to what experiences or goals they will approach or avoid, and the degree of effort they will exert in that respect" [19]. Motivation is viewed as highly unpredictable and changeable, being subject to divers influences [20]. In education, there is a consensus that motivational messages impact student motivation level and have a positive influence on their class performance

The term "***Motivation to learn***" is defined by Marshall, H. [21] as the meaningfulness, value, and benefits of academic tasks to the learner regardless of whether or not they are intrinsically interesting. According to Brophy, J. [22], motivation to learn is a competence acquired through general experience, but stimulated most directly through modeling, communication of expectations, and direct instruction or socialization by significant others (especially parents and teachers).

Motivation can be Intrinsic or extrinsic. ***Extrinsic motivation*** is doing or not doing something because of external benefits or consequences (i.e., reward or punishment) [23]. An "***Extrinsically***" motivated student performs "*in order to*" obtain rewards or avoid punishments external to the activity itself," such as grades, stickers, or teacher approval [24]. They also perform because of pressure, reward, incentive, among other external reasons [25].

Intrinsic motivation is basically self-motivation [26]. This internal motivation involves values [27] and is frequently linked with achievement [28]. A student who is "***Intrinsically***" motivated undertakes an activity "for its own sake, for the enjoyment it provides, the learning it permits, or the feelings of accomplishment it evokes" [29].

Condry, J. et al. [30] discuss that, when students were confronted with complex intellectual tasks, those with an intrinsic orientation used more logical information-gathering and decision-making strategies than did students who were extrinsically oriented. Students with an intrinsic orientation also tend to prefer tasks that are moderately challenging, whereas extrinsically oriented students gravitate toward tasks that are low in degree of difficulty. Extrinsically oriented students are inclined to put forth the minimal amount of effort necessary to get the maximal reward [24].

Numerous researches have been undertaken in order to monitor and manage student motivation. Keller, J.M. [31] Introduced the ARCS model as a method for improving the motivational appeal of instructional materials and is based on four dimensions of motivation. These dimensions were derived from a synthesis of research on human motivation and are known as ARCS: Attention (A), Relevance (R), Confidence (C), and Satisfaction (S). ARCS model focuses on using motivational messages that are intended to enhance faculty-student interaction, which leads to enhancing student motivation [32]. Ciampa, K. [24] argues that the list of elements that make an activity both intrinsically and extrinsically motivating for a learner include: challenge, curiosity (cognitive & sensitive), control, cooperation, competition and recognition.

Moreover, Bobis, J., et al. [33] propose a model for mathematics instruction to enhance student motivation and engagement. Part of their research questions were: What teaching strategies might motivate middle-grades students to engage more in mathematics? Bobis et al. proposed an upgraded version of Martin, A.'s motivation wheel framework [34], by conceptualizing the wheel into adaptive, impeding, and maladaptive dimensions. Their framework allows educators to identify a set of common factors. Those factors underpin in particular student's motivation and engagement. The motivation wheel also allows to identify what aspects need to be targeted for intervention. From another perspective, Fogg [14] introduced principal motivators for designing behavior change in the Fogg

Behavior Model (FBM): (1) Pleasure vs. Pain, (2) Hope vs. Fear, and (3) Social Acceptance vs. Rejection.

After discussing motivation in this section, we present next relevant research studies to KSMS and persuasive education.

VI. Persuasive Technologies for Education

We argue that persuasive technologies and persuasive design can be efficiently integrated in self-learning systems. We believe that persuasive technologies have to be considered in all aspects of the target learning system. Therefore, we propose to integrate persuasive design and persuasive technologies in a framework of three layers. Following is a description of the framework and the guidelines we adopted on each layer (Figure 1):

1) Learning Structure: in this layer we consider the ease of use for the KSMS proposed system, as well as the ease of registration and subscription to all proposed pedagogical activities. We also take into consideration the impact of celebration, and the success/failure perception to ensure an efficient motivating roadmap for the proposed learning progress structure. Thus, the learning progress will be designed to consider small achievable goals. To those goals, specific behaviors are defined as target behavior for the persuasive strategies or component to integrate or include in the solution. The challenge is then to guide and help the final user – the learner, to continuously feel successful by achieving a sequence of small goals that lead to the defined target one.

2) Learning Medium & Infrastructure: at this layer, we are adapting the learning scenario, content and medium to learner context information gathered throughout used devices. The main design driver at this layer is ensuring reduction and facilitating the interaction with KSMS. In this layer, we integrate the ARCS model to ensure user engagement in using the KSMS learning system, and also in keeping focused on the learning goals to progress in his/her learning. We also enhance the context awareness in order to propose content and learning scenarios that match more the real world of the learner. Some technical constraints and limitations make the social learning difficult to occur. In fact, the bandwidth is limited in the provided mobile network using 2G technology. We adapted the solution to use data collected by devices to create virtual classroom or learning groups that are formed by neighbor users. We believe that throughout those learning groups we can stimulate social learning and provide the learner to interact with peers and even act as a teacher when helping other.

3) *Learning Content & Scenarios:* at this layer, we propose an integration of persuasive technologies in the content and in the way the learner will receive the content. Our analysis of the content leads us to consider target learning skills as target behaviors. Thus, the main goal is to make the final user (in our case, the learner) exercise those target behavior according to their needed frequency. A high consideration is given to the learner context and to the real world learning mapping opportunities, in order to make the KSMS's learning experience more relevant and then more efficient. In fact, the Geographical Positioning System (GPS)'s data is for instance, a great source of context understanding. We propose to use the GPS data to retrieve information about the environment (sunny, raining, culture, known products, etc.), and then map it in the content so we can give examples of raining vocabulary when it is raining, for example. Other sensors and technologies are considered, especially the Bluetooth and ad-hoc Wi-Fi, to stimulate social learning even when there is no Internet connection. Moreover, when a kid is well performing in a task, he will be prompted to share his knowledge with neighbor kids having problems to perform that task. In this way, the intent will be not only stimulating the teacher role (and by the way this is a way to replace the ordinary teacher), but we also give the first well performing pupil to identify and control his own learning.

We base our persuasive design mainly on FBM. We consider different classes of behaviors regarding the three layers. To build strategies for bringing the learner to target behavior, we monitor his ability, motivation and trigger. This principle is applied either for behaviors related to the use of KSMS, to the learning engagement and perseverance or to the target skills defined in the target curriculum. We then use Behavior Wizard methodology to implement the persuasion strategy [35], by defining the behavior state transition and mapping it to the proposed grid. Fogg, B. and Hreha, J. [35] proposed fifteen cells in his BehaviorWizard: five columns for behaviors types (New behavior, Familiar behavior, increasing behavior, decreasing behavior and stop behavior), and 3 rows for behavior frequency (DOT: one time, SNAP: period of time, PATH: from now on). We use the BehaviorWizard to design the transition path of behaviors after breaking them down into a combination of small and more specific ones.

In this section, we presented an overview of the persuasive design integration to KSMS persuasive learning system. A synthesis of guidelines and fundamentals adopted in designing persuasive technologies that will be embedded in the target mobile learning system KSMS.

VII. Conclusion and Future Work

ICT and persuasive technologies can contribute significantly to resolve the school's access problem. We presented throughout this paper our vision on delivering education to where there is no access to school and teachers, taking advantage of persuasive technologies. This activity is part of the KSMS project presented in the paper. We also discussed the persuasive design framework and guidelines we adopted for KSMS. We are working on tuning the framework and finalizing the implementation of the defined solution before evaluating the results with the industrial partner in real settings. DATAWIND has partnered with the Indian government, as well as other countries, to begin providing its low-cost tablets to an estimated number of 220 million kids, especially those suffering from a school access problem.

ACKNOWLEDGMENT

KSMS project was funded jointly by MITACS-CANADA and DATAWIND Inc. throughout a partnership with LICEF research center.

REFERENCES

[1] Fogg, B.J., Persuasive technology: using computers to change what we think and do. Ubiquity, 2002. 2002(December): pp. 2.

[2] Behringer, R. and Øhrstrøm, P., Persuasive Design in Teaching and Learning. International Journal of Conceptual Structures and Smart Applications, 2013. 1(2): pp. 1-5.

[3] Gram-Hansen, S.B., D. 3.3 PLOT Persuasive Learning Design Framework: Persuasive Learning Designs. 2012.

[4] Winther-Nielsen, N., PLOTLearner's Persuasive Achievement: Force, Flow and Context in Technology for Language Learning from the Hebrew Bible. HIPHIL Novum, 2014. 1(2): pp. 78-94.

[5] Nakajima, T. and Lehdonvirta, V., Designing motivation using persuasive ambient mirrors. Personal and Ubiquitous Computing, 2013. 17(1): pp. 107-126.

[6] Lucero, A., et al., Persuasive technologies in education: Improving motivation to read and write for children. Lecture notes in computer science, 2006: pp. 142.

[7] Ardt, K., et al., Report on primary education in bangladesh: Challenges and successes. Bangladesh Bureau of Education Information and Statistics (BANBEIS)/Bangladesh Ministry of Women and Children Affairs (MWCA), 2005.

[8] Kim, P., Miranda, T. and Olaciregui, C., Pocket school: Exploring mobile technology as a sustainable literacy education option for underserved indigenous children in Latin America. International Journal of Educational Development, 2008. 28(4): pp. 435-445.

[9] Kim, P.H., Action research approach on mobile learning design for the underserved. Educational Technology Research and Development, 2009. 57(3): pp. 415-435.

[10] Achoka, J.S.K., Odebero Sephen O., Naiyo Julius K., and Mualuko N., Access to basic education in Kenya : inherent concerns. Educational Research and Reviews, 2007. 2(10): pp. 275-284.

[11] UIS, U.a., A growing number of children and adolescents are out of school as aid fails to meet the mark. POLICY PAPER 22 / FACT SHEET 31, 2015. : http://www.uis.unesco.org/Education/Documents/oosci-global-report-en.pdf. (last accessed March 2016)

[12] Kam, M., et al. Designing e-learning games for rural children in India: a format for balancing learning with fun. in Proceedings of the 7th ACM conference on Designing interactive systems. 2008. ACM.

[13] Behringer, R. and Sinclair, G., IWEPLET 2013 Proceedings. EuroPLOT Retrieved December, 2013. 8: pp. 2013.

[14] Fogg, B.J. A behavior model for persuasive design. in Proceedings of the 4th international Conference on Persuasive Technology. 2009. ACM.

[15] Marczewski, A., The Intrinsic Motivation RAMP. 2013.

[16] Plass, J.L., et al., The impact of individual, competitive, and collaborative mathematics game play on learning, performance, and motivation. Journal of Educational Psychology, 2013. 105(4): pp. 1050.

[17] Lerkkanen, M.-K., et al., The role of teaching practices in the development of children's interest in reading and mathematics in kindergarten. Contemporary Educational Psychology, 2012. 37(4): pp. 266-279.

[18] Hirvonen, R., et al., The developmental dynamics of task-avoidant behavior and math performance in kindergarten and elementary school. Learning and Individual Differences, 2012. 22(6): pp. 715-723.

[19] Keller, J.M., The use of the ARCS model of motivation in teacher training. Aspects of educational technology, 1984. 17: pp. 140-145.

[20] Keller, J.M. and Kopp, T.W., An application of the ARCS Model of Motivational Design. 1987.

[21] Marshall, H., Motivational strategies of three fifth-grade teachers. The Elementary School Journal, 1987.

[22] Brophy, J., Socializing students' motivation to learn. Advances in motivation and achievement, 1987. 5: pp. 181-210.

[23] Ryan, R.M. and Deci, E.L., Self-regulation and the problem of human autonomy: does psychology need choice, self-determination, and will? Journal of personality, 2006. 74(6): pp. 1557-1586.

[24] Ciampa, K., Learning in a mobile age: an investigation of student motivation. Journal of Computer Assisted Learning, 2014. 30(1): pp. 82-96.

[25] Konheim-Kalkstein, Y.L. and Van den Broek, P., The effect of incentives on cognitive processing of text. Discourse Processes, 2008. 45(2): pp. 180-194.

[26] Deci, E.L., et al., Motivation and education: The self-determination perspective. Educational psychologist, 1991. 26(3-4): pp. 325-346.

[27] Sanacore, J., Turning reluctant learners into inspired learners. The Clearing House: A Journal of Educational Strategies, Issues and Ideas, 2008. 82(1): pp. 40-44.

[28] Spittle, M., K. Jackson, and Casey, M., Applying self-determination theory to understand the motivation for

becoming a physical education teacher. Teaching and Teacher Education, 2009. 25(1): pp. 190-197.

[29] Lepper, M.R., Motivational considerations in the study of instruction. Cognition and instruction, 1988. 5(4): pp. 289-309.

[30] Condry, J. and Chambers, J., Intrinsic Motivation and the Process of Learning. In the Hidden Costs of Reward, edited by MR Lepper and D. Greene. 61-84. 1978, Hillsdale, New Jersey: Lawrence Erlbaum Associates, Inc.

[31] Keller, J.M., Using the ARCS motivational process in computer-based instruction and distance education. New directions for teaching and learning, 1999. 1999(78): pp. 37-47.

[32] Robb, C.A. and Sutton, J., The Importance of Social Presence and Motivation in Distance Learning. Journal of Technology, Management & Applied Engineering, 2014. 31(1-3): pp. 1-10.

[33] Bobis, J., et al., A model for mathematics instruction to enhance student motivation and engagement. Motivation and disposition: pathways to learning mathematics, 73rd yearbook. Reston: National Council of Teachers of Mathematics (NCTM), 2011.

[34] Martin, A., Building classroom success: Eliminating academic fear and failure. 2010: A&C Black.

[35] Fogg, B. and Hreha, J., Behavior wizard: a method for matching target behaviors with solutions, in Persuasive technology. 2010, Springer. pp. 117-131.

[36] www.Datawind.com (last accessed April 2016)

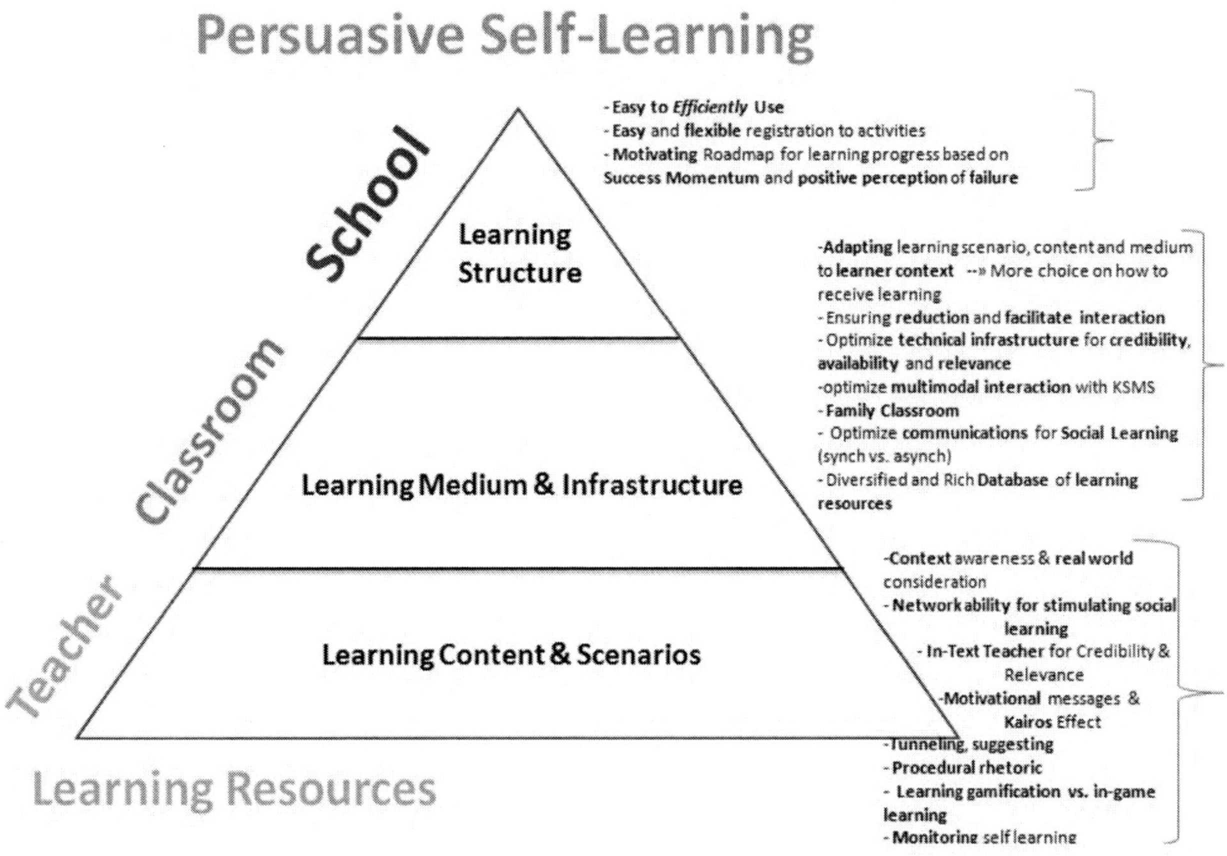

Figure 1. Implementing persuasive technologies in KSMS

AmITest: A Testing Framework for Ambient Intelligence Learning Applications

Nikolaos Louloudakis, Asterios Leonidis and Constantine Stephanidis
Foundation for Research and Technology – Hellas (FORTH) - Institute of Computer Science
N. Plastira 100, Vassilika Vouton, GR-700 13
Heraklion, Crete, Greece
e-mail: {luludak, leonidis, cs}@ics.forth.gr

Constantine Stephanidis
University of Crete, Department of Computer Science
Heraklion, Crete, Greece
e-mail: cs@csd.uoc.gr

Abstract— **As the Ambient Intelligence (AmI) paradigm emerges and develops, applications in education are attracting increasing attention. For maximum educational efficiency, extensiveness and adaptation to the needs of their users, AmI systems in education need to be easily programmable. Considering that their users are primarily non-computer professionals, giving them the ability to program those environments is a task difficult by itself, as those environments are of high architectural and computational complexity. In addition, it is of high importance that those environments work as expected, making the testing and the validation of their behavioral aspects a crucial part of the development process. In this paper, we propose AmITest, a framework that effectively allows the testing and the validation of behavioral programs written by users in a simple, yet direct and effective way. AmITest is part of a complete end-user development suite named AmIClass, which allows the effective programming of AmI educational environments by non-computer professionals.**

Keywords-visual programming; end-user testing; ubiquitous environments; smart learning environment; ambient intelligence testing

I. INTRODUCTION

As Information Technology evolves, the traditional interaction paradigm where humans are just the operators of stationary machines is revolutionized by the concepts of Ambient Intelligence [1] and Pervasive Computing [2] that introduce innovative ecosystems in which humans are surrounded by ubiquitous technological artifacts (e.g., sensors, actuators, smart devices, etc.) and computational units, that enrich their environment in a smart, transparent and unobtrusive way. In such environments (i.e., AmI Environments), ubuquitous artifacts can reason, collaborate and interact proactively in order to improve the quality of life of humans, by satisfying their needs and offering assistance in their daily activities.

The list of the application domains whose users could be benefited by such intelligent environments is rather endless, ranging from the automation of repetitive tasks (i.e., daily routines) in order to offer more spare time to their inhabitants for other activities, to improving the overall quality of life of specific groups of people (e.g., people with disabilities, elderly, etc.) by assisting them with their daily activities. Such a domain with promising potentials is the domain of education, particularly regarding the concept of Just-in-Time Learning [3] (i.e., the provision of learning material at the right time, the right place and the appropriate format).

An Intelligent environment that promotes learning by offering to its users educational material when and where they are ready to espouse knowledge the most, based on the current task at hand and the available technological artifacts that could be used in order to make the information as easily adoptable as possible (e.g., sensors, actuators, interactive devices, etc.), is called a Smart Learning Environment (SLE) [4].

A key requirement of SLEs is that their behavior and interaction policies need to be easily programmed by their end-users, who most likely will not be computer professionals. In this respect, Leonidis et al [5] have proposed AmIClass, a framework for end-user visual programming aiming primarily to users that are non-computer professionals. An important aspect is that such environments are of high architectural and computational complexity. Therefore, not only programming is a challenging task, but also the proper testing and validation of the behavior of those environments is of utmost importance. Towards such objective, this paper proposes the AmITest Framework, a testing framework for AmI environments, with its main focus on SLEs.

AmITest aims to support the users that define the behavior of the SLE (i.e., SLE programmers), rather than the end-users of the SLEs themselves (e.g., teachers, students, school principals, etc.). The programming expertise of AmITest users however may vary greatly ranging from motivated teachers who want to modify the intelligent environment they work into, to experienced IT professionals who determine in detail the behavior of the environment and the contained learning facilities. To accommodate both groups, while considering that the majority of the target users will not be experts, AmITest makes the testing process as straightforward as possible, by offering a visual programming tool for the end-users to define their tests. The AmITest framework is a novel part of the AmIClass Framework [5] that provides testing capabilities using the dynamic scripting language of AmIClass in order to test the artifacts of the SLE being tested as subject.

The AmITest framework is mainly consituted of two main components: (1) *The ClassScript Testing Agents*, a framework for testing and validating the behavior of SLEs defined in an imperative domain-specific language named ClassScript and (2) *The Tests Management and Deployment Suite*, a suite that facilitates end-users to visually program a number of tests regarding the AmI environment behavior using a building block-based Graphical User Interface (GUI). These components interoperate in order to provide the best programming options to the end-users so that they can configure parts of the behavior of the system (e.g., articulate user input for a certain scenario, transcript the behavior of a fictional user, etc.) and validate whether the intended behavior meets the original expectation.

The paper is organized as follows. Section II describes relevant approaches to the AmITest framework. Section III outlines the requirements that should be met to apply successful testing of a SLE. Section IV describes the implementation details. Section V presents a proof-of-concept scenario. Section VI focuses on the biggest challenges met in order for AmITest to do efficient testing, and Section VII concludes the paper by discussing the current status of the framework and discussing a list of potential improvements and additions.

II. Related Work

AmITest focuses on the creation of tests that aim to validate the behavior of an SLE. The behavior itself is defined in AmIClass using the ClassScript language [5], a dynamic, untyped language used specifically for the definition of the behavior of particular artifacts inside an SLE, and macroscopically, the behavior of the SLE as a whole [5]. AmITest introduces a library that enables testing of ClassScript. AmITest is based on similar testing frameworks for untyped languages, and in particular on two testing frameworks for the JavaScript programming language [6], Jasmine [7] and QUnit [8].

As aforementioned, non-computer professionals will mainly be asked to program and test the behavior of an SLE, thus mechanisms that facilitate programming by such users with little or no experience are supplied, including visual tools that can be easily learnt and used in order to design programs and validation tests [9]. This paradigm is effectively used in order to provide programming capabilities to systems that target non-professional users in various systems with diverse objectives. AmIClass [5] enables the definition of the behavior of SLEs via visual programming even by novice users (e.g., teachers). Scratch [10] is a visual programming environment primarily targeted to users in ages between 8 and 16 years old, with limited to none programming experience, that aims to teach them programming while working on meaningful projects such as animated stories and games via a visual programming editor. Virtuoso [11] is a visual tool for creating educational games aiming primarily non-professional users, based on Valve's game engine. TouchDevelop [12] is a system for developing applications directly from a mobile device through the cloud using a custom visual editor that adapts its functionality based on the knowledge and programming skills of its user. App Inventor [13] is a platform from MIT which provides a web-based visual programming tool for designing mobile applications online. Automator [14] is a visual scheduling tool providing capabilities of repetitive automation tasks in the Mac OSX platform.

All the aforementioned systems facilitate programming of various kinds to users with very little or no programming experience via employing the visual programming paradigm. However, only AmIClass targets AmI environments where common testing techniques (i.e., Unit Testing) may not suffice as most of them lack the necessary testing and validation mechanisms to allow the verification of the behavior of the programs by their end-users.

AmITest aims to address those pitfalls as it not only supports testing of the behavior of an SLE, but also offers both visual and script editing facilities to accommodate users with different levels of expertise. Consequently, any user will be able to program her own test cases and test the behavior of the SLE easily. Text-based scripting support for end-user programmers is inspired by many well-established incarnations in the domain of electronic games development, with languages such as Lua [15] and JavaScript [6] having played an important role in the widespread adoption of extensible game engines (such as Unity [16]), and even further, to the introduction of games that players can freely customize (e.g., the game "Second Life" offered the Linden Scripting Language [17] through which players were able to create in-game elements).

III. Framework Requirements

Considering that SLEs are complex systems with a considerable number of collaborating artifacts composing them, it is necessary to validate the behavior of each artifact individually, but also the SLE behavior as a whole.

In order for the proposed system to efficiently test the functionality of each individual artifact and the behavior of the SLE as a whole, each artifact should have installed a lightweight service, the *ClassScript Testing Agent* (CTA), which facilitates the orchestrator of the testing operations done in the artifacts, and works as the delegate of the *Tests Management and Deployment Suite (TMDS),* which is responsible for the definition of the testing actions on each artifact. The CTAis practically a service communicating with the Service Mediator Agent of the AmIClass framework and is responsible for the installation, deployment and execution of the test scripts on that artifact.

Each artifact should also implement a lightweight Application Programming Interface (API) called *ISchoolArtifact* in order to allow the system execute certain operations necessary for testing, such as requesting the form of the information provided from each artifact (i.e., the information schema), accessing that information to determine the status of the artifact, etc,.

As aforementioned, artifacts of an SLE interoperate with each other in a distributed manner [18], as they are different remote sub-systems that coexist inside the SLE. To satisfy the increased communication needs stemming from both the "normal" SLE operation and the testing purposes, the proprietary FAmINE middleware [19] was used. The *ISchoolArtifact* interface is defined as a FAmINE component and via that interface the distributed systems can communicate with each other.

Finally, since the testing framework will be a part of the AmIClass Framework, each artifact should meet the requirements of AmIClass as described in [5].

IV. System Architecture

The AmITest system is an integral part of the AmIClass suite, thus it follows a similar architectural structure from an engineering perspective. The AmiTest framework consists of: (1) the delegate ClassScript Testing Agents (CTA), which get installed on every artifact and are responsible for the installation and local execution of the testing scripts, and (2) a master web-based suite, the Tests Management and Deployment Suite (TMDS*)*, responsible for the creation, overview and management of the testing procedure. The overall architecture is depicted in Fig. 1 below.

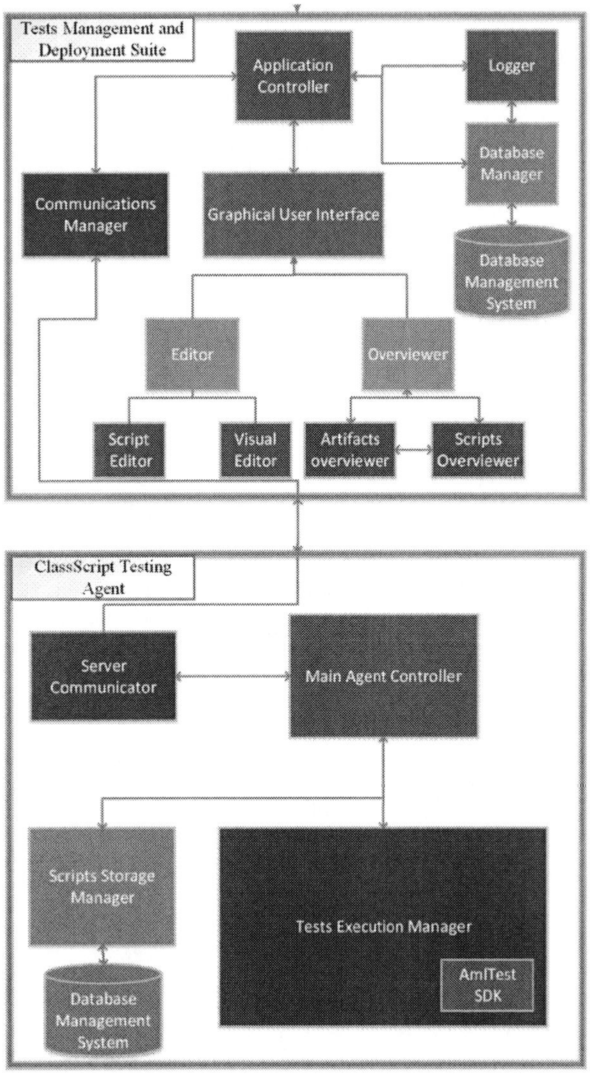

Figure 1. Architecture of the AmITest framework

In Addition, CTA is responsible for managing any locally installed scripts (i.e., update, delete). Before its initial execution, each script is cached locally to minimize its startup time since for every subsequent execution there will be no need to retrieve it from the main repository. The CTA also ensures that the local version is always the latest one, thus on any update it replaces the old version with the new.

The Standard Development Kit (SDK) of AmITest is a native library of the AmIClass framework – part of the language implementation, and the test scripts of the AmITest framework are ClassScript language scripts. Therefore, they are executed by the installed AmIClass interpreter without any modifications. The SDK consists of three specially-purposed APIs: the Artifacts API, the Invoker API and the Tester API.

The Artifacts API handles the information retrieval of the data structures and the actual data of an artifact. Upon launch, it loads the information schema of the underlying artifact, and then periodically collects any data used from the test scripts to validate its behavior and provides them to the Tests Management and Deployment Suite for updating the artifact's overview, enabling test editing, and for logging purposes. Its objective is two-fold: (1) provide the server-side TMDS with information that will assist and enhance the development process of the end-users, and (2) retrieve and use the artifacts data for assertions checking when validating the behavior of a component or of the SLE as a whole.

The Invoker API let programmers schedule valid invocations of a function or triggering of events, in order to check whether the correct behavior has been applied based on the respective "expectations" (i.e., assertions) of the artifact(s) of the SLE. Considering that the Invoker API will mainly focus on the invocation of asynchronous functions, a mechanism that address any dirty object instances existence has been considered. The Invoker API is designed and implemented based on the Promises pattern. A Promise is a pattern which represents the result of an asynchronous, long running and potentially, but not necessarily, complete operation, using an object instance which represents the promised result of the operation. This concept is common on asynchronous programming, and various frameworks implement it for both typed and untyped programming languages, such as C++ Promises [20] and Javascript Promises [21].

The Tester API is responsible for the evaluation of any assertions, named Expectations, relevant to that artifact or the overall SLE. The most common use of Expectations is in combination with Promises, in order to apply checks on the data of one or more artifacts within an SLE: considering that the testing process is an asynchronous task by itself, artifact-specific promises are used to ensure that expectation checking on the artifacts will be performed when the objects are in a ready, clean state and not before. Such an example is depicted in Fig. 2; when all the necessary events are handled by the respective components -the promises are satisfied-, only then the expectations will be evaluated. The Tester API offers a variety of checking options, such as numerical and string checking, shallow and deep object equality comparison, regex checking, etc.

All the components of a CTA are orchestrated effectively via the Main Agent Controller, which orchestrates all the components aforementioned for a proper functionality. The controller is responsible to enable all the components required for any actions needed to be done, such as script installation, script execution, server briefing about the scripts and the artifact status etc.

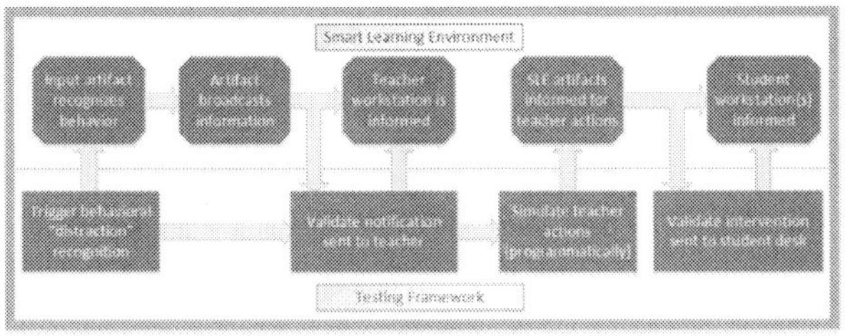

Figure 2. Flow of Information across core SLE (blue boxes) and AmITest (green boxes) components

A. *The Tests Management and Deployment Suite*

The Tests Management and Deployment Suite (TMDS) is responsible for the management of all the testing scripts that exist in the SLE. The suite has two main components: the *ClassScript Integrated Development Environment (CIDE)* and the *Management Suite (MS)*. CIDE is an environment for the development of the scripts that define the behavior of the artifact (i.e., its business logic) and testing scripts that will validate it. MSis a Graphical Suite that facilitates the overview, remote installation, supervision and execution of any testing scripts and consists of the following components: the Application Controller, the Graphical User Interface, the Database Manager, the Logger and the Communications Manager.

The Application Controller is the main controller of the server-side application, which orchestrates all the operations of every component with respect to the testing procedure. The Graphical User Interface is the main Graphical Component of the system, and consists of the Test Scripts Editor and the Overviewer components.

The Test Scripts Editor provides the end-users with an environment where they can create new scripts from scratch or edit existing ones, either visually or via textual scripting since both modes are interoperable. In Visual Editing Mode, the end-user can create and/or modify existing tests using a visual tool of building blocks (based on a Google's Blockly project [22]), as depicted in Fig. 3. This mode is more suitable for users with very little or no programming experience giving them the capability of creating effective test scripts. This tool will eventually generate valid ClassScript code (as shown in Fig. 4) and any artifact will be able to execute it directly using its installed ClassScript interpreter. In Scripting Mode, the end-user can write the tests for the application directly in the ClassScript language, using an integrated WYSIWYG text editor. This mode increases the expressiveness of the scripting tests, it is considered to be more difficult for novice users, but more powerful for users with some programming experience. The system though attempts to assist the end-user programming as much as possible, providing auto-completion capabilities along with syntax highlighting capabilities.

The Overviewer is the graphical tool that presents the overview of the Artifacts and the Scripts existing in the SLE. In particular, apart from their aggregated statistics, for each SLE it provides an overview of the installed, deployed and/or currently executing behavioral and testing scripts. This component also consists of two smaller components, the Artifacts Overviewer, responsible for the overview and management, from a testing perspective, of the various artifacts present in an SLE (e.g., activation and deactivation of facilities) and the Scripts Overviewer, responsible for the overview and the management of the scripts installed in the main repository, or cached locally in every artifact. The end-users can use this component in order to install more scripts on each artifact, but also to monitor a script's execution, its outcomes or even interact with it in real-time (e.g., inspect its status, breakpoint or stop it etc.).

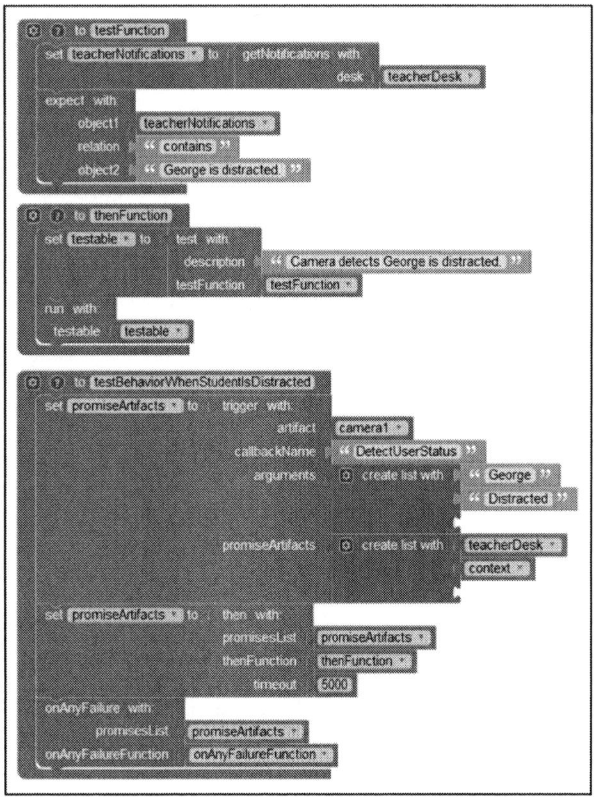

Figure 3. Definition of a test using AmITest Visual Editor

TMDS also contains the Database Manager component for the manipulation of the database operations regarding the test scripts and any relevant information about them (e.g., logging information, information schema, history, etc.). This component is responsible for all the Create-Read-Update-Delete (CRUD) operations of the Database Management System (DBMS) held in the server where the application is installed. The Logger is a component responsible for managing the logging operations, and works in close collaboration with the Database Manager component.

Finally, the suite contains the Communications Manager, a component for the two-way communication between the artifacts and the Suite on the server. This component receives all the data needed in order to inform the Suite Graphical User Interface, logging data, scripts data, etc., and propagates any commands to the artifacts including user-oriented commands (e.g., resulting from the interacting with the Suite, such as new scripts installations, scripts executions on an artifact, etc.) or system-oriented commands (e.g., predefined reaction of a fictional user to a certain event, etc.).

V. Proof Of Concept

A. *Test Case Scenario*

AmISchool [23] is an ambient educational test bed which consists of a number of artifacts: four touch-enabled AmIDesks [24][25], an interactive teacher workstation, a large projection screen, a Heating, Ventilation, and Air Conditioning (HVAC) controller, alights control system, a sophisticated vision-based user tracking system [26] and various AmI-oriented learning applications [23][27][28]. It employs the ClassScript framework [5] in order to enable the definition of learning plans (i.e., scripts) that control its behavior by the teachers themselves, thus it provides the context for our test case scenario.

Mrs. Smith is a 42-years old history teacher, with very limited programming experience mostly related to formulas creation in a spreadsheets processor to calculate her students grades, who teaches the 5th grade in that school. After a few unsuccesfull attempts, shehas managed to define and validate the general behavior of the classroom both in terms of physical conditions and privacy; she has created scripts that instruct: (1) the classroom to automatically turn on the lights when students are present and control the room's temperature to maximize students' convenience, (2) the AmIDesks to initiate the login procedure when a student is sitting in front of them and show the contents of her presentation if the relevant application is on the foreground on her workstation.

Today, she wants to use for the first time the available Student Attention Monitoring and Intervention system, which in case of inattention can actively intervene, thus she needs program eventually validate a simple intervention that will aim to motivate a distracted student. Therefore, she instructs the vision component to track the gaze of each individual student and notify the teacher if inattention is detected. Upon notification, she wants to be able to either virtually poke that student or activate a quick educational mini-game to regain attention and increase interest for participation.

B. *SLE Behavior Programming and Testing*

The SLE behavior is defined using the ClassScript's visual editor, while the AmITest framework facilitates its simulation and validation via the Tests Management and Deployment Suite. In order for Mrs. Smith to validate the behavior described above, she can use the AmITest framework in order to simulate the actions of virtual students in order to and validate if the SLE performs as expected. For that to be achieved, firstly she defines two auxiliary testing blocks (i.e., functions), one that checks whether the teacher's workstation displays a notification when inattention is detected and another that validates that whenever the teacher launches a mini-game in a student's desk, then that game is the only active application (Fig. 3 and Fig. 4 present those functions in the user-friendly visual format and the automatically generated ClassScript code respectively). Afterwards, she creates a virtual student, in order to simulate a student distraction behavior for SLE behavior validation purposes. This virtual student will simulate a distraction after a few seconds in order to trigger the overall detection and reaction process, as depicted in Figure 2.

```
function testBehaviorWhenStudentDistracted() {
  $executor.trigger($camera1, "DetectUserStatus",
                ["George", "Distracted"],
                //Artifact promises passed as argument (array)
                [$deskOfTeacher, $context]).then(function() {

    $tester.test("Camera detects George is distracted.", function() {
      $teacherNotifications = $deskOfTeacher.getNotifications();
      $tester.expect($teacherNotifications).toContain("George is distracted.");
    }).run();

    //Definition of SLE's reaction to student's distraction
    $executor.invoke($deskOfTeacher, "StartGame",
                  [$deskOfGeorge, "TheSubtractionGame", "Easy"],
                  [$deskOfGeorge, $context]).then(function() {

      $tester.test("Starting game for George:", function() {
        $gamesOnDeskOfGeorge = $deskOfGeorge.getGamesRunning();
        $tester.expect($gamesOnDeskOfGeorge.getKeys()).toContain("TheSubtractionGame");
      }).run();
    });
  // Expect for the tests to be executed properly within 5000 ms.
  }, 5000).onAnyFailure(function() {
    $tester.fail("Test failed! Could not start game to address George's distraction.");
  });
};
```

Figure 4. Portion of the automatically generated ClassScript code to test SLE reaction to a student's lapse of attention

Upon programming of the classroom's behavior and the testing methodology, Mrs. Smith launches the validation process. She uses the TMDS component of the AmITest framework to create an instance of that test and execute it right away in order to check whether or not the SLE behaves as expected.

VI. Challenges

One of the most challenging issues in order to perform testing operations is the complexity of the system; there is a considerable number of distributed, interoperating components, applying operations asynchronously between their operations most of the time, but also acting asynchronously between each other. Considering the artifacts as isolated units and testing them that way would be incorrect, as there is a high level of dependency between the artifacts.

What we attempted though was focusing mainly on isolating and performing assertions on the values of the artifacts, thus practically checking all the individual components operated as expected. For instance, if a student gets distracted during a lecture, then the teacher should be offered the opportunity to motivate her to participate. In order to validate that these operations function as intended, one could observe the situation of the class, something that it is not possible in a simulation scenario. On the other hand, this observation could be done via value checking of all the affected artifacts. Therefore a complete test would assert that: (1) the status of the teacher's workstation would change from "classroom overview", to "inattention detected" and eventually to "mini-game launched" and (2) the AmIDesk of the distracted student would disable interaction with every application but the mini-game initiated by the teacher.

To support such tests, we have implemented a sophisticated monitoring mechanism through which we ensure that value checking (i.e., Expectations) is performed only after the necessary handling actions have completed (i.e., Promises).

VII. Conclusions and Future Work

This paper has described a testing suite for Smart Learning Environments in order to check the validity of operations programmed by end users in a Smart Learning Environment. The suite aims primarily at non-programming professional users, and supports testing via scripting and Visual Programming. Even though well-established user-friendly visualization techniques have been currently applied (e.g., Blockly), following the iterative approach of the User-Centered Design (UCD) process [29], both educators and experienced developers of AmI servicers will be actively involved in the design process of the visual tools, through preliminary evaluation sessions and participatory design sessions, to maximize their usability for both groups. Whereas, upon the release of version 1.0 of AmITest, we plan to conduct an extensive in-vivo full-scale evaluation experiment both with HCI experts and educators in order to examine and improve the usability of the AmITest editing facilities.

Finally, as regards our future plans for the overall framework, we have already laid the foundations to extend its application to support testing, in a scalable and effective way, in other domains beyond its initial target domain (i.e., SLEs), such as Smart Homes, Technologically-enhanced Cultural Monuments, Smart Cities, etc.

References

[1] J. Krumm, Ubiquitous Computing Fundamentals. Boca Ragon: Chapman & Hall/CRC Press, 2010.

[2] F. Adelstein, Fundamentals of Mobile and Pervasive Computing. New York: McGraw-Hill, 2005.

[3] G. M. Novak, Just-in-time Teaching: Blending Active Learning with Web Technology. Upper Saddle River, NJ: Prentice Hall, 1999.

[4] M. Chang, and Y. Li. Smart Learning Environments. Springer, 2014.

[5] A. Leonidis, M. Antona, and C. Stephanidis, "Enabling Programmability of Smart Learning Environments by Teachers." Distributed, Ambient, and Pervasive Interactions Lecture Notes in Computer Science, 2015, pp. 62-73.

[6] D. Crockford, JavaScript: The Good Parts. Beijing: O'Reilly, 2008.

[7] P. Ragonha, Jasmine JavaScript Testing: Leverage the Power of Unit Testing to Create Bigger and Better JavaScript Applications. Birmingham: Packt, 2013.

[8] D. Sheiko, Instant Testing with Qunit. S.l.: Packt Publishing Limited, 2013.

[9] M. Maleki, R. Woodbury, R. Goldstein, S. Breslav, and A. Khan. "Designing DEVS Visual Interfaces for End-user Programmers." Simulation 91, no. 8 (2015), pp. 715-734.

[10] M. Resnick et al, "Scratch: Programming for All." Communications of the ACM Commun. ACM 52, no. 11 (2009), pp. 60-67.

[11] O. Gray and M. Young, 2007. "Video Games: A New Interface for Non-Professional Game Developers". In ACM International Conference on Computer-Human Interaction (CHI 2007), USA: San Jose.

[12] N. Tillmann, M. Moskal, J. De Halleux, and M. Fahndrich, "TouchDevelop: Programming Cloud-connected Mobile Devices via Touchscreen." Proceedings of the 10th SIGPLAN Symposium on New Ideas, New Paradigms, and Reflections on Programming and Software - ONWARD '11, 2011, pp. 49-60.

[13] D. Wolber, "App Inventor and Real-world Motivation." Proceedings of the 42nd ACM Technical Symposium on Computer Science Education - SIGCSE '11, 2011, pp. 601-606.

[14] B. Waldie, Automator for Mac OS X 10.6 Snow Leopard. Berkeley, CA: Peachpit Press, 2010.

[15] R. Ierusalimschy, Programming in Lua. Rio De Janeiro: Lua.org, 2006.

[16] W. Goldstone, Unity 3.x Game Development Essentials: Game Development with C# and Javascript. Birmingham, UK: Packt Publishing, 2011.

[17] R. J. Cox, and P. S. Crowther, "A Review of Linden Scripting Language and Its Role in Second Life." Lecture Notes in Computer Science Computer-Mediated Social Networking, 2009, pp. 35-47.

[18] E. Mangina, J. Carbo, and J. M. Molina, Agent-based Ubiquitous Computing. Paris, France: Atlantis Press, 2009.

[19] I. Georgalis, Y. Tanaka, N. Spyratos, and C. Stephanidis, Programming Smart Object Federations for Simulating and Implementing Ambient Intelligence Scenarios. In C. Benavente-Peces and J. Filipethe (Eds.), Proceedings of the 3rd International Conference on Pervasive and Embedded Computing and Communication Systems (PECCS 2013),), Barcelona, Spain, 19-21 February 2013, pp. 5-15. Portugal: SciTePress.

[20] A. Williams, C++ Concurrency in Action: Practical Multithreading. 1st ed. Manning Publications, 2012.

[21] D. Parker, JavaScript with Promises. O'Reilly Media, 2015.

[22] "Blockly | Google Developers." Google Developers. Accessed January 25, 2016. https://developers.google.com/blockly/.

[23] A. Leonidis et al, "A glimpse into the ambient classroom." Bulletin of the IEEE Technical Committee on Learning Technology 14.4, 2012, 3.

[24] M. Antona et al, Ambient Intelligence in the classroom: an augmented school desk. In the Proceedings of the 2010 AHFE International Conference (3rd International Conference on Applied Human Factors and Ergonomics), Miami, Florida, USA, 17-20 July 2010. CRC Press [CD-ROM].

[25] C. Savvaki et al, "Designing a Technology–Augmented School Desk for the Future Classroom." HCI International 2013-Posters' Extended Abstracts. Springer Berlin Heidelberg, 2013, pp. 681-685.

[26] G. Galanakis, X. Zabulis, P. Koutlemanis, S. Paparoulis, and V. Kouroumalis, "Tracking persons using a network of RGBD cameras." In Proceedings of the 7th International Conference on PErvasive Technologies Related to Assistive Environments, ACM, 2014, 63.

[27] M. Korozi et al. "Ambient educational mini-games." Proceedings of the International Working Conference on Advanced Visual Interfaces. ACM, 2012.

[28] G. Mathioudakis et al. "Ami-ria: real-time teacher assistance tool for an ambient intelligence classroom." Proceedings of the Fifth International Conference on Mobile, Hybrid, and On-Line Lerning (eLmL 2013). 2013.

[29] D. A. Norman and S. W. Draper. "User centered system design." Hillsdale, NJ, 1986.

The Role of Smartphones in Teacher Training Mediated Through Photo-elicitation

Antonio Bautista
Faculty of Educacion
Complutense University
Madrid. España.
e-mail: bautista@edu.ucm.es

Laura Rayón
Faculty of Education
Universidad de Alcalá.
Alcalá de Henares. Spain
e-mail: laura.rayon@uah.es

Yolanda Muñoz
Faculty of Education
Universidad de Alcalá
Alcalá de Henares. Spain
e-mail: yolanda.monozm@uah.es

Ana María De las Heras
Pedagogy Department
UDIMA
Madrid. Spain
e-mail: annita19834@gmail.com

***Abstract*- In this paper, we advance the results of a study on the use of smartphone functions in the permanent training of primary-school teachers supported by photo-elicitation processes. The study began in January 2015 and will end in December 2017. Three teachers participated from the primary schools Jaime Vera in Madrid and La Paloma in Azuqueca de Henares (Guadalajara), Spain. To date, the smartphone functions used for photo elicitation by these teachers to reflect on difficulties in their practice include: taking photos of classroom situations that are judged difficult by teachers; viewing these photos; recording an audio track of sessions reflecting on the content of these images; playing back the recorded audio tracks to transcribe their content and identify the theories and beliefs on which participating teachers' decisions are based and, finally, storing all this information in the cloud (Dropbox, Drive, at the rest).**

Keywords- teacher education; photo-elicitation; digital hybrids; smartphones.

I. Introduction

We begin this section by explaining two conceptual elements. Both are essential to understand the functionality of the phones in teacher training. These are: the reflection on own practice, and photo-elicitation as a means of signification.

A. *Reflecting on teaching practice*

Extensive theorising exists on the value of professionals' critical reflection on their own practice in order to improve their work [3] [6]. Teachers can be helped to improve their work once they are aware of their beliefs, theories, attitudes, values and so on. To do so, teachers must be "forced" to make these explicit. This occurs because they are questioned about what they do, and this is achieved by reflecting on his practice as a teacher. This reflection is included and is one of the three moments of a loop or cycle of Action Research [2]. Each is made up of a procedure consisting of the three following phases:

1- Planning the teaching or specifying within a document the aims, cultural content, materials and so on that the teachers are going to work on or will need over a period of time.

2- Executing the plan and recording certain moments of it. The plan must be followed and information must be recorded on what occurred during the process. Because it is difficult to reflect on the action while it is taking place, reflection has to take place afterward. To avoid forgetting things or missing relevant details the action must be recorded.

What technological tools are needed to help teachers record their actions and reflect upon them? Those whose primary function is producing information; in other words, audio recorders and cameras that can be found on one of the current digital hybrid devices: smartphones. We propose that mainly teachers should follow this procedure, taking photos of those moments so that later, outside the classroom, they can verbally analyse the content. Therefore, we focus on the languages of verbal and photographic representation.

3- Analysing, questioning, discussing and reflecting on what happened. After having carried out the plan, one must reflect on the value of what took place; we encapsulate it using photo elicitation, for which it is also necessary to use the information reproduction functions that all digital hybrid devices contain. The result of this phase leads to new knowledge on the decisions taken, on the whys or wherefores of the latter and consequently new knowledge of the theories, beliefs and so on that underlie them.

This generated knowledge gradually enriches or improves the work plan for the following action inquiry loop and consequently enhances the teacher-tutor's training.

B. *Photo elicitation as a means of reflection*

Eliciting means drawing something out of oneself, arousing an experience, establishing a bridge between the past and the present using a photo [1] [4]. It consists of capturing an image so as to describe it later. Several procedures exist in the field of education: one is that directed by the teacher and the photos she or he takes; another, when students take the pictures, and finally, a mixed procedure in which everybody takes photos. This means the photos are taken by users to be screened later so users can describe what they represent and explain what they have experienced.

In this sense, we consider that photo elicitation is a good procedure for understanding the tangible and intangible aspects of human beings' lives – in our case, the three primary school teachers who aim to improve their teaching practice. At the point of reflection within the action inquiry loops, photos taken by the participants are shown (in our case, only the teachers) on different teaching moments as a base document on which to question, query or wonder about some aspect of the content depicted. This is how we have used one of the underused action inquiry procedures called observational and narrative, McKerman said: that an underdeveloped resource in the conduct of curriculum action inquiry is the use of the still photograph [5].

In Section 2, we explain the objectives and the methodology that we followed. Finally, in Section 3, we present the conclusion and future work.

II. The Aims and Research Method

This research has two objectives:

a) Identify the functions required on a smartphone in the training of primary teachers based on photo elicitation processes.
b) Know whether the photo-elicitation sessions help teachers change their teaching practice.

The data needed to achieve the above aims are being gathered through a supported discussion group in two session types we call photo elicitation and audio reflection.

Photo elicitation sessions. These are held every two weeks. During this time, the teachers take photos of events, tasks, dilemmas, conflicts, behaviours and so on that they consider most relevant and interesting in the life of their classroom and other spaces in the center. After each fourteen-day period, the above-mentioned meeting takes place. It lasts about 75 minutes with each teacher separately and takes place when they have some free time during the school day in their respective schools. To do so, the photos taken by each teacher are shown and the teacher, the research group members and student representatives comment on the reasons that led her or him to take each photo. Next, the other group members formulate questions or doubts on the content of the images and the reasons provided by the teacher and students, either on the decision taken at a specific classroom moment, or on the tasks undertaken by students, etcetera.

Audio reflection sessions. An audio recording is being made of the photo elicitation sessions with a two-fold research purpose. Firstly, to analyze each teacher's statements and respond to the questions posed in the first aim of the project, regarding the different uses of the smartphone. Secondly, to codify and create the information provided in the photo elicitation session to be used in the second aim. As stated in the summary above, the discussion group which conducted this reflection consists of the teacher who is the center of the training process, the members of the research team who were present during the prior photo elicitation session, and some students when they appear in the photos. The parents gave permission to use the photos in which their children appeared as long as such use was confined to teaching and research purposes.

III. Conclusion and Future Work

Regarding the *first aim*, the smartphone functions that the three teachers used are:

- *Taking photos* of classroom situations the teachers considered complex and conflictive, such as dilemmas, difficulties emerging from the students and so on.
- *Storing photos in the cloud* (Dropbox, Drive, at the rest).
- *Viewing* those photos in the photo elicitation sessions with the aid of a projector.
- *Recording audio files* of the reflection sessions on the content of the images projected.
- *Storing the audio files in the cloud* (Dropbox, Drive, at the rest).
- *Playing the recorded audio files* to transcribe their content and identify the theories and beliefs that lie behind the decisions of the participating teachers.
- *Storing the texts transcribed in the cloud* (Dropbox, Drive, at the rest) for later analysis.
- *Reading the transcriptions for the analysis* of theories, beliefs, attitudes and so on, on which the teachers base their behaviours and decisions, and communicate such analyses so that the teachers are aware of them, can reflect on their value and consequently decide whether they should change any of the latter.

Concerning the study's *second aim*, based on the results as of late November 2015, it can be stated that teachers are changing the way they design and approach teaching situations. This is because, according to the analysis of the transcriptions of the photo elicitation sessions, the teachers are becoming aware that they base their actions and decisions on five different aspects of their person:

- Theories: rational ideas or arguments, with a scientific basis.
- Beliefs: ideas or arguments with no scientific basis.
- Attitudes: forms or kinds of willingness to do or respond to something.

- Habits: routines they use in certain situations.
- Emotions: feelings about a situation that guide decisions.

The teachers have shown a disposition to change once they become aware that the above five components influence their motivations and decisions, both to improve the school tasks in the classroom and to address the personal difficulties of their students.

Finally, we should indicate that all of the smartphone functions that the teaching staff required in the discussion or photo elicitation processes (those that take place when viewing the image of a photo taken by the teacher and projected on-screen) were used to record moments in the classroom, to bring some quietness to the educational practice in order to slow down the analytical processes. These pauses made it possible to describe and interpret the content reported by the participating teachers, allowing them to reflect and comment on their theories, beliefs, attitudes, habits and emotions so that, once aware of them, the teachers uncovered those that are incongruous with their idea of education or unsuitable for working with that unique and unrepeatable group of students in a specific context.

In the future, we want to deepen the possibilities for smartphones to locate, select and project a part or element of a photograph. We think that the analysis of these details of an image can help teachers to evoke their theories and beliefs. Also, we want to use smartphones to store and play music during sessions photoelicitación. We think that both, the projection of detail and background music, can improve the evocation of the beliefs and emotions that have promoted the decisions taken in their classrooms.

ACKNOWLEDGMENT

A project subsidised by the Ministry of Economy and Competitiveness of the Spanish Government, within the R&D&i State Plan, reference EDU2014-57103-R.

REFERENCES

[1] M. Clark-Ibañez, "Inter-City Children in Sharper Focus. Sociology of Childhood and Photo Elicitation Interviews". In Visual Research Methods, Gr. C. Stanczak, Ed. Los Ángeles, CA: Sage, pp. 167-196, 2007.

[2] J. Elliott, Action-research in education. Madrid: Morata, 1990.

[3] J. Gimeno, The curriculum: a reflection on practice. Madrid: Morata, 1988.

[4] D. Harper, "Talking about pictures: a case for photo elicitation". Visual Studies, Vol.17, Nº 1, pp.13-26, 2002, doi:10.1080/14725860220137345

[5] J. McKernan, Curriculum action research. Madrid: Morata, pp. 121, 2008.

[6] D. A. Schön, Educating the Reflective Practitioner. Barcelona: Paidós-MEC, 1989.

AUTHOR INDEX